WORTHY

ALSO BY
JAMIE KERN LIMA

Believe IT: How to Go from Underestimated to Unstoppable

•••

WORTHY

How to Believe You Are Enough and Transform Your Life

Simple Steps,
Life-Changing Results

Jamie Kern Lima

HAY HOUSE, INC.
Carlsbad, California • New York City
London • Sydney • New Delhi

For the 80 percent of women who don't believe they're enough, the 75 percent of female executives who deal with imposter syndrome, and the 91 percent of girls and women who don't love their bodies. For the 73 percent of men who feel inadequate and the 100 percent of men who come from a woman and likely have at least one girl or woman in their lives whom they care about. When you believe you're fundamentally not enough and unworthy as a person, it's a lie. The time to unlearn that lie has come. Together let's leave no girl, no woman, no person left behind in knowing they are worthy!

CONTENTS

A NOTE TO THE READER

My HOPE IS the stories, lessons, and ideas in this book help give you the inspiration and tools to transform your life, and I want to ask you that if at any point while you are reading, you feel you know someone who could benefit from the messages and tools in it, please share this book with them. Together, let's leave no girl, no woman, no person behind in knowing they are seen, valuable, and fully worthy.

While we may have varying beliefs, identities, and life experiences, I believe that we all share this life together, that we are all divinely connected, and that we are all worthy of unconditional love. This book is written for you, because no matter how similar or different you and I might appear on the outside, I believe there's a very good chance we share so many similarities on the inside. And for us to enter this quest of transformation together, it will only work if we show up fully, authentically, and unapologetically ourselves. So that's what I'm going to do on these pages, and my hope is that we both truly do this together.

I don't believe it's an accident you're reading this book right now, and I want to honor and celebrate you for beginning this transformative journey! And while I can't wait to discover the impact it will have on your life, I also want you to know that just by purchasing this book, you've already made a tremendous difference in the lives of others. **100 percent of my author proceeds from this book are donated** to Feeding America and programs dedicated to building self-worth in girls and women.

WHEN I IMAGINE a world where every girl and woman believes she's worthy, I imagine the powerful force for good we can be together to help heal ourselves, generations, and humanity through love. If you think of someone, or many people, who needs the stories, tools, and takeaways from *WORTHY* as you're reading it, please share it with them. Please be my teammate and join me in spreading the message and impacting as many lives as possible. I can't do it alone, and I am so grateful for your help, working together with me in this meaningful movement.

Also, I would love to invite you to post photos or your favorite images, pages, quotes, and experiences related to this book on social media using the hashtag #WorthyBook or #JamieKernLima so I can see and then repost yours on my page! If you'd like weekly inspiration and encouragement on your worthiness journey and beyond, I'd love to invite you to join my free email newsletter at JamieKernLima.com.

NoteWORTHY: This book and the exercises in it can be read alone, in partnership with a friend or a mental health professional, or as part of a book club. You can also create your own Worthy Circle: a group of two or more people who gather together as a book club or simply as a group, live or virtually, to celebrate and support building self-worth together. See WorthyBook.com/Resources for resources on how to join one or create your own.

You can also find more free tools and resources to complement your experience through this book, making it even more fully immersive, on WorthyBook.com/Resources and JamieKernLima.com or by scanning the QR code here.

Please note, this book is not meant to replace therapy, medication, or mental health treatment.

You Become What You Believe You're Worthy Of

D O YOU REMEMBER the first time, perhaps as a little kid sitting in a classroom, that you knew the answer but decided not to raise your hand? With a slight pit in your stomach caused by the new and daunting awareness of other people's opinions, you debated raising your hand and going for it . . . until you decided not to. And just like that, in a single moment, you began to live in a way that was incongruent with your soul's fullest expression.

You doubted. You held back. You hid. You played it safe. You questioned whether you were wrong, even though you knew you were right. You questioned if you were smart enough. You questioned if *you* were enough.

And now, fast-forward to today, are you still the person who's not raising your hand when you know the answer? Are you still hiding? Just in case you're wrong. Just in case you fail. Or because you want to stay in your comfort zone of certainty. Now you're an adult who knows the answer, but inside are you still that same little kid who doubts it? Maybe you're sitting silently in work meetings, or in your daydreams, knowing you have a wild idea that just might be genius? Or are you languishing in an unhealthy friendship or relationship, knowing you're worthy of more but not quite believing it enough to leave? Perhaps you're the boss, but you're holding back from taking chances because deep down inside,

1

you're afraid you're not strong enough to be a leader. Did you finally get that big break, that big promotion, that big increase, but you feel like an imposter so you're playing it small?

Maybe you really despise that other PTA mom, but you betray yourself and spend your precious free time hanging out with her. Maybe you're hustling and burned out while hiding that what you really need is rest. Maybe you're struggling with a health issue and are losing faith in your body, your worth, and your Creator. Do you feel unseen at your core and tell yourself the lie that life is better that way? Maybe you're working *in* a business but know you were born to *run* one? Maybe you're in an intimate partnership where your worthiness goes unrecognized, but you're afraid to be alone so you're dimming your light and hiding from your truth? Maybe you're calling busyness a badge of honor, when you're really using it to numb your feelings? Maybe you've been living by someone else's story of success for you because you're confusing approval with love? Maybe you've decided that other people have already done what you can do, better than you could do it, so you've been canceling yourself out of your own calling? Or maybe you've been showing up as who the world tells you to be, people-pleasing, for so long that you don't even remember who you are anymore?

Self-doubt, unworthiness, and fear cause us to dim our soul's light. And start playing it safe. Holding back. Hiding. Speaking only part of our truth. Living only half of our life. Expressing only part of our soul's true essence. Craving the perception of belonging over authentic connection. Craving validation and significance in a way that's defined externally. Because we start to believe that these are the only paths to love, to belonging, and to worthiness.

If any of these ring true for you, if you know in the deepest part of your being that you're only living as *part* of who you are, but holding back and doubting or hiding *all* of who you are, then you're probably feeling an inexplicable void in your life. An aching longing for something that's missing. An emptiness created when others, or even you yourself, don't know and therefore can't embrace the full, authentic you. A disconnection from joy, when no matter what you achieve, it doesn't bring the feeling of fulfillment you'd hoped it would. An unremitting feeling that you're not quite enough. A lack of feeling truly alive that you can disguise from the world with the ease of a smile.

You're living your life hiding in plain sight.

OKAY, SO MAYBE you are thinking, *Whoa, we're going this deep right off the top of the book?* Yep, we're going there, because your time is precious. And this one beautiful life we each have is precious. I'm not showing up to play small, especially because I'm going to ask you to show up fully too in the pages to come. I wrote this book with the purest intention to give you everything I've got, as an expression of love, from my soul to yours. Each of us is on a journey toward believing, then to truly knowing in every ounce of our being that we are fully worthy, exactly as we are. This is one of the most critical parts of achieving what Oprah Winfrey powerfully describes as "the highest, truest expression of ourselves."

You, exactly as you are, are enough, valuable, and fully worthy of love and belonging. There's nothing you have done or could ever do to change that. But let's go there later, because chances are, if you're anything like I've been for most of my life, you might not believe this quite yet.

Speaking of Oprah, and speaking of hiding in plain sight, I want to share one of the greatest moments of my life, a moment that almost didn't happen, and one that came after four years of me hiding because I didn't believe I was actually worthy of it. Oprah was my mentor-from-afar, the one I spent every weekday as a little girl, then later as an adult, watching on TV. The one I dreamt of meeting my entire life and had this knowing deep inside that somehow I actually would.

"This is what I know 100 percent for sure," Oprah said as she held up my first book, *Believe IT,* live to the camera. "You don't become what you want, you become what you believe." I did everything in my power to keep my jaw from dropping open, to not pee my pants, and to believe this moment was real and actually happening. You see, it almost didn't happen. In fact, many of the most significant moments in my life almost never happened. Because for years, while my soul dreamed wildly big, bold dreams and imagined moments like this one with Oprah, I never thought they could actually happen. Because I didn't believe I was worthy of them ever actually happening. In fact, and maybe you can relate to this, **I've spent most of my life feeling like I was not enough and doubting myself out of my own destiny.**

If not-enoughness feels like your hidden twin, then we just might be long-lost triplets.

No matter how vividly we visualize our goals and dreams, perhaps in relationships, or in our careers or our health, no matter if we even take action toward making them happen, if deep down inside we don't actually feel like we are deserving or worthy of those dreams and goals, then we won't achieve them. We'll stay stuck and never go for them, we'll talk ourselves out of them, we'll give up too soon or somehow sabotage them along the way. With some self-worth, but not strong self-worth, we might allow ourselves to feel worthy of achieving a big goal or dream, but when we do, we'll arrive still feeling empty, unfulfilled, and like something is missing. Has this ever happened to you? If you've ever experienced a sense of *not-enoughness*, even if you know it's a lie (because it is!), and you want to overcome it for good, this book is for you. **If *not-enoughness* feels like your hidden twin, then we just might be long-lost triplets.** If you struggle with self-doubt and not feeling worthy, even if no one knows it but you, this book is for you. And I believe one of the bravest and most important journeys we are on in this lifetime is learning the truth, which is that we are more than enough, and knowing and believing it in every part of our beings. If this resonates with you, **I've got your book and I've got your back.**

See, I believe **the moment you learn to trust yourself, and believe that you are worthy, is the moment your entire life, the past and future generations of your family, and our entire world change for the better.**

It's only when you believe you're worthy of it . . . whether it's of having a healthy relationship, of receiving unconditional love, of celebrating your body, of sharing your ideas, of being in the room, of being on the stage, of leading the team, of having soul-filling friendships, or of living out your biggest hopes and wildest dreams . . . that your greatest life and greatest destiny start to unfold.

> *The moment you learn to believe you are worthy, your entire life, the past and future generations of your family, and our entire world change for the better.*

AS OPRAH HELD up my book, I tried desperately to be present, to stay in my body, and to focus on the thousands of people watching us live. She and I were teaching a class together called "The Life You Want." *Please help me serve at the highest level I can*, I prayed over and over, because I've learned over the years that having an intention that's bigger than myself is the only way to get out of my own head. Before she even held up my book, I was already struggling to believe that I really was teaching a class with the person I had considered my mentor my entire life. It was the first time she and I had done anything professionally together.

What Oprah and I knew, which the live audience didn't know, is that nearly five years earlier, when I met her in person for the first time and we had lunch together shortly after, she gave me her personal phone number and I didn't call her for almost four years. Yep, Oprah, the one person I would have done anything to meet, the person I spent thousands of afternoons as a little girl watching from my living room all alone, the person who inspired much of my career, had given *me* her direct cell number and I didn't call it for almost four years! Why? Well, I thought I knew why for a long time.

See, as the months, then years, passed, I told myself stories that made sense. Stories like *You're not ready to call her yet*, or *Everyone probably wants something from her. Play it cool so she knows you don't*, or *You don't have the perfect thing to say to her yet. When you do, you'll know, and then it will be time to call*, or *If she gets to know you, she'll discover you're not as interesting/smart/funny/successful/cool/talented as she might think you are*, until one day I realized the *real* reason I hadn't called Oprah, and I wasn't

> *I believe one of the most prevalent forms of cancel culture is one that no one talks about. It's us canceling ourselves before we even try.*

proud of it. I hadn't yet called her because deep down inside I didn't believe I was worthy of it. I didn't believe I was worthy of being her friend.

Have you had moments like this in your life, where you sabotaged an opportunity? Or didn't go for it at all because you didn't think you had what it takes? Maybe this is a recurrent theme for you in your life right now. If it is, you're far from alone.

I believe one of the most prevalent forms of cancel culture is one that no one talks about. It's us canceling ourselves before we even try.

When I realized the real reason I hadn't called Oprah for four years, I felt a knowing: feeling unworthy wasn't aligned with who I truly am and with the person I was created to be. See, my soul knew I was worthy, but I let my thoughts and my mind's deep belief about my own unworthiness overpower my soul's knowing. Without realizing it, I was letting my thoughts and feelings of unworthiness sabotage something I dreamed of my whole life. When I had this realization, almost four years after the day I got her number, I decided **it was time to turn down the volume on my doubting mind and turn up the volume on the power of my knowing**

soul. I decided to trust myself. The part that knows I am worthy. (And you are too!) And I dialed the number.

I'LL SHARE MORE about that call later, but first, fast-forward to May 2022 when I was teaching the class live alongside Oprah. I had been preparing tirelessly for months for this opportunity. But like all of our biggest moments, we've really been preparing our entire lives for them, whether we know it or not. Because as Oprah teaches and I fully believe, every step, failure, victory, mishap, trauma, growth, blessing, lesson, and moment of grace has always been happening *for* us, to prepare us so we can show up in each coming moment exactly as we're destined to. Even our setbacks are almost always setups for the path we're destined to take. As the live class began, I led the *Oprah Daily* audience through exercises on how to build resilience, embrace rejection, stop hiding, and learn to confidently step into *all* of who they are. Oprah and I shared stories and teachings. I was in such a state of flow that it felt like I was moving inside a space that had been divinely orchestrated.

It's time to turn down the volume on your doubting mind and turn up the volume on your knowing soul.

Then as Oprah held up my book again, and I tried not to fall out of my chair *again*, she said something that sent shockwaves that felt like truth through my body. Words that I believe capture the ultimate path so many of us are on, even if we haven't discovered it yet. Words that capture why I wrote that book, and even more powerfully why I wrote this one. Words I believe that, if we embrace them, can change the course of our entire lives. She said, "You don't become what you want. You can have the greatest heart desire, and really work so hard, so hard, so hard. But if you don't believe you are **worthy**, it will not come. That is the magic formula."

IN MY LIFE, I've been learning to believe I am worthy in stages, through ups and downs, big moments of knowing and small steps toward believing. In our human experience, believing in our worthiness is often a lifelong pursuit, and one of the most important ones we'll ever take. See, if I hadn't pursued building my self-worth, many of the moments in my life's story so far would never have happened.

You don't soar to the level of your hopes and dreams, you stay stuck at the level of your self-worth.

The stories in the press about me usually say something like "Denny's waitress builds billion-dollar business." And while that's true, my real story is about a girl who didn't believe in herself and learned how to. A girl who felt unworthy, and often still does to this day, but who is hell-bent on learning to believe she is. A girl who was placed into adoption at birth, but decided she was chosen and was born not only on purpose but with purpose. A girl who knows in her soul that at our core, we're all enough, and we're all worthy of love.

I'm a girl who knows that where we come from doesn't have to determine where we're going, and that making bad decisions in our past doesn't mean that *we're* bad. A girl who knows that the labels that others put on us and that we put on ourselves are removable, not permanent. A girl who faced thousands of rejections for years when she was building her business but chose to trust her gut and keep going anyway. A girl who had a knowing she'd one day meet Oprah and learned that we become what we believe when I finally did. A girl who had to learn she was worthy of being in the room, of launching a business, of being called CEO, of learning not to *wait on her weight*, of learning to love herself, and learning to believe she's worthy of receiving love. A girl who knows we are not our past mistakes, we are our present and future intentions.

––––––

HERE'S WHAT I know to be true: If we don't believe we're worthy of starting the business, of being in a loving, committed relationship, or of having healthy, empowering friendships . . . If we don't believe we're worthy of a seat at the table, of writing the book, of running for office . . . If we don't believe we're worthy of rest, of celebrating our body exactly as it is, of soul care, of *doing* less and *being* more . . . If we don't believe we're worthy of showing up on social media authentically, of leading the team, of breaking the generational cycle, or of sharing our story with others . . . If we don't believe we're worthy because we've made too many mistakes, we've already failed too many times, or because someone told us we weren't worthy and we believed them . . . If we don't believe we're worthy of all of these things we want and deserve, we'll never get them.

In life, you don't soar to the level of your hopes and dreams, you stay stuck at the level of your self-worth. You don't rise to what you believe is possible, you fall to what you believe you're worthy of.

In your goals and career ambitions, you don't achieve everything that you're qualified for or capable of—you plateau at what you believe you deserve, and whether you know it or not, at the level of success where you've established your own internal identity. In your romantic relationships, the level and depth of intimacy, vulnerability, and love can only be as strong as the level and depth of vulnerable, intimate love you have for yourself. It's the same with your friendships. And in these relationships in your life, the level of pain you'll allow another person to cause you, whether it's through hurtful words or actions, often hovers right around the standards you have

You don't rise to what you believe is possible, you fall to what you believe you're worthy of.

for the level and frequency of hurtful thoughts, ways, and words you think and say to yourself. And it's the same with your body. **Your body can feel like a source of shame or like a miracle in motion, all depending on your relationship with worthiness.**

If you're an entrepreneur, boss, or leader of a team, building strong internal self-worth is one of the best business moves you can make. We act on our identity, so when you're the boss you can have the title and even the stellar business results, but if deep inside you still struggle with self-worth, imposter syndrome, and believing you're enough, it will eventually show in your leadership and your business decisions. You'll second-guess yourself, you'll hold back, you'll sabotage yourself or your company in your decision-making. Building your self-worth is the best business decision you'll ever make for your company, your team, and your leadership. **If you want to double your business, double your self-worth and watch what happens.**

When you change what you believe you're worthy of, you change your entire life.

SEE, WE CAN have big goals and dreams, we can study, get knowledge, get the biggest degrees on the wall, become activists, use our voices . . .

In life, you don't get what you want, you get what you believe you're worthy of.

we can know with passion and clarity what we believe in and believe for, we can make vision boards and we can even distinguish ourselves among the rare group of people who actually take action toward getting what we want in life . . . but if we don't believe deep down inside that we're worthy of it, it will never happen, or if it does, we won't be able to sustain it. Because **in life, you don't get what you want, you only get and maintain what you believe you're worthy of.**

When deep down inside we don't believe we're worthy of what we want, hope, and dream for, we will find a way to lose it or for it not to happen at all. We will sabotage the opportunity. We'll put a decent guy in the friend zone. We'll ghost a new friend who has pure intentions. We'll make a million excuses why we're not yet ready to make a career move, don't have the resources or the time or the talent. We'll focus on our problems instead of our potential because our problems can be an easy way to justify playing life small. **We might think we have a *net-worth* problem, when what we really have is a *self-worth* problem,** as when deep down inside we don't believe we're worthy of abundance, we sabotage ourselves to make sure that we don't get it. We'll dim our light to make others comfortable and to fit in. We'll tell ourselves stories like, *Once I get to my goal weight, then I'll be enough; once I get more experience, then I'll apply for the promotion; once the kids get through school, then I'll focus on building a healthy relationship.* We'll sit in the audience watching, all while knowing we're born to be on the stage. We'll walk into the room, all while hiding in plain sight. And we'll start living our lives this way. We'll talk ourselves out of our potential, out of our talent, out of our knowing, out of trusting ourselves, out of our gifts, out of the relationships we deserve, out of getting unstuck, out of making our health a priority, out of asking for the raise, out of launching the idea, out of accepting a mentor's offer, and if we're not careful, out of becoming the person we're born to be. All because we don't truly believe we're enough, or worthy of it, exactly as we are.

IF ANY ONE of these examples hits home for you or feels like a past or present version of you, then this book is for you. If you struggle with not believing you're enough or truly worthy of walking into the big meeting room, of being called a good parent, of wearing the swimsuit, of receiving unconditional love, of looking in the mirror and seeing everything that's beautiful, of speaking up, of sharing your story, of

Do you have some self-doubt to destroy and a destiny to fulfill?

asking for help, of resting, of setting boundaries, of showing up in the world as you authentically are and as *all* of who you authentically are, this book is for you.

I wrote this book for you if you have some self-doubt to destroy and a destiny to fulfill.

And I'm so honored to invite you into the pages of this journey together. And I'd like to start it by imagining together . . .

See, I can't help but imagine what our world would look like if it was full of women who decided to believe they're worthy. When I imagine a world full of women who feel worthy, I imagine the earth shaking with the jolt of possibility when we all wake up in the morning. Imagine with me . . . what would a world full of women who decide to believe they're worthy feel like? The potential that would be unleashed, the power of possibility unfolding. Imagine the generational cycles broken, imagine the unhealthy relationships that would end, imagine the businesses that would be launched, the body shapes and sizes that would be celebrated, imagine the rest that would be taken without guilt. Imagine the cellulite that would confidently be jiggling with joy. Imagine the seats that would be filled up in the boardroom, imagine what the list of Fortune 500 CEOs would look like, imagine the mental and physical health that would be prioritized, imagine how our government would lead, imagine the injustices that would end, imagine how children's storybooks would be written, imagine who little girls would grow up dreaming of being, imagine the time and capacity that would be freed up when self-doubt is silenced, imagine . . .

Imagining this is why I wrote this book. With the intention of you not just imagining what your life would be like if you truly felt worthy, but actually learning how to believe that you are. Because you are. And in your soul, you know that you are. Most of us are born into a world—and even into loving, well-intentioned families—that whether knowingly or not, teach us to believe that we're not. I believe that if we choose to, it's possible to unlearn what we've been taught that doesn't feel right in our soul, take our power back, and decide today is the day to forge a new path ahead. If you feel me, say out loud wherever you are, "I'm ready!"

Don't think I didn't see you not say it. Listen, if you're not gonna be bold here along with me, how are you gonna be bold out there when things get hard? I'll say it with you. We'll say it together out loud. Who cares what anyone around you thinks? Okay, ready? Let's loudly proclaim it: "I'm ready!"

You don't become what you want, you become what you believe you're worthy of: in life, in love, in friendships, in your career, and in your hopes and dreams.

ONE OF THE greatest parts of your journey to believing you're worthy is learning to stop hiding. Learning, for the first time, or for the first time in a long time, the courage to start raising your hand. Or to be the person who leads and encourages others to raise theirs. To discover the true essence of your soul, of the real you, and to start *living* as the real you. Not your achievements, but your innateness that is full and whole and enough. And blossoming toward a new freedom and fulfillment that springs alive when we live in alignment with the true nature of the person we were born to be. And knowing in every ounce of our being that the person who we truly are is enough. And is worthy of love.

When you venture to stop hiding in plain sight, trust your inner knowing, live in congruence with your soul, ignite your purpose, and show up in this world as *all* of who you are, that's when you truly *feel* fulfilled and truly *feel* alive. That's when you live **in alignment with your assignment**. That's when you become who you were born to be. That's when you're able to fully live in and express the joy and the beauty and the gifts and the ideas and the possibilities of your soul. That's when you can wake up every morning and ask yourself one of life's most powerful questions: **What will you do with the power that is YOU?** And then with that power fully tapped into, and because you're no longer hiding it or hiding from it, **you bravely, boldly live the answer.**

THROUGHOUT THESE PAGES, I hope you'll laugh, connect, see, and be exactly YOU every step of the way. And like my good friend Sarah Jakes Roberts says, we didn't come here to look cute. We're gonna go deep. As deep as you're ready to. This book might feel like it's too much at times, or perhaps it will feel like you arrive at the end way too quickly. We'll examine our own self-worth, delve into the lies that keep us doubting ourselves, unlearn those lies, and embrace the truths that wake up worthiness. We'll begin our transformation into living authentically and fulfilling our destinies. There are some chapters packed with tactical tools you can apply to your life right now that have led to breakthroughs for me, like how to redefine rejection, how to rethink the labels you put on yourself, and how to take risks when you have a million reasons why you're afraid to. There are some chapters you might find to be deeply personal and stir up a lot of thought and emotion. Some chapters might evoke the feeling of heavy reflection, and others might spark joyful, wide-eyed, soul-filling delight. I know how precious the gift of your time is, and I can promise you I'm not taking a second of it for granted. In this book, I'm all in with you, right by your side, and we're really gonna go there together, okay! Soul to soul. Light to light. Love to love.

In this book, you're invited to embark on an expedition into the essence of who you are. At times it might feel like a courageous crossing, a treacherous trek, a laugh-out-loud fun-filled flight, or even a soul-savoring safari. Each chapter might be a destination you visit for a day or sit with for a while. The one thing I'll ask of you is this: in every story, every lesson, every silly embarrassing overshare, every vulnerable soul-stirring revelation, and every deeply challenging question, trust yourself to know if it is for you. And if it's not right for you, or you're not ready to consider it yet, then skip that part. And you will know, your soul will know, at each turn of this book, the parts that are for you in this moment of your journey. You'll know if the timing is not right to open up to yourself in ways that might feel like too much. And you'll know if the timing is *just right*, and the words feel like they're written exactly for you!

What will you do with the power that is YOU?

You may want to have a journal or pen and paper handy while reading. And as we begin this journey together, all I ask is that you trust yourself fully. Take the things that feel right for you and leave the rest. Perhaps for another day, or another person you share this book with.

I believe in divine timing and that our steps are divinely ordered in life, and I don't believe it's a coincidence or accident that you're reading these words right now. Similarly, in this book I'm leading you on an intentional journey, one transforming step at a time. Each chapter lays a key piece of the foundation, that then builds on the next. All crafting a deeply personal worthiness journey intended to expand how you see and unconditionally love yourself. From *seeing* the importance of and critical difference between self-confidence and self-worth, to *unlearning* the lies that lead to self-doubt and embracing the truths that wake up worthiness, to *transforming* your connection to yourself and multiplying your unconditional self-love, to *knowing* and truly believing in your innate value and worthiness.

As we begin this journey, I want to invite you to come with me, through these pages, as who you truly are. Not as the role you play at home or at work, not as who you have to be when you're the leader in the room, not as who other people want you to be, not as the version of you that the world rewards, not as the socially conditioned belief systems you've built. But as the person who sheds all of that and is willing to show up soul-first. Coming soul-first is safe here, knowing this truth: **There is nothing you can do or say or be that could ever make you unworthy of love. I believe we are all here to love. To receive it, to give it, to live it, to be it. And our greatest journey on this earth is to learn how and to truly believe we're worthy of it.**

My intention in the pages of this book, is that you experience the true feeling of *home* that fills your soul. And there's no greater feeling of home than living in alignment and congruence with your soul. With the true nature of who you are and who you were born to be. Fully worthy. And yet, when we aren't living the truest expression of our souls, it can feel like we're strangers in our own lives, as if we're living our lives away from our real home.

Our souls are our true home. The words in this book are a love poem from my soul to yours. Let's live in our souls, together on this journey. As we get started, I want you to feel like I'm welcoming you right into my home. When I imagine opening my front door to see you, I will really *see* you. And you can really *see* me. And when you walk in, I'm wearing my favorite cozy sweats, no makeup, unwashed hair in a messy bun (but I did use some dry shampoo in it because I knew you were coming!), and I give you a great big hug while my dogs are jumping on you and kissing you as if they'd never been through training school. I have your favorite warm drink in a coffee mug ready to greet you. That mug says WORTHY on it. Because you are. After I hand it to you, imagine seeing a sign right in front of you on the wall as you walk inside. It's how I want you to feel when you walk into my home, or into my hug.

The sign says:

Come as you are
Heal where you need
Blossom what you choose
Journey toward your calling
Stay as long as you'd like
You belong here
You are worthy
You are loved
You are love

I love you.
Jamie

Are you ready to get started? I'm ready if you are! As you're about to turn the page, I'm imagining reaching my hand out to yours right now . . . here we go . . .

PART ONE

SEEING

*Self-Confidence, Self-Worth,
and Self-Revelations*

CHAPTER 1

The One Thing That
Transforms Everything

*She said, "I'm just not giving up. The woman I'll be a few
years from now is counting on me." And the world shifted.*

— NAKEIA HOMER

HAVE YOU EVER been longing for *that thing* to happen, the thing
you're sure would *finally* make you happy and fulfilled, whether
it was landing a certain job, reaching some level of achievement, getting
married, having kids, hitting that goal weight? Have you thought, *When
I finally get the promotion, when I finally make a certain salary, when I
finally get the dream house, when I finally get the external recognition I'm
craving so deeply, when I finally feel celebrated by others, when I finally hit
that milestone . . . then I'll be enough. Then I'll finally feel fulfilled and
happy and . . . worthy!*

Have you ever had an experience when you actually got *that thing*
you'd been longing for? It probably felt amazing, right? Did you experience joy and elation? Did *that* thing *finally* happening solve all of your
feelings of emptiness and leave you with lasting fulfillment forever? Or
did you experience a temporary high, followed by a slow descent back to
unfulfillment? Be honest and really think about it. Did it feel incredible

for a year or two? A month or two? A few weeks, or maybe even a few days or hours? And then what?

Or maybe you're still waiting on *that* thing to finally happen, so you can then surely finally feel happy and fulfilled.

MOST OF MY life, I believed if I could just accomplish *that* thing, then I would finally feel enough. I thought that if I became successful enough, based on the world's definition of what success looks like, then I would eventually have these feelings of worthiness and love. That I wasn't capable of just feeling them on my own, that I needed to earn them and achieve them.

This belief drove me to spending most of my life hiding in plain sight, feeling unworthy. I imagined that one day I would achieve enough, get physically fit enough, eat healthy enough, pray enough, do the right thing enough, be attractive enough, become funny enough, please everyone else enough, be celebrated enough, be selfless enough and resolve all of my perceived flaws, and *then* I would be worthy. *Then* my feelings of self-doubt would be resolved. I also used to think I was all alone in feeling this way.

After decades of life experience, and the blessing of growing a company that served millions of people across the US and eventually the world, I finally understand that I'm not alone in these feelings. The sense that you're not enough and therefore you're undeserving of love is as close to universal as a feeling and a fear can be.

Through meeting so many of my greatest heroes in real life, many of whom have accomplished more than I could imagine, I learned they still have these exact same fears. And they work daily to overcome them. It was then that I had a huge epiphany. Waiting on x, y, or z to happen and then expecting to feel happy, fulfilled, and worthy is never going to happen. **Nothing actually changes, even when things change all around you, unless things also change within you.** That is why embarking on the journey of truly learning to believe you're worthy will impact every other part of your life in a way that accomplishments, relationship status, job titles, gold medals, cosmetic surgery, material possessions, or the number on the bathroom scale never can.

So what does make us feel truly fulfilled? That's what this chapter is all about. And just FYI, we're gonna get tactical here and I am going to share some foundational tools that will help set up many of the lessons in the book to come. So get ready, class is about to be in session, but like I said earlier, we didn't come here to look cute. Your time is precious, so let's roll up our sleeves together and dive in, as these concepts are core to the wild journey of unlocking worthiness we're going to take together!

Self-Worth and Self-Confidence

Your self-worth is the foundation of your fulfillment. And without it, you'll never feel truly fulfilled. But before we go any further, I want to clarify the difference between self-worth and self-confidence. They're two very different things, but we so easily confuse them. And many of us spend our entire lives focused only on things that build our self-confidence, not realizing they do nothing to build our self-worth, which is a huge reason that when we finally do get *that* thing, and the next thing, we're still left feeling unfulfilled.

Self-worth is the internal, deep-rooted belief that you are enough and worthy of love and belonging, **just as you are**. On the other hand, *self-confidence, while also an internal trait,* is generally linked to your assessment of how you compare to the outside world. It is the feeling of assuredness, certainty, and competence in one or more specific areas of your life. *Self-confidence* is how you evaluate yourself based on your qualities, skills, and traits. It's also how strongly you believe in your ability to meet life's challenges, your willingness to try and go for it, and to succeed. *Self-confidence* is linked to external things that can fluctuate often, so your self-confidence can also fluctuate often. It can rise and fall based on mood, comparisons, circumstances, performance, and approval from others. *Self-worth* is believing you are enough, lovable, and valuable innately and exactly as you are, regardless of how you evaluate your traits and independent of what's happening around you.

There are also several other commonly used terms that are easily confused with *self-worth* and *self-confidence*, including *self-esteem* and *self-love*. To avoid confusion and for maximum clarity, in this book we'll focus solely on the terms *self-worth* and *self-confidence*. While both *self-confidence* and *self-worth* are important to your overall well-being, to maintaining healthy and fulfilling relationships, to building physical and mental health, and to enjoying greater success in the areas that matter to you most, it's *so* common to confuse the two. Which is why so many of us who struggle with feeling unworthy, or as if we're not enough as we are, hope to fix our lack of *self-worth* (which is deep, internal, not dependent on the external), with things that only help our *self-confidence* (which fluctuates depending on the external). And no matter how much we achieve, how many personal or career goals we accomplish, how large our following on social media is, how great our outfit looks, or how svelte a figure our most recent fitness or weight-loss goal leaves us, we're still left with the same feelings of *not-enoughness* deep down inside.

When we achieve everything we set out to accomplish, we help boost *self-confidence*, which is important and wonderful! But we haven't done the work to help bolster *self-worth*, which is different.

Self-confidence is what you show on the outside.
Self-worth is what you feel on the inside.

Self-confidence is based on mastery.
Self-worth is based on identity.

Self-confidence is what you can do.
Self-worth is who you are.

Self-confidence is believing you're skilled enough.
Self-worth is believing you ARE enough.

Self-confidence fluctuates based on your environment.
Self-worth is stable through every environment.

Self-confidence is fragile.
Self-worth is foundational.

Self-confidence is the belief in your abilities as a person.
Self-worth is the belief in your value as a person.

Self-confidence is "I'm striving to earn love."
Self-worth is knowing "I am love."

Self-confidence gives you drive.
Self-worth gives you peace.

Self-confidence is optional.
Self-worth is essential.

Self-confidence eventually surrenders.
Self-worth ultimately prevails.

Self-worth is your foundation.
Self-confidence is the house you build on top of it.
Your house will only ever be as secure as the foundation it's
built upon.

The common misconception is that building self-confidence will give you feelings of innate love, *enoughness*, and value, and it simply doesn't. Only self-worth does that. Both self-confidence and self-worth play a very important role in your journey to ultimate fulfillment in life, and while it's important to continuously build and strengthen both, it's also so important to understand and differentiate between the two. So often people focus on self-confidence alone and don't understand or aren't aware of how critical a role self-worth plays. With strong self-worth, when you go after your pursuits, and build self-confidence, and achieve and grow and contribute to the world and to others, you can do it all on the foundation that you're worthy, whole, lovable, and enough. When it comes to the meaningful pursuits in your life, only a foundation of strong self-worth can ensure these three important things—first, that you don't stay stuck because you feel unworthy or not enough to go after them. Second, that you don't sabotage your success along the way. And third, that when you do achieve the things you want in your life, you're able to actually enjoy them and feel **fulfilled** in the journey.

Self-worth is your foundation. Self-confidence is the house you build on top of it. Your house will only ever be as secure as the foundation it's built upon.

Your **self-worth** is independent of what's happening on the outside. It's independent of your strengths and weaknesses. It's independent of your successes and failures. Your **self-confidence** fluctuates easily based on circumstances that are often external.

Self-confidence can shatter when we face a painful failure, a setback, or rejection. When we have self-confidence without strong underlying self-worth, we're less likely to take risks. We don't want the pain associated with losing our self-confidence and feeling like we have nothing left. Strong self-confidence without strong self-worth often keeps us stuck—afraid to take chances, afraid of rejection, and afraid of potential failure. Almost everything around us in life—every product, every consumer message, every goal we're told to strive for—all simply build self-confidence alone, which can be fragile and volatile. But when we have strong self-worth, it gives us a resilient core that is much more difficult to diminish.

What might seem counterintuitive at first is that when you have strong self-worth and believe you're enough exactly as you are, you don't become complacent and lose ambition. It's actually the opposite. The stronger your self-worth is, the less complacent you are, because you're no longer affected by most of the reasons causing you to stay stuck. There's a famous saying in boxing that a boxer gets 30 percent better after they win the title. Because their self-confidence boosts and identity boosts simply from winning the title. I would venture to bet the opposite is true too—that after a loss, the toll on a boxer's confidence would diminish performance. But either way, their performance fluctuates along with their confidence in response to external circumstances. The beauty about strong self-worth is that it doesn't fluctuate easily in response to external wins or losses.

With strong self-worth as your foundation, you become unwaveringly resilient, and that is how you become unstoppable on your journey of becoming all of who you're born to be.

Self-Confidence Without Self-Worth

Whether you're in a highly celebrated or public role, or you're a behind-the-scenes kind of person, even if you have all of the self-confidence in the world, you're equally likely to hide in plain sight, or not show up to others as your true authentic self, when you're lacking deep self-worth. Even when it's undetectable to anyone else. When you walk into a room, and even talk to everyone in that room, but know that no one truly sees the real you. That you're showing up, in a way, disassociated from the real you. I like to call this showing up as your "representative" rather than your full self. That representative might even change based on what room you walk into. Whether it's the boardroom, the classroom, or your own living room and bedroom. **Every time you show up inauthentically, or as your representative, or as the person you think will make other people happy, you tell yourself you're unworthy as your true self.** This leaves us feeling unseen and disconnected, even if we're the ones deciding not to be seen for who we truly are. And this is much more likely to happen when at our core we don't believe we're enough and worthy of love innately.

Self-confidence without self-worth looks like abundant approval on the outside and lack of fulfillment on the inside. Self-confidence without self-worth feels like success on the outside but failure on the inside. It's why you can win the Ironman or walk on the moon or win the Olympic gold medal, only to return home and, shortly after, feel incredibly unfulfilled. It's why you can finally achieve that fitness or health goal, or get the huge promotion at work, and still wonder why you don't feel the love or lasting fulfillment you hoped you would.

> *Every time you show up inauthentically to make others happy, you tell yourself you're unworthy as your true self.*

When you improve self-confidence, you're bolstering your opinion of your own traits and abilities. When you improve self-worth, you bolster the deep belief within you of your own value as a person. Learning this distinction makes it easy to understand how all of the solutions most people advise us to do, and that we've gone after, haven't ever worked the way we had hoped. They're usually solutions derived from external sources, which are important to help us grow in our confidence, but don't actually help us grow in our own core belief about our worthiness.

Achievement Doesn't Lead to Love or Fulfillment

All things we strive for, in any area of our life, all come down to one simple thing. We hope they'll make us feel enough and loved. Don't believe me? Sound too simple? Let's break it down.

After their most basic needs are met and they're financially secure, why is it that most people still want even more money? To buy things? Why do they want those things? To feel important, to gain external admiration, or for the positive emotions they expect to experience when they have them? Why do they want that? Because underneath all of it, they want to feel enough and loved, and they believe that acquiring *these things* will give them *these feelings*. Often people get married when they don't want to, make decisions to avoid feeling like they will be abandoned, have kids when they're not ready, and take jobs they dislike all to get their families' or society's approval, to fulfill the same hope and need to feel *enough* and loved. So many of us spend the majority of our lives on the unhealthy diet trend of the moment and

Self-confidence without self-worth can feel like success on the outside but failure on the inside.

spend countless hours and money to try to look a certain way. Others take harmful drugs to enhance their muscles or trade the maximum amount of their time on this earth for the maximum amount of money, prestigious cars, and job titles they can acquire. All with the underlying belief that the closer we get to an aesthetic ideal, the more we'll be enough and loved. And these beliefs are often reinforced as truths by well-intentioned people around us, and just about every advertisement we see. None of these things we spend so much time striving for actually leads us to the true feeling of being enough, truly loved, or truly fulfilled. But these beliefs don't foster fulfillment because they aren't truths at all, they are all based on the same lie: that you need to achieve, to do more and be more in order to feel love.

It's very common to believe this lie, but it's a never-ending dead end when it comes to worthiness. Don't get me wrong—the journey of going after your hopes, ambitions, and dreams is a beautiful path to building self-confidence. And it's a key part of living the highest, fullest expression of yourself. It can make you feel confident, strong, and many other positive emotions and feelings, but never worthy.

"You need to achieve in order to be worthy of love" is a lie that is often reinforced by well-intentioned friends and colleagues who only ask us what we're *doing* and what we're up to, instead of how we're *being* or how we really are. Well-intentioned family members only want to know how our job or career is going, if we're dating or married yet, and what we're doing next. When we deliver answers that demonstrate achievement in any of these areas, they are often met with an approving smile, congratulatory words, and recognition that can be confused with love. We receive similar messages in other areas of life: you're a good parent if your kids get into a good school, get a good job, get married, and start a family. And if your kids do none of those things, even if they're wonderfully happy, the concern and pity that others show reinforces the message that you must have done something wrong as a parent and you should be worried about your children. Similarly, social media projects the notion that everyone else is happy because in their posts they seem to be doing so much, achieving so much, traveling so much, and having so much fun. And the more exciting their lives look, the more they are rewarded with likes and comments. This cultural obsession with achievement can certainly stimulate the economy, but when generations are taught that hard work, career progression, recognition, and monetary achievement are the ultimate goal, it doesn't foster learning innate worthiness or true fulfillment.

FOR MOST OF my life, I believed the lie that if I could achieve what our culture calls success, if I could look a certain way, if I could please everyone else and check all of the boxes, then I'd be fulfilled. Then, after spending decades of my life striving for *it all*, I got a whole lot of *it all* and nothing changed. Because as I arrived at each new destination, and crossed each celebratory finish line, **I still took *me* with *me*.**

I learned firsthand that no amount of money or fame actually helps you feel more enough and more loved. Nothing actually changed, because the core of my own self-worth was always the same—and almost always low. My self-confidence increased, my bank account increased, the approval and praise I got from others increased. But none of those things impacts self-worth. And none leads to true fulfillment.

Let me repeat that: **No matter what you accomplish or what finally happens in your life, you still take YOU WITH YOU!** Meaning, if you're still standing there with the same circumstances inside, there's nothing outside that can fill up the inside, at least not for long. We so often spend our whole lives delaying our happiness and worthiness under the false pretense that when we finally get this or that, then we will feel fulfilled.

It's fun to win and often so fun to celebrate a victory, but it doesn't change how "enough" you feel. So the real work is learning how to believe and feel enough and fulfilled right now, exactly as your circumstances are, and exactly as you are . . . as the **you** that **YOU** take with **you**. The you that's innate. The you that doesn't need any icing on the cake because it knows it's already sweet and filling enough.

THE JOURNEY OF unlearning all of the lies our conditioned belief system believes and learning how to hear our own knowing, trust ourselves, and believe we are truly worthy exactly as we are is one of the greatest and most important journeys we will ever take, if we choose to, in this lifetime.

If you're someone who, perhaps, is a lifelong student like I am, and you love personal growth and development, here's something that might be a huge aha moment for you. Perhaps you've read countless books and perhaps even attended events where you identified the limiting beliefs that have been holding you back in your life. For example: "I'm not attractive enough," "I'm not funny or interesting enough to attract a potential partner," "I don't have enough money," "I don't have the right education," "I'm too young or too old," "I'll never become wealthy," "I'm an imposter," or "My business won't ever succeed," etc. Then perhaps you practiced tools and methods to replace those limiting beliefs with empowering ones. Well, here's the thing, almost all of the most common limiting beliefs are tied to self-confidence or external circumstances. Building confidence and learning to believe the things you hope and dream of are actually possible for you in your life is an important endeavor. But there is a big problem and missed opportunity in how most people, life coaches, thought leaders, and even many of the most sought-after experts approach overcoming limiting beliefs and creating the life you desire.

They almost always focus solely on how overcoming limiting beliefs will only lead to better self-confidence. People are left with the impression that if they build their skill sets and grow their confidence, that's enough, but they completely miss a critical step: if you only begin to confidently believe those things are *possible* for you, but don't innately believe you are *worthy* of them, you likely won't keep them if you get them. Even more important, you'll never feel fulfilled in life if you don't ALSO overcome limiting beliefs around self-worth. Perhaps you have limiting beliefs (or stories you believe to be true about yourself) such as "I don't come from the right family" or "I'm not good-looking enough" or "I'll never make a ton of money" or "I'm a bad mom" or "I've made too many bad decisions" or "I'm scared to try and take a risk" or "I break promises to myself and never stick to a workout routine" or "I'm an imposter and not deserving of this CEO title." If you do the work to overcome those limiting beliefs and replace them with new empowering beliefs, it will boost your self-confidence and improve your life greatly. But it won't lead to fulfillment in life. It's just one piece of the equation.

See, you can do all the work overcoming limiting beliefs and building a confident identity around how smart you are, talented you are, hardworking you are, how you keep promises to yourself and others, how devout your spiritual practice is, how you live your values and treat others well, and how you put goodness out into the world. And when you do all these things, they're so important for an improved, beautiful, strong self-confidence and external identity . . . but if your internal identity around self-worth doesn't feel valuable, enough, and worthy of love exactly as you are with or without all of those things, then you can achieve them all but you'll still never feel fulfilled.

If you or someone you know, love, or care about continues to achieve it all, accomplish it all, work on all the things that we know lead to a greater sense of self-confidence but STILL feels unfulfilled and can't figure out why . . . this is why. Because you're growing in the areas and beliefs about yourself and your own identity that boost self-confidence, but not in the ones that boost self-worth. You can accomplish all your self-confidence-building pursuits successfully, build great assuredness and skill, and achieve goals that align with a high external identity, but you will still only reach a level of fulfillment and sustainability that reflects your own internal identity around worthiness. You can achieve all the things that make it look like you're a success, but if your internal identity and self-worth still tell you you're not enough or not worthy of love and belonging, then you'll feel imposter syndrome when you reach a goal, you'll feel like it's never enough no matter how much you accomplish, you'll feel unworthy of love and not understand why you feel empty in a relationship. You can live out and experience every great thing in the world and feel unfulfilled the entire time because your deep sense of self-worth has debilitating cracks in the foundation.

The Path to Fulfillment

I love a great visual! And where you fall on the one below impacts all areas of your life. Take a look at this chart that explores the relationship between self-worth and self-confidence on the path toward fulfillment.

Later in this book, I'll share a powerful tool around gaining *ultimate fulfillment* in life. But first, it's important to note where you fall on this WORTHY *Self-Worth* and *Self-Confidence* Chart right now in your life.

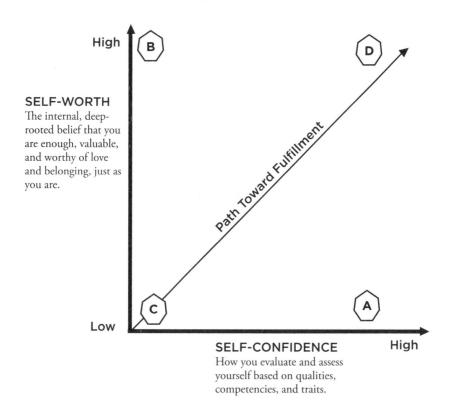

WORTHY
Self-Worth and Self-Confidence Chart
©Jamie Kern Lima

SELF-WORTH
The internal, deep-rooted belief that you are enough, valuable, and worthy of love and belonging, just as you are.

Path Toward Fulfillment

High

Low

SELF-CONFIDENCE   High
How you evaluate and assess yourself based on qualities, competencies, and traits.

When you see this chart on self-worth and self-confidence, I want you to consider how almost every effort, action, focus, and goal falls under the self-confidence category. But notice on the chart that no matter how far to the right you succeed on the self-confidence (horizontal) scale, you will only progress up the path toward fulfillment to the level you rise and soar on the self-worth (vertical) scale.

Self-Worth, Self-Confidence, and Your Identity

Your identity is the story you tell yourself about yourself, and the story you believe. No matter our intentions, we always find ourselves returning to behaviors, actions, and decisions that reinforce our beliefs about who we are. This is why so many people do such deep work overcoming limiting beliefs in their life. Because if they don't, those limiting beliefs will hold them back from believing their hopes and dreams are possible.

The more self-worth and self-confidence you have, the more fulfilled, emotionally and physically well, and happy you feel. Research shows that self-worth is one of the best predictors of personal happiness. One study from the Berkeley Well-Being Institute shows that worthiness is a better predictor of happiness than nineteen other emotional processes including strong personal relationships and gratitude.

Let's take a look at four examples of where people fall on this chart, and in particular what happens if you have either self-confidence or self-worth without the other. And as you read each description, note where they visually fall on the chart.

Person A is very high on self-confidence but low on self-worth. They're incredibly successful on the outside, likely a high achiever with career or financial success, but whatever they achieve, it never feels like it's enough, and they are perpetually unfulfilled. Perfectionists are often A's.

Person B has very high self-worth but very low self-confidence. They likely feel a deep sense of peace and love, yet don't feel competent or confident in their own skills and abilities that indicate external measures of success. They may or may not have any drive to achieve more, but are at peace either way, regardless of the outcome of their external pursuits or even if they choose not to have external pursuits.

Person C has low self-worth and low self-confidence and may be at the infancy of their journey of awareness around, and commitment to, building one or both.

Person D has a strong inherent self-worth and assesses themselves to have high levels of skills and attributes. This person has high ambition and drive, but because they also have strong self-worth, they're not trying to fill a void of not being enough, lovable, or worthy through external accomplishments. They remain unshakable internally, even through the highs, lows, risks, rewards, successes, and failures of their external ambitions. They feel a deep sense of self-worth as well as self-confidence.

Where would you place yourself on this chart right now? Take a moment and mark where you feel you truly are right now. Then, mark where you'd like to be in your life.

Next, consider where your close friends, family members, and colleagues might fall on this chart. Are they aware of the ways their current levels of self-confidence and self-worth impact all areas of their lives?

If this is a huge aha for you, and if you know someone else right now who has been hustling and hustling, thinking that if they could only accomplish those things in the self-confidence column, then they would finally love themselves, then they would finally be enough, please pause and share this book with them. No girl, no woman, no person left behind in learning how to foster true self-worth. Because we're in a society that tells us if we could only be person **A**, we would be happy. And that's a lie.

See, I've been person **A** for most of my adult life. Thinking if I could just achieve enough, commit to my fitness routine enough, read enough books, contribute enough, fit into that one pair of jeans, please enough people, become the world's definition of success enough, *then* I would finally *be enough*. And then that's when I would finally be happy. And it's all a lie. Because no amount of success on the self-confidence scale leads to true fulfillment.

When I received Oprah's cell number, then didn't call her for over four years, I was living as an **A** on the Worthy Chart. I felt confident in my skills, talents, and abilities. I had just been named to the *Forbes* list and was one of a small number of women who had started an idea in their living room and built it into a company as large as IT Cosmetics had become. I was passionate about my personal and our company's philanthropic efforts. I felt confident in my life's purpose of helping women truly believe they're enough. But still, deep down inside, I didn't yet feel like I was enough. As I was sitting there having lunch with Oprah and talking about many vibrant topics for more than four hours, I had high self-confidence, but deep down inside I didn't have strong self-worth. And I didn't yet understand the difference between the two. So, when she shared her phone number with me, I failed to seize the blessing and didn't call her for four years. That's what low self-worth will do to us. It makes us feel undeserving and not valuable enough or lovable enough as we are. It convinces us to sabotage opportunities and possibilities because we don't believe we're worthy of them.

AS I'VE APPLIED this revelation and concept to my own life, along with the lives of many others I've begun so passionately sharing it with, it's been eye-opening how widespread the misconception of confusing self-confidence with self-worth is, and just how detrimental it is in guiding so many people toward an unfulfilling life. Even people who have the privilege of access to therapy, coaching, and education, and even people who coach others on or teach personal fulfillment for a living.

I was recently having lunch with a friend who has incredibly high self-confidence and by all external measures is successful financially, socially, and in his decades-long career. In our conversation, he was reflecting on his past career success in the corporate world and sharing how painful a recent setback had been in his business. He had made a decision that had cost him both money and notoriety. Mid-conversation he blurted out something that made my jaw hit the floor.

"I used to be somebody," my friend declared.

"WTF!" I exclaimed. (Sorry, Grandma.) "What do you mean you used to be somebody? Everybody is somebody. You've got some major work to do around worthiness right now." I was very direct with him.

He instantly stopped short and just stared at me. After a few moments of silence, his eyes began to tear up ever so slightly. Even though he was someone who many others turned to for advice, it was apparent that he still believed that external validation would lead to worthiness. A mistake that is so easy to make. Plus, he was now in a spot in his life where he had low self-worth and, for one of the first times in his adult life, low self-confidence at the same time. He had been living his life as an **A** on the Worthy Chart: very self-confident with a lot of external success, but because he never felt fulfilled, he had spent his entire life striving for even more success, hoping worthiness and fulfillment would eventually come. Now, given his recent external setbacks, he was living as a **C** on the chart, and was low in both areas. When he said the words *I used to be somebody*, it broke my heart. And because of his beliefs around unworthiness, he was breaking his own.

So many of the things we worry about, so many of the things we let hold us back, so many of the lies about our worth we waste time believing to be true, don't actually matter. Life is way too short to believe the lie that they do. The more and more conversations I have, where I listen to someone explaining how unworthy they feel and how they hide it from the world, the more I'm resolved to spend this one beautiful life believing I'm worthy and valuable, exactly as I am. And I don't want to leave anyone else behind on their own journey of worthiness. I want you to know that you are valuable and worthy of love, right now, in this very moment, exactly as you are. You are SOMEBODY. Nothing on the outside, nothing you fearfully fail at or victoriously achieve, no past mistake you've made, nothing anyone else says or doesn't say about you, can change that. They can't give it to you, and they can't take it away. It already IS. And is already TRUE. And the SOMEBODY that is you is fully worthy.

Self-Worth and Its Impact on Your Most Important Relationships

When you confuse self-confidence and self-worth, it can also affect the level of depth of connection you experience in your relationship with yourself, your friends, and your peers, and often in your intimate relationships as well.

Self-worth-related issues are often the kind of issues that couples keep from each other. Most people only share when they're facing issues that fall into the self-confidence category. But when it comes to the issues of self-worth, most of us either aren't aware of them or don't want to acknowledge, share, or discuss them with our partners or anyone else. We not only keep them to ourselves, but we also bury them deep inside. Though buried, they're still there and they impact all areas of our life.

The first and most important person you have to be honest with about self-worth is yourself. And let's talk about perceptions around the idea of self-worth and self-love for a moment. Sometimes we don't focus on learning to love ourselves because we worry it seems selfish or self-centered or even narcissistic. This couldn't be further from the truth. In fact, narcissism is not about self-love at all, it's actually the opposite and is one of the most shame-based of all personality disorders. Narcissism actually comes from deep feelings of unworthiness and shame. It is driven by self-hatred. All the grandiosity, superiority, and entitlement that's often displayed with it—that could be mistaken for self-love—are actually attempts to compensate for low self-regard.

Cultivating self-worth inside of you is one of the greatest ways to show love to others.

Cultivating true self-worth is one of the most generous pursuits not only for your own fulfillment in life, but for your capacity to show love to others. Research shows that without self-love we're more prone to addictions, self-sabotage, unhealthy relationship patterns with our body and with others, co-dependency, people-pleasing, and other self-destructive behaviors.

Our kids, too, often neglect their self-worth. With parents and others they trust, they will usually share their struggles that fall into the self-confidence category, around external circumstances, or their own perceived abilities, external experiences, or competencies. But they often don't share their deep beliefs around whether they feel innately worthy of love and belonging. If something or someone hurts their self-confidence, they'll tell us, but if something or someone hurts their deep sense of self-worth, they often won't. If you are a parent, this is one more reason to do the work of truly understanding and building self-worth in your own life, so you can better equip your little ones to know how to nurture and continue building theirs too.

Similarly, in marriage, if your partner is having some problem that's tied to external, achievement-based, skill-based, or even confidence-based issues, they'll be more likely to share it with you than if they're struggling with a deep, internal self-worth issue. In our society, it's much more acceptable, if not expected, that men will hide their self-worth issues. Then the pain of those issues transmits in endless, often hurtful ways to themselves and those around them, whether through disconnection, disassociation, or sabotage. What's most often the case is neither partner is aware of the true underlying issues tied to self-worth, and that two partners live inside a relationship with no idea why it feels so disconnected, lonely, or like the other person is hiding something, when in fact they're both hiding from themselves and their own awareness. **You can only experience the depth of love, intimacy, and connection with another person as the depth you love and intimately connect with yourself.**

I've embraced my own self-worth in stages, through the awareness and tools that I'm sharing with you in this book. That's how I eventually, finally, got up the courage to call Oprah. From there, I gradually believed I was worthy of teaching alongside her. And now we have a beautiful friendship. I recently invited her over for lunch at my house—we called it a *Worthy Weekend*. I know she loves these special English muffins, so I had them overnighted from a small bakery in Napa for her, and she knows I love cozy blankets, so she brought me her favorite blanket as a gift. Now don't get me wrong, I'm still tempted to freak out right before she arrives, I still feel butterflies in my stomach, and I still immediately have to practice many of the tools in this book to remember, then know, that just like you and every one of us is, I am fully worthy and enough, exactly as I am. Even at a *worthy weekend* lunch with Oprah.

Soaring Self-Worth

When you improve self-worth and your inherent belief that you are worthy as a human exactly as you are, it gives you the knowing that you are innately valuable and *enough*, regardless of any achievement, compliment, award, or circumstance. Research shows building our worthiness can impact everything from our mood to the quality of our relationships to our job satisfaction.

Remember, you can build your self-confidence like a house on top of the foundation. Strong self-worth, knowing you are enough exactly as you are, is that foundation holding your house up and allowing you to actually enjoy the pursuit of building it. **True self-worth can give you a stable, dependable, unwavering, unshakable sense of mental and emotional armor that, unlike self-confidence, isn't easily swayed by feelings, thoughts, behaviors, experiences, and the external forces life inevitably throws your way.** Self-worth gives you a foundation of unwavering strength and resilience, even if the house comes crashing down in a storm of blows to your self-confidence in the form of setbacks, failures, rejections, and changes to external circumstances. Self-worth helps you endure all of these. So, let's get busy building it!

CHAPTER 2

Change Your Relationship
with Rejection, Change Your Life

I've missed more than 9,000 shots in my career. I've lost almost 300 games. Twenty-six times I've been trusted to take the game-winning shot and missed. I've failed over and over and over again in my life. And that is why I succeed.

— MICHAEL JORDAN

WHAT WOULD YOU do in your life if you had absolutely zero fear of rejection or failure? If there were such thing as having a master's degree in rejection, I'm pretty sure I have one. I've spent most of my life feeling and fearing countless rejections and failures. Many of my most painful rejections have come from the voice inside my own head, telling me I'm not enough and don't have what it takes. Every time someone asks me about the successes I've had in my life, I can't help but think about how they almost didn't happen. Had I not changed my relationship with rejection and failure, I never could have mustered the courage to get back up every time I got knocked down when growing my business. After one, or twenty, or a hundred rejections, I would have quit. Had I not changed my relationship with rejection, I never could have pursued finding my birth mom, who placed me into adoption the day I was born. I never could have asked Paulo, the man who would one day become my husband, if he wanted to study together, knowing he might say he wasn't interested. I never would have taught a course alongside Oprah, because I wouldn't have believed I was worthy of it.

Mark Leary, a professor of psychology and neuroscience at Duke, has conducted research on the fear of rejection. Leary says, "Whether one considers a romantic rejection, the dissolution of a friendship, ostracism by a group, estrangement from family members, or merely being ignored or excluded in casual encounters, rejections have myriad emotional, psychological, and interpersonal consequences. People not only react strongly when they perceive that others have rejected them, but a great deal of human behavior is influenced by the desire to avoid rejection."

Fear of rejection and fear of failure are two of the biggest reasons people hold back from taking a chance, stay stuck, never share their ideas, talk themselves out of pursuing their dreams, and never reveal who they truly are and how they truly feel.

Rejection and Failure

First, I want to clarify that rejection and failure are not the same— but we fear and react to failure and rejection similarly, and we can use the same strategies to change our relationship with both of them.

At our core, we all want to be loved and to belong, and for so many of us, we equate rejection or failure with the exact opposite of love and belonging. We equate them with pain and exclusion. And they certainly can feel like that if you choose to let them. And the key is the word *choose*. What if I told you that you could actually embrace and look forward to rejection and failure? Would you think that was even possible? My guess is you would probably dismiss that idea and think I'm making up some BS. Except I'm not.

Everything in life simply carries the meaning we attach to it. That meaning creates the emotions we feel around it. And the emotions we feel then create our life experience. When you change the meaning

you assign to something, and truly believe that meaning, everything shifts. Disappointment becomes divine trust. Self-loathing becomes gratitude. Rejection becomes resiliency. Self-worth solidifies.

My husband, Paulo, grew up believing that if he didn't know the answer to something, he had failed. If he couldn't win at a sport, then he didn't want to keep playing at all. On his worst days he decided that losing a game meant *he* was a failure. He worked really hard to unlearn this. Paulo loves tennis, pádel, and pickleball, and he's had to work really hard to assign new meanings to the activity of playing. He had to learn not to let playing poorly steal his joy or love of the game. These days, failing to win the match no longer means he shouldn't play or that he's a failure. It now means he's a competitive player who loves the game so much he can't wait for a rematch!

In contrast, my friend Sara Blakely, founder of the billion-dollar company Spanx, was raised by a dad who had the family make it a practice to sit around the dinner table and share one thing they failed at that day. In that environment, failure was honored as important, because it meant they weren't afraid to take risks. As they went around the table, one at a time, family members of all ages would share one thing they had tried and failed at that day. Is it any wonder that Sara courageously started a company with only an idea and $5,000, and was willing to take risks, enduring setbacks and rejections, and stick with it until it succeeded?

> *When you change your relationship with rejection and failure, you change your entire life.*

When you change your relationship with rejection and failure, you change your entire life.

You have the power to transform rejection and failure from experiences you dread to ones that you embrace fearlessly. When you acquire the tools to change your relationship with rejection, you can apply them to any area of your life.

I CAN SIT here right now and tell you that while I have plenty of issues and challenges in my life, fear of rejection or failure isn't one of them. I am fearless when it comes to rejection. Absolutely fearless. Not afraid of it one bit. I wasn't always that way, not even by a long shot.

I have a skin condition called rosacea. It shows up in the form of bright red patches that are rough in texture all across my cheeks, and sometimes my forehead as well. When I'm having a bad flare-up, it gets bumpy also. It's hereditary and there's no cure. After seeing several dermatologists and trying multiple prescription creams that didn't work, I went through a season in my life of feeling down.

In my late twenties to early thirties, I was working as a TV news anchor, and the rosacea flare-ups started getting so bad that the makeup wouldn't stay on my skin. I would be live on television, and the hot high-definition lights would cause the makeup to start separating, revealing the red patches I was desperately trying to cover. The producers in my earpiece would often alert me live during the newscast to say, "Something's on your face." I feared losing my job.

I never left the house without makeup. When I did, strangers at the coffee shop or grocery store would often ask me, "Are you feeling okay?" or they would say, "Wow, got a bad sunburn, huh?"

One day I was rushing to get my errands in and stopped by the grocery store, makeup-free. In the produce aisle, I noticed a woman who looked to be in her late twenties staring at me. She too was makeup-free and had a lot of hyperpigmentation, patches all across her face that were several shades darker than the rest of her skin. She gave me a smile that said to me, *Thank you*, without saying a word.

It was a huge light-bulb moment for me. I realized that by showing up with bright red rosacea across my face, I made her feel less alone with her patches of hyperpigmentation fully exposed. In that moment, her courage and my courage met. In a world that tells us to hide any part of us that is rejected by societal norms, we accepted each other. We deemed each other approved. Beautiful. Worthy. Smiling, we held eye contact for a moment, then went about the rest of our day.

In that moment, I changed the meaning I had been assigning to my rosacea. Before, I had labeled it with words like *embarrassing, shameful, unattractive, flawed.* That day I decided to assign an entirely new meaning to it. One that was about something so much bigger than me. I decided my rosacea was a superpower. And that every time I bared it publicly, it would help reverse shame around how others might be feeling about their own perceived imperfections. Every time I walked out into the world barefaced, makeup-free, I marveled at the idea that it might make one other person that day feel more *enough* and more liberated. I literally, in every ounce of my being, changed the meaning I attached to my own "flaw."

IN MY FIRST book, *Believe IT,* I shared in detail the journey of growing my company, IT Cosmetics, from my living room, and facing years and years of countless rejections. I want to share a very small, select part of that journey now, but through a totally different lens.

During the years of countless rejections building IT, one of the things most of the beauty stores told me while saying *no* to carrying my products was that "women will never buy makeup from images like the ones you're using, showing real skin challenges. Women will only buy makeup from images that show unattainable aspiration." They always used those words *unattainable aspiration,* meaning nobody could ever actually look like that. They wanted me to use photoshopped, faked images of flawless skin. But I knew in my gut that I could create a company that made women feel the way that the other woman and I felt in the grocery store that day. If I could truly SEE other women, if we could SEE each other, then it could be so much bigger than just a company. It could be a powerful and much-needed message and movement. This approach was needed and could be healing.

After years of hearing *no* and "you're not the right fit," I ended up getting a *yes* and one shot to appear on the TV shopping channel QVC in a ten-minute segment. I would be on the live real-time broadcast, being shown to 100 million homes, and I needed to sell around $10,000 of product per minute for all ten minutes I was given in the segment to hit their sales goal or I would not be invited back. Everything was on the line in this one shot. The third-party consultants I'd hired all told me the same thing I'd been hearing from most beauty stores: that in order to have even a slim chance of succeeding on QVC, of hitting their sales targets and being invited back, I needed to produce my ten-minute spot using models with flawless skin. That was what had worked for many of the other makeup brands. When I suggested showing my bare face with its bright red rosacea, and casting models who also had what the world told them were embarrassing skin challenges, like acne or hyperpigmentation, the consultants were mortified at the idea. They gave me the best advice they knew, which was not to do that.

Now, at the time I was given this one big shot on QVC, I had been receiving hundreds of rejections by potential retailers for years. No one thought my idea of showing real women as models would work, and they weren't willing to bet on me. My company was on the verge of bankruptcy. But I knew what I had felt in that moment in the grocery store.

And when I walked into the QVC studio to get my one shot, and the on-air lights went on, and the ten-minute countdown clock started, I was shaking. And to be fully transparent, I wasn't just shaking, I was sweating and praying the sweat hadn't soaked through the two pairs of Spanx I had on under my dress, in an attempt to absorb it.

See, in that moment, if I took a huge risk and followed my gut telling me to show the world my bare skin and other real women's skin issues, I might fail to hit their sales goal. And if the product didn't sell with everything on the line, my company could end up bankrupt. But I decided that I would be brave. That I might be rejected by viewers who vote with their wallets and not welcomed back by QVC, but I would know I was one of the brave ones willing to trust myself. And I decided that even though most of my life I had never left the house without makeup, I was going to reveal my skin "flaws" on national television because I no longer attached negative meaning to them. I attached positive, empowering meaning to them. The third-party consultants adamantly disagreed with my decision. But it felt right in my soul.

AS THE RED on-air light turned on indicating we were broadcasting live, and the ten-minute clock started ticking down, 9:58, 9:57, I was literally shaking like a leaf on the outside, but unwavering on the inside. I remember the moment my bright red bareface "Before" shot came up on national television. I remember walking over to the models, all real women of all ages, shapes, sizes, skin tones, and skin challenges, and calling them beautiful—and meaning it!

A few minutes in I didn't know how sales were going, but I knew they hadn't cut me off early or eliminated my time yet. Right before my one big shot, I learned that you're not actually even guaranteed your ten minutes. Since QVC is broadcast to 100 million homes, stakes are high, so if you're a minute or two into your presentation and you're not hitting sales targets, you might still think you have eight minutes left, but then all of the sudden they might cut your time, and you see only a minute left on the clock. Which means, you're done. Failed to hit the sales goal. You're outta there. You know, *just that* kind of pressure.

We got down to the one-minute mark and I remember the host saying we were starting to run low in some shades: "We began with six thousand two hundred of these. In the deep shade we have two hundred remaining; in the tan shade there are just two hundred left." Then, just at the moment that our ten-minute clock was about to run out, the giant *Sold Out* sign came up across the screen!

I started crying on national television, and they cut from me and went to a Dyson vacuum or something. My husband came rushing through the double doors of the studio. All he could focus on was overwhelming relief, and I remember him throwing his arms up in the air victoriously and loudly proclaiming, "We're not going bankrupt!" With tears streaming down my face, I proudly proclaimed, "Real women have spoken!"

THAT ONE MOMENT turned into us being invited back again and again. We ended up doing more than 250 live shows a year on QVC and building the biggest beauty brand in QVC history. And every moment I was live on TV, I felt the exact same connection with the viewer at home that I had with that woman in the grocery store produce section. And every day I thought of her. She mattered more to me than the culturally learned belief system that my rosacea is embarrassing and a flaw. Or that it's a reason I'll be rejected and unlovable. I changed the meaning I gave to it, and it became the exact reason I was accepted and loved. By customers, but first by myself.

But the story could have turned out very differently because retail stores, department stores, and QVC had said *no* and "You're not the right fit for us or for our customers" to me for years. And even once we had great sales success in the business, there were still never-ending rejections that came in various forms. Just like rejection in our personal, day-to-day life is always happening, especially if we show up fully for our lives, our friendships, and our dreams.

Let's revisit the question that I opened the chapter with: **What would you do in your life if you had absolutely zero fear of rejection or failure?** Now, let's get to that place, okay?! Because when you acquire the tools to change your relationship with rejection, you can apply them to any area of your life.

Changing Your Relationship with Rejection

Here's the process of how to change your relationship with rejection in your own life right now. I'm going to explain it very simply, but remember to give yourself grace. It takes a while to unlearn old patterns and habits, and to create new ones. Even to this day, I have to practice these tools to stay as sharp as I can with them. I believe it will be a lifelong effort, because I've learned it's just too easy to fall back into fearing rejection or failure, especially if you're the only person in your peer group or family to be putting in the work of gaining awareness, changing old patterns, and reclaiming your power around rejection and failure.

The Process: The Four Rs to Transcending Rejection

1. Reveal: Identify your current default definition(s) you give to rejection/failure when it happens. Or the one(s) you use to talk yourself out of even trying. These are often disempowering and happen automatically without intention.

2. Redefine: Create new, empowering definitions that you're going to assign to rejections/failures when they happen or when you're tempted to not try, out of fear of them happening.

3. Revisit and Reframe: Revisit and reframe rejections of the past. Assign new meanings to these past rejections/failures that still feel significant in your life.

4. Revel: Revel in rejections ahead! They no longer faze you! Think: Dear rejection, you might be big, but my resiliency is bigger!

Reveal

Okay, let's go there, are you ready? I'll go first. For most of my life, my internal reaction to a rejection has been, *Yep, that confirms it yet again, I'm just not enough.* Or *I don't have what it takes.* Or *I'm not smart enough,*

clever enough, cool enough, funny enough, or [fill in the blank] enough.
Sometimes it's been a version of how I'm insufficient or unworthy.

Okay, now it's your turn, ready? When someone rejects you, or you put yourself out there and it doesn't go your way, or you try and fail, or you never try at all out of fear of rejection or failure, what is the first thing you think? Imagine this scenario and really feel it, then notice what's the first thought that goes through your head when you're rejected or fail at something, perhaps without you even being aware of it? Get really, really honest here. It's just you and me.

Make a mental note, or even better, write down whatever comes to your mind first. It might help to imagine a scenario where you're getting rejected or when something you try fails, and then while imagining that situation, take note of what you think about yourself. This is your *current definition* of rejection.

I once asked this question while on stage speaking to a crowd of over a thousand people: I asked them to shout out the first true thing they think when they're rejected or fail. The answers were so vulnerable, raw, and real that I started crying. And I noticed several people in the audience began crying too. This was a business conference! But this question caught so many of them by surprise because it wasn't one they had ever considered. It was like there was an awful soundtrack playing in their minds on a daily basis that they weren't even aware of the impact of.

It goes to show that it doesn't matter if you're a seasoned CEO, the leader of a team, the leader of a toddler in your home, or all of the above, everyone deals with self-doubt.

As human beings, we are wired to avoid pain at all costs. It's a survival mechanism. And when we feel not enough, or unworthy, or unlovable, we feel massive amounts of pain. And when we mentally link all of this pain to the idea of rejection or failure, then we're reluctant to take risks. We stay stuck and play life small. If we never put ourselves out there, we don't risk the perceived pain that comes with rejection or failure. If we never go after our dreams, we don't risk embarrassment and dejection when they don't work out. But rejection and failure only mean those things because we've decided they do. And we can undecide that. Just like I undecided my rosacea was an embarrassing flaw and instead assigned a new meaning to it. It was an empowering gift. And I taught myself to believe it.

Redefine

Assigning a new meaning to rejection and failure is one thing that changes everything. You have the ability to decide that rejection and failure don't have to cause you pain. When you assign a new meaning to those experiences, and you believe it, the fear goes away.

When you assign a new definition to each failure and rejection, you can choose one that frees you from taking rejection personally. This is a HUGE benefit. When you take rejection personally, it not only causes you great pain, it also complicates your relationship with the person who delivered the rejection, when in fact it might not have been personal on their side at all. Taking rejection in your work personally can have negative consequences on your career or company and its potential success.

In the journey of building IT Cosmetics, I got hundreds and hundreds of rejections, and honestly, some of them felt like they just had to be personal, rather than based on the assessment of our actual product, but even then, I chose never to take them personally. Instead of getting defensive or offended each time I got another rejection, sometimes from the same person more than once, because I had changed my definition of rejection I was able to not take the rejections personally and instead respond in a way that actually created momentum for my company.

Here's what I mean. Even if a store buyer said NO as in *not now, not ever*, with not even a crumb of encouragement, I would thank them, and then follow up with an email the next day, expressing excitement that one day when we ARE in their stores, our products would bring so much value to their customers. I communicated zero resentment and full conviction that it would in fact be a YES one day, and in my mind, I decided to believe that day would surely come. And when they rejected me again, I did the same, every time. When we got an exciting press placement or had a new product launch, I would send them an enthusiastic email reminding them yet again, that one day when it *is* a YES, we will bring so much value to their stores and their customers. Now, while some of these people may have thought I was weird, what I was doing created seeds of momentum without them fully realizing it. Sometimes these same people rejected me over and over, and sometimes for years. But eventually, I was able to turn every single NO into a YES. Yep, every single one. I was able to grow IT Cosmetics into one of the largest luxury makeup companies in the country. And I was only able to do it because I became fearless about rejection, I trained myself to associate no pain with it, and I didn't ever take it personally. I did this by creating new definitions of rejection in my life. That with enough repetition I was able to believe to be true.

I have a few go-to definitions I assign to the rejections and failures that still happen to me often, to this day. Whether it's a business idea that is rejected by a potential partner, or a friend who doesn't invite me to speak at their event, or a harsh critic online whom I've never met. As a best practice and now automatic habit, when I face rejection or fail at something, which happens frequently, instead of defaulting to my old belief that it means *I'm not enough*, here are some of my go-to ways to redefine the meaning that I assign to a rejection, and fully believe:

1. Rejection is God's (or the Universe's) **protection**.

2. I haven't been rejected. My Creator **hid my value from them** because they're not assigned to my destiny.

3. Rejection and failure are victorious! They're a reminder I'm one of the **brave ones** willing to go for it!

When something doesn't go my way, my old response to rejection pops into my head: *You're not enough.* I catch it in real time and imagine myself deleting it. Or hitting the Mute button. Or smashing it out of the park with a baseball bat until I can't see it anymore like a grand slam home run. Then I instantly replace it with one of these new definitions I choose to believe. I remind myself of one of these new definitions, saying it to myself louder and imagining it more boldly than the negative thought that preceded it. I imagine it coming in and through my body as the truth. And I believe it. The more I've done this, the more it has become habit. And the more I look back at past rejections and failures and how they panned out, the more I also know these definitions aren't just positive thinking, they're actual truths.

Here are some examples of how I've applied these new definitions in my life. Notice the patterns of how and when I applied them and see if they resonate with you too, as we dive into your new definitions of rejection and failure, and how to apply them to transform your life.

Rejection Is God's Protection

Perhaps you and I share this first, very common scenario. Think of someone you once dated and loved, with whom things didn't end as you'd hoped they would. Looking back with the benefit of time, perhaps now it's clear that you would have been settling if you stayed in the relationship. Or maybe they did you *so* wrong. Over and over. You, your friends, and your family knew they weren't good for you, but you kept hoping it would work out anyway. While the breakup may have hurt back then, how glad are you NOW that you didn't stay together? Rejection is protection!

In my journey of building IT Cosmetics, a potential investor once passed on investing in my company, and when I asked why, he told me, "I just don't think women will buy makeup from someone who looks like you with your body and your weight." In that moment I had so desperately wanted this potential investor to say yes. Especially because at the time we were nearly out of money, and I wasn't sure how our company was going to stay alive. I thought he was going to be my saving grace.

And the truth is that we were so close to going out of business, if he'd believed in me and given us a chance, I would have probably sold him the majority of my company for very little money. If he'd partnered with us, helped us stay afloat, and advised us how to get into all of the retail stores that had been rejecting me, I might have ended up owning just a tiny piece of the company. Well, rejection is God's protection. Because he didn't say yes, we figured out how to keep going and succeed anyway, and by the time I sold my company six years later, I was still the largest shareholder.

By the way, six years after the investor said those hurtful words to me was the first time I heard from him again. It was the day we sold IT to L'Oréal. Because they're a public company, they disclosed the purchase price of $1.2 billion—their largest US acquisition to date. It made the press everywhere, and that once-potential investor must have seen the headlines. That day the news was announced, he reached out to me to say, "Congratulations on the L'Oréal deal, I was wrong."

Remember in the movie *Pretty Woman*, where Julia Roberts's character goes into the fancy store and the salespeople won't help her? The moment the would-be investor called to congratulate me on the deal, what I wanted to say to him was the same words Julia's character said to the store clerk the day she returned to the same store, this time dressed in nicer clothes with bags from other fancy stores hanging off her arm. I wanted to say to him, "Big mistake . . . huge . . . HUGE . . . In fact, I can give you 1.2 billion reasons why it was a huge mistake," but I didn't. I just thanked him. And I thanked God for both the open doors and the closed doors in life, as I have truly grown to trust both. In that moment when that once-potential-investor had congratulated me, I couldn't help but smile and remind myself, rejection is God's protection.

Sometimes, depending on which feels more applicable in the moment, I use a variation on this definition that is one of my favorites as well. For this one, I imagine my Creator saying to me:

"You weren't rejected. I hid your value from them because they're not assigned to your destiny."

Picture God saying: "You weren't rejected. I hid your value from them because they're not assigned to your destiny."

Think of a heartbreak you've gone through: that friend who didn't include you or appreciate you, that person who didn't like you for whatever reason, a setback that felt insurmountable, the job you wanted badly but didn't get, the times you took the risk and failed, that person who betrayed you, and all the painful rejections you've experienced. Imagine your Creator saying to you right now: *You weren't rejected. I hid your value from them because they're not assigned to your destiny.*

These are the words I imagined my Creator saying to me recently when a newer friend in my life betrayed my trust, and clearly didn't value our friendship the way I did. When I gave this particular betrayal this meaning, and believed it, it helped me process it quickly and kept it from penetrating my self-worth. Learning to do this is transformative. This is now one of my all-time favorite definitions that has changed my life and helped me feel free.

Rejection Is a Reminder That You're One of the Brave Ones!

Many times in my life, while crying under a blanket, I've googled and read about some of my heroes and the endless rejections and failures they've endured on their journeys. What I've concluded is that every single person who has ever been brave enough to go after a dream, to share their talents or gifts with the world, to build a business, to become a thought leader, or to help move humanity forward in any type of positive way has faced countless rejections and failures. Every single one. They're just the brave ones willing to keep going anyway.

I've decided I am going to believe this truth: that every time I face another rejection or failure, it's an exciting reminder that I'm one of the brave ones willing to go for it! I'm not one of the majority who's going to live sitting on the sidelines of life, scared to try, while criticizing others who do. I'm one of the brave ones! And every time I'm rejected or fail at something, I've trained myself to feel joy. And to feel this inspirational, wholehearted, soul-filling gratitude. I've convinced myself that the victory isn't in the outcome, it's in being one of the brave ones taking the chance. And that every failure is simply a reminder of this victory.

This might sound wild, but I actually truly believe it now. Because I also know it's true. For me and for you too. Here's to being the brave ones, willing to go for it!

I often share this lesson with my kids in words they understand. I tell them, *The people who succeed the most are often the same people who fail the most. Because they're the ones who try the most.*

There are endless new meanings you can assign to rejection and failure that are also true. The important thing is they feel true to you. A few more:

- Rejection is redirection. It's simply pointing me in the way of something better that's soon to come.

- Thank you for this rejection/failure because I trust it's happening *for* me not *to* me.

- Thank you for this rejection/failure because I know it's helping me build the resilience, the muscle, and the strength to carry the weight of my future successes when they happen.

Here's the deal, when you have a vision on your heart, not everyone is going to get it. Not even the experts. Not even the people you respect. And oftentimes, especially not even your friends and family. Because God didn't give the vision to them, He gave it to you. So don't be surprised if you feel misunderstood or underestimated, or if others aren't as excited for your dream or vision as you are. He didn't give it to them, He gave it to you. You are a steward of it. You are a steward of your own potential. You are a steward of your hopes and dreams. Don't take it personally or like some indication of its worth, when someone else doesn't validate your vision, or appreciate it or believe in it or think it will be successful. Only you know what you know. Only you see what you see. Only you feel what you feel. Only you've been given the divine download and now you are a steward of what to do with it. Of how strongly to believe in it. Of how willing you are to fight for it. Of how persistently you get back up every time you get knocked down. You are the steward. You are the owner. It's all in you and it's all up to you.

Revisit and Reframe

You can apply your new definitions of rejection and failure to past experiences that might still feel significant in your life today. Doing this has helped me make peace with past situations and let go of lingering pain and resentment. And it's helped me see where I come from and the things I've gone through as empowering versus disempowering. Even if to this day, they might not feel fair or make sense. Even if they are things that I wouldn't ever want to happen again to me or to anyone else. I now see everything I've gone through as things that were FOR me, that taught me lessons, that exposed me to painful experiences that I made it through and am now able to help others make it through only because I learned how to. It's not about denying things that have happened in the past, but rather about assigning a meaning to them that transforms them into peace and empowerment.

The people who succeed the most are often the same people who fail the most. Because they're the ones who try the most.

I was adopted the day I was born, and my parents who raised me chose to work long hours, leaving me alone after school for long stretches every day. There was a season in my adult life where I struggled with beliefs around being abandoned. For years, these beliefs manifested in very hurtful ways in my life. I never wanted to abandon anyone else, so I stayed in toxic relationships with boyfriends and friends, and I let people mistreat me. Later, as a boss, my greatest weakness was not firing people soon enough, when they merited it, because I didn't want to abandon them. But when I decided to do the work of changing the story I was telling myself about being abandoned and rejected, it shifted my perception of my own identity and strengthened my self-worth, which led to me making clearer and wiser decisions in all areas of my life.

Instead of choosing to believe I was rejected, I chose to believe I was chosen. On purpose! I was chosen by my birth mom to live—what a gift. I feel a tremendous sense of gratitude that my birth mom chose to carry me, to go into hiding, and then to bring me into the world. Her life would have been much easier if she chose not to. But she chose to. She chose me. I was chosen by my adoptive mom and dad to be raised. And I feel the deepest sense of divine orchestration that my mom and dad who adopted and raised me, chose me as their baby. And I feel a tremendous sense of awe that I was chosen by God to come into this world on purpose. See, my birth mom and birth dad were together just one time ever. Then never again. And in that one time, in that one single moment, I was created. But I don't believe I was an accident. And I don't believe, no matter the circumstances around your conception, that you were either.

When I decided to change my story, I changed my life. I now don't just believe; I know I was chosen. And this belief and knowing has helped my relationships flourish. My friendships, my marriage, my professional relationships, and my relationship with my families, all of them. I'm not a victim, I'm a victor. God chose me on purpose, with purpose. My journey happened *for* me; I was chosen to live, and chosen to be chosen.

Research shows that when people reflect on difficult painful experiences with the goal of finding meaning, or something positive that's come from it, they're happier, make better decisions, give better advice, and solve problems more effectively. When I started practicing this tool of changing the meaning I assign to things, it changed everything for me. It's not a seeing-the-glass-as-half-full thing. It's actually believing the glass is half full. Because we become what we believe.

NoteWORTHY: Apply these tools now: on paper, in a journal, or by downloading the free *Rejection Reframing Worthy Worksheet* at WorthyBook.com/Resources, let's dive deep into these questions:

What are your go-to default definitions of rejection and failure that you're now aware of and would like to replace?

What's your new definition or definitions of rejection and failure that you're going to intentionally choose to believe every time they happen to you? Spend as much time as you can considering this idea and writing down your new definitions.

What's one story or rejection that's happened to you in the past, that you need to rewrite today to tell yourself a different story? And commit to remembering this new true story every time you think of this past experience.

And the most exciting question: How do you anticipate these new definitions impacting your life?

Revel

Once you've identified your new, empowering definitions of rejection and failure, you start to fear them less. You start to tap into your own courage more. And the more you build this practice of applying your new definitions to your life, the less you'll sabotage opportunities, and the more confidently you'll pursue your ideas, needs, hopes, and dreams. And you can start this today, right now!

In fact, maybe today is the day you're going to make the decision to keep going with that thing you were about to give up on. Maybe today is the day you're going to decide to write the first page of your book. To register the domain for your business. To get back on the dating app. To tell the person you want to be more than just friends. To launch the podcast. To forgive someone or ask them to forgive you. To tell that person it's not okay to speak to you that way. To post a no-makeup selfie on social media. To wear the swimsuit with pride, even if it's just inside your own home, in front of your partner, or in front of the mirror with yourself. Maybe today's the day you're going to send an email right now asking for a promotion or a raise or a leadership position in your company or church or volunteer group. Maybe you're going to pick up a paintbrush again and share your art with others. Maybe you're going to show up as who you truly are at your next family gathering, knowing you might be judged but at least **you'll be free.**

Idea: Let's be rejection partners. Let's see who can rack up the most. Can you imagine how abundant our successes will be, and how incredible our lives will be when we do? You are fully worthy and valuable as you are, and the number of rejections, failures, and even triumphs and successes don't change that. Changing your relationship with rejection and failure is one of the greatest tools to restoring a strong identity and belief in yourself. Even if you're the first in your peer group or family to do this, make the decision today to assign a powerful meaning to rejection and failure in your life. When you do, you change your life for the better, forever.

CHAPTER 3

You're Not Crazy, You're Just First

*The world will ask you who you are, and if
you don't know, the world will tell you.*

— CARL JUNG

MOM AND DAD, I have this product idea. It's a pet rock. I think I can sell these and make millions." For those of you who are too young to remember, the Pet Rock came out in 1975 and was enormously popular. The creator, Gary Dahl, became a millionaire. But can you imagine the conversations he must have had when he came up with the idea? Can you imagine the doubt and laughter that came his way?

Or what about the moment witnesses gathered on the beach to watch the Wright brothers make yet another attempt to fly a machine into the air after hundreds of previous failures? Can you imagine the names they were called, or how misunderstood their genius likely was? Or the person who invented the Shake Weight, you know, that product commercial where the guy holds that dumbbell-like weight in front of his abdomen and shakes it back and forth rapidly to get a workout. Note, you should have seen my grandma's face the first time she saw that commercial, because, well, it can look like a lot of things other than shaking a weight. Who knew that invention would be such a huge . . . climactic success? These innovative people were probably all called words like *crazy* at some point along the way, but they were just first. And so are you.

Confession: I've been called *crazy* most of my life. Most often by people who loved me and used it as a term of endearment because they didn't know what else to say. I was the one who thought differently. The one who always had the big, wild ideas to challenge or fix the world's problems. The one who dreamed of going to faraway places and was willing to work enough jobs to make it happen. The one who never felt like I fit in, even when I tried desperately to. The one who believed that where I come from doesn't have to determine where I'm going. And challenged my family with questions like, *What's stopping people like us from having success like that?* The one who got teased for being the only person at my party not drinking alcohol on my twenty-first birthday, because I was scared to death of repeating the generational cycle of addiction.

After years of being called words like *crazy*, I couldn't help but to start wondering if I was. I began trying desperately to feel like I belonged and did whatever I could to feel less alone and more enough. I mastered dimming my own light to make people around me feel comfortable. But I was left feeling empty and even more alone. Then, in my twenties, I swung the pendulum in an entirely different direction and spent a few decades overachieving, confusing the world's approval and celebration with love. But neither overperforming nor dimming filled the void of *not-enoughness* I felt inside of me.

When they called me words like *crazy*, I told myself it just meant I was misunderstood. But I secretly wondered if they were right. In my twenties, following all the rules the world told me to, I planned to get married before I was ready. Then I started having panic attacks. I fell into depression. My adoption, coupled with divorces in my family, means I actually have five families, and no one in any of those families had ever gone to therapy that I was aware of or even spoke about mental health. In the environment where I was raised, the solution was to avoid talking about hard things, to bury them deep down inside until they went away, or just to ignore that they existed at all. I was the first one in my families and peer group to seek therapy. Between the health insurance my job gave me and my savings, I figured out how I could afford to go, and I was in so much anguish that I couldn't afford not to.

The first appointment I had with my therapist changed the course of my life forever. After explaining to her all the ways I felt different and like I didn't belong, I also let her know I had big, bold dreams and wild ideas, and I felt like I had more potential than the person I was allowing myself to be. I told her that I felt like I was made to do different things from what I needed to do to belong, and that I was dimming my own light on my ambitions and even my personality because I felt like something was wrong with me. And now I was supposed to be marrying someone I loved, but I was scared. How could I know if marriage was right for me, when I'd seen it be wrong for so many people in my family?

After my therapist diagnosed my panic attacks and depression, I point-blank asked her: "My whole life I've been called crazy. Or different. Or too ambitious. Or strange. Or out there. Am I crazy?"

She replied, "No, you're not crazy. But I'm really glad you're here." She proceeded to explain how when we're the first one in our peer group, family, or community to challenge the status quo, it can feel very isolating. When we're the first or only one to feel differently, we can feel othered. When we don't morph who we truly are to fit in and we show up authentically, it can be worrisome to others who live in a comfort zone where fitting in is the path to acceptance. When we're the first to break the mold of our conditioned belief system, it can come with loneliness, stress, and trauma. She then explained how when we live out of alignment with who we truly are in order to fit in, we actually live divided. And that division can also come at a great expense to our mental and physical health.

It all made so much sense. And then it hit me, like a light bulb so instantly hot that it burst: *I'm not crazy, I'm just first.*

I FELT THIS aha moment in my soul, a truth that had just set me free. Like the weight of self-judgment had just been lifted off my shoulders for the first time in my life. **I'm not wrong, I'm just first. I'm not bad, I'm just first. I'm not broken, I'm just first. I'm not a mistake, I'm just first. I'm not off course, I'm just first.**

I'm the first me. And you are the first you. And if we bravely live as our authentic essence, we are first.

If you live your life authentically, you're automatically first. Because there is only one of you in the entire universe. So, if you're wondering if you're actually first, you are. Or at least you are every day in which you're true to your one-of-a-kind self.

Because there is only one of you in the entire universe, just one person in existence with your thoughts, with your life experience, with your DNA, with your fingerprints, with your unique heartbeat (yep, we actually each have a unique heartbeat), and even with your individual tongue print (yep, we each have unique tongue prints too!), then every thought, decision, and action you choose for the rest of your life is coming from someone who is first.

When you dare to live fully authentically as the first you, it can easily be confused with feeling odd or misunderstood or awkward or lonely or not enough. And when we feel these things, the biggest temptation is to hide and change who we truly are so that we feel like we fit in. In fact, this is most people's strategy their entire lives. Because they don't realize they're just first, so they think they're inadequate and need to change who they are or show up as another version of themselves to be loved. But: **being first isn't what's wrong with you, it's what's right with you!**

What are the parts of you and your personality that aren't crazy, they're just first because they're uniquely you?

It takes courage to be the real you, and it's also the only path you'll ever find to true freedom. It takes risk to be the real you, and it's also the only possibility of experiencing true purpose. It takes vulnerability to be the real you, and it's also the only place you'll experience true love.

Showing up in this world as ALL of who you are tastes like freedom.

The people who dare to be first, who courageously embrace their innate firstness, are the ones who can change the course of their families forever. They're the ones who decide to stop people-pleasing and actually say how they feel. They're the ones who learn to stop doubting their own uniqueness and decide to embrace who they truly are. They're the ones who might set different examples for their kids than their families set for them. The ones who might challenge injustices and liberate truth. They're the ones who might say, "I want more for myself, my family, and my world," and then dare to believe it's possible. The ones who break addictions and generational cycles. The ones who say, "This doesn't make sense in my soul. I'm challenging that belief system." They're the ones who help heal others, by first healing themselves. They're the ones who courageously share their ideas

What if the thing you thought was wrong with you is actually one of the greatest things that's right with you?

and offerings, no matter the criticism that might come. They're the ones who change things in their families, for generations to come. They're the ones who change industries. They're the ones who change the world. When I realized this truth, it helped me change the meaning I attached to how I felt about who I was. It helped me reestablish my own identity. From one that was disempowered to one that was emboldened. From one that felt ashamed of who I was, to one that felt liberated for all that I am.

Be Authentic, Even If It Means Standing Alone

Maybe you're the first in your family or peer group to dream big, to vote or love differently, to dare to take a risk, or to break a generational cycle. Maybe you're the first to want a life or belief system that's different from the one you were raised around. When you're the first, it can be so tempting to feel like something is wrong with you. Or like you were made defective. It becomes tempting, and for many people a habit, to show up in rooms, in your job, and even in relationships dimming your light and hiding in plain sight. To live your life as only part of who you are, but not as all of who you are. We crave belonging and fear being alone, but we often don't realize that **standing all alone, authentically, is less lonely than standing with others who have no idea who we truly are.**

How many times have you felt like you were desperately overworking to try and feel *enough*? Showing up as the person you thought others wanted you to be, to get their stamp of approval. Showing up as your "representative" thinking that this representative is who you need to become to be successful. This is living in a divided state. Divided from your true self. And that can take a toll not only on your joy, but also your physical and emotional health, as well as your connection with others in your personal and professional relationships.

In one study 40 percent of people reported they censor what they say because they worry that voicing their opinions would create distance between them and the people they care about. But voicing opinions, when they're authentic, creates connection. Psychologist Serena Chen, who is the chair of the psychology department at UC Berkeley, defines authenticity as "when people feel like they can be their true self. The authentic person is comfortable in their own skin. . . . They've vulnerable. They're not afraid to look silly or to admit mistakes." Chen adds that authenticity is correlated with well-being and satisfaction with life, plus when we're authentic, we don't alienate people. On the contrary—it's good for bonding and generating closeness.

We need to stop hiding who we are from others and from ourselves.

If you're like me, and you've spent most of your life only showing up as part of who you are, or showing up the way you know others want you to in the situation, then, like me, you'll have a lot of unlearning to do. There are so many lies that make hiding attractive, and so many truths that make hiding feel justified. And unfortunately, there are so many ways hiding hurts us in our lives.

While we often learn that the things that make us different from everyone else are the things we should fix or hide, the lesson I've learned firsthand so many times is that those things that make you authentic and different are actually the things you should embrace and expand the most. I know this feels counter to what most of us have learned.

When we courageously take steps toward unlearning the lies and gaining awareness of the truths, and assessing the impact of living our lives in ways that are inauthentic, disconnected, numb, people-pleasing, and out of alignment with who we truly are, we begin our journey of going from unseen to seen. From invisible to visible. From disconnected to connected. From doubting ourselves to trusting ourselves. From craving love to realizing we already are . . . love.

MY GOOD FRIEND Ed Mylett, entrepreneur and best-selling author, shares an incredible business and sales analogy that applies to life even if you aren't in sales. He says, "People don't have to believe in what you're actually selling, they just have to believe that YOU believe in what you're selling." Worthiness works the same way. Here's what I mean. People don't have to understand you or believe in you to connect with you. They just have to believe *you* understand you and *you* believe in you. And if you know, deep down inside, that you're showing up as someone different from who you are, then you will emit an energy that reveals that you don't believe in yourself. Because you're not being you. And this means you'll not be able to feel a true connection with someone else, because you know, and they feel, that you're not you. In other words, you have to be you, and know you're being the real you, to have true human connection. You have to feel worthy of being who you truly are. Otherwise—no matter how fancy or perfect or conformed you show up—you'll always feel disconnection and so will they.

There's also the other extreme that you see all over social media, where people reveal extremely shocking or vulnerable things in a way that doesn't feel believable. It's still a form of hiding who you truly are, but behind the confusing persona of someone who overshares and "reveals it all." Showing up fully and revealing who you truly are with the intention of connection and love is very different from confusing attention with love and trying to reveal things in hopes of calling for attention. Showing up authentically in hopes of true connection is very different from ploys to get attention in hopes it will lead to a feeling of validation or significance. People also sense your intention behind things—you can't fake that either. Sometimes you can in the short run, but never in the long run.

In relationships, in business, and in life, while authenticity alone doesn't automatically guarantee success, inauthenticity guarantees failure.

WHEN YOU SHOW up in life as the authentic you, remembering that *you're first* can be a great tool. It can also be another great definition of rejection. When I was building my first company and countless beauty retailers told me no one would buy makeup from images of real women, here is one way I would reframe every rejection in my mind: instead of *This "no" means I'm never going to make it*, I told myself, *My idea isn't bad, I'm just first!* When, after years of Nos, we finally got one big shot and those expensive consultants told me to do what most every other successful beauty brand was doing instead of taking a chance on my unique vision, I reminded myself that it only felt risky to them because I was first.

I eventually did over 1,000 live shows myself on QVC, and in that eight-year journey I saw that very, very few of the thousands of brands and on-air presenters ever hit the sales numbers needed to make it past one show and be invited back. When I look at what it was that the very few who made it had in common, it wasn't that they had the best product or the most adored, well-known, or well-funded brand. It wasn't how good a deal or discount they were offering. The only thing that the very few who made it over the years had in common was that they were authentic when selling on camera, and they were the same on-air while selling on live TV as they were off-air, behind the scenes even while no one was watching. This was consistent no matter what personality style they had, or even how likable they were. You cannot fake authenticity, and authenticity is truly the only way to form deep, true connections, in person or through a screen, with friends and in business.

Because at IT Cosmetics we stayed the course—we were authentic, we were novel, we were first at what we were doing—it meant we were misunderstood among beauty industry insiders for many years . . . until we weren't. It meant we were outsiders until we were celebrated. It meant we were considered strange for many years, until we were copied over and over. It meant we endured countless rejections, until we were all of the sudden courted. It meant we were broke and barely getting by, until we were outselling everyone else. It meant we were underestimated until we became unstoppable. It meant we heard over and over *your idea is never going to work*, until we heard *you're number one in the industry*.

There's an **until** waiting for you too . . .

I've never been afraid to march to the beat of my own drum and I'm starting to really like the sound of it.

— TRENT SHELTON

Reframe Your Individuality

What if the thing you thought was odd or quirky or unique or *wrong* with you is actually one of the greatest things that's *right* with you? When you reframe your uniqueness as a great thing, a strength, an adventure, an exclusive qualification, courageousness, a novel gift, you start to reframe your own perception of it and start to associate your own identity with those more empowering words. It's a powerful tool to boost not only your belief in yourself but also what you hold to be true about your own identity and worth. When you change the meaning you attach to the part of your uniqueness you previously may have been tempted to hide, you change your life.

> *If you're comfortable with yourself and know yourself,*
> *you're going to shine and radiate, and other people*
> *are going to be drawn to you.*
> — DOLLY PARTON

If you're like me, you've been called words like *strange* or *odd* or *crazy* or [fill in the blank], and if you haven't yet, you might experience being called them when you start showing up fully as who you are. Try replacing these words with words like *first* or *trailblazer* or *visionary* or *brave* or *unique* or *one-of-a-kind* because they actually begin to impact who you believe you are. See, one of the strongest forces in our human nature and belief system is the need to remain consistent with our own identity or with how we identify ourselves. This means that if you believe something to be true about who you are, your brain scans and highlights proof around you that reinforces that belief. So when you label your uniqueness with words that are disempowering, you then live out those words and that identity; if you label your uniqueness or firstness with words like *crazy, weird, strange, unlovable, outcast, broken, flawed*, then you will hide that part of you at all costs or, worse, will identify with those words and believe that's who you are. You'll form a negative, limiting belief around your uniqueness. But when you reframe your uniqueness as a great thing, a strength, an adventure, an exclusive qualification, a celebration of your courage, a novel gift, you reframe your own perception of it and start to associate your identity with those more empowering words.

If you're lucky enough to be different, never change.

—TAYLOR SWIFT

When we live our life hiding from our firstness and uniqueness, believing it's a negative thing, dimming our light, underestimating our own abilities, playing it small, confusing approval for love, or people-pleasing our way off our path, we actually risk talking ourselves out of our own truth and never becoming the person we're born to be.

I HAVE TWO questions for you that only you can answer:

Who would you be, if you lived your life embracing your firstness and all of who you authentically are? How freeing would it be if you decided to live the answer?

Take off your armor; dare to be vulnerable, dare to unwrap yourself, and dare yourself to be yourself.

— MARIA SHRIVER

You, right now, exactly as you are, are first. You are the only person in the entire universe who has your fingerprints, your toe prints, your irises in your eyes, yep, there is no one else like you with these. And those are just a few of the characteristics on the outside. Your unique characteristics on the inside, and in your thoughts and emotions, are infinite. When you are authentic to who you truly are, you are first. And while it's tempting to hide, play it safe, be small, dim your light, or show up like everyone else in hopes they'll love you, you can't experience deeply connected, true love unless you're truly you. Hiding your uniqueness might feel safe, but you won't ever be able to impact and serve the world the way you're created to.

There is only one of you and there will only ever be one of you, so be you. Be the best you. Be the most fully alive you. The quirkiest you.

The most outspoken you. The silliest you. The bravest you. The boldest you. The fully loving you. The most spectacular you there has ever been. Be the one, true, only ever you . . . who is FIRST.

P.S. I wrote a poem called "You're Not Crazy, You're Just First," from my soul to yours, that I would love to share with you. Please listen to it here as part of this free, fully immersive book experience at WorthyBook.com/Poem or scan the QR code to experience it on video here.

CHAPTER 4

You Have Greatness Inside You

*Just because your past didn't turn out how
you wanted it to, doesn't mean your future
can't be better than you ever imagined.*

— UNKNOWN

WE ALL HAVE greatness inside of us. Part of our life's journey is learning to believe that for ourselves. Then we have to unlock it and unleash it, which won't happen until we believe we're worthy of it. When you ghost your own greatness, you risk doubting yourself out of your destiny.

There are so many reasons why we doubt our own greatness, some taught to us and some we invent. We believe other people have special talents and gifts, but not us. We believe success is something that happens to other people, but not people who've made the kind of mistakes we have, have a past like we do, or come from the wrong [fill in the blank]: family, neighborhood, religious background, etc. **Many people live their entire lives talking themselves out of their own truth, never becoming the person they were born to be.**

It's never too late to turn this around. It's never too late for a fresh start. You're never too young or too old to begin. It's never too late to begin your own journey to worthiness. Nothing that has happened in your life, or in your past, disqualifies you from it. It's never too late to see your own greatness and learn to embrace it, to own it, and to share it with the world. In fact, I believe it's what you were created for. The problem is that we so often let our past mistakes, misfortunes, unfair setbacks, and labels paralyze us and keep us stuck.

If people have heard of me, it's generally because of the story of my success in business. In particular, my story of enduring many years of hundreds of rejections and setbacks growing IT Cosmetics. After teetering on bankruptcy many times trying to keep the business alive, I eventually grew that business to over 1,000 employees. The company eventually got so large that I wanted to expand its mission globally, which required a much larger team, and which is why eventually, in 2016, I sold it to L'Oréal. It was the largest US acquisition in their history, and they made me the first woman to hold a CEO title of a brand in their more-than-100-year history. It was a hard-fought journey to success, but what was even longer and harder was the journey I've gone through my entire life and continue to go through even today. The journey to feeling worthy. A journey that, along the way, has taught me that your past, and especially your past mistakes, don't define you. Labels, harsh words, or names we and others put on us, aren't permanent. I learned that **where you come from doesn't have to determine where you're going. And that your past can only hold you back if you live there. I learned this by feeling stuck for a long time, then learning how to break free.**

I'm going to share some deeply personal things with you in this chapter. I've actually deleted them a few times, then added them back. See, these are things I've only shared with a few of the closest people to me. These are truths many in my family will learn for the first time in this book. But I know that part of my life's calling is to help others feel *less alone* and more *enough*. That mission is bigger than me and bigger than any fear I feel of being judged for what I am going to share in this chapter. So. . . *deep breath* . . . here we go.

I WAS RAISED by a loving, hardworking superhero of a mother, Nina, and an alcoholic father, Mike, who loved me the best he could within his own capacity. I craved my dad's love most, and it was the hardest to get. Most mornings, the only thing he wanted on waking was to have a beer ready to crack open. I would often wait by his bedside with a can of beer ready in hand, hoping if I gave him what he wanted, he would give me the time and love I craved. Most mornings, he thanked me for the beer and said good morning, and that was the end of the exchange. Others I cherished, when he taught me how to ride a bike or took me to the local pond to paddle on a blow-up boat together, which would often hit a rock and start to deflate mid-ride and we'd have to frantically paddle back to shore on a half-blown-up boat. We always made it back to dry ground, just in the nick of time. And I remember, even as a little girl, always somehow knowing we would.

As I grew up, school came easily to me, but I often lived in my imagination and was almost always dreaming about how to get what I didn't have enough of: attention, validation, the feeling of worthiness. My parents divorced when I was six and both remarried. Thankfully my new stepdad Dennis and stepmom Laura were both kind and loving. I lived primarily with my mom and Dennis, who both worked long hours, often seven days a week. I was alone a lot, and, as I mentioned, my closest friend growing up was Oprah on my living room TV. Oprah showcased other people's stories, helping me feel less alone in my own thoughts and dreams and struggles. In a now-famous interview with Barbara Walters, Oprah once shared how she always knew she *was born for greatness in her life.* These words struck a chord in the hearts of many girls and women across the country who couldn't put words to their own knowing that they did too, including me. Those words felt true to me. I often imagined hosting a show just like Oprah one day and sharing other people's stories with the world. But I also believed that dream was too far out of reach. I was surrounded by messages that reinforced how *things like that didn't happen to people like me.*

AS A TEENAGER, I began to hang out with a troublemaking crowd. And not the valuable kind of troublemaking that moves society forward. Since my parents were usually working, I spent a lot of time home alone, and I gravitated toward wanting to help friends who didn't have good situations in their homes. At the age of twelve, I let one of my friends who was dating a much older guy store his guns in the attic of our house. My parents never knew. Then, at fourteen, I started dating my first serious boyfriend, who, along with his friends, made a practice of stealing cars and selling their parts. They targeted a specific year of Honda Accords because you could jump-start the car with a screwdriver in the ignition. I didn't approve of my boyfriend's car theft hobby, but I went along for the ride anyway, and often found myself on joyrides with my boyfriend at the wheel and a carful of friends I barely knew. My parents never had any idea of what I did when I was "just hanging out with friends."

One afternoon, my fate took a turn for the worse. My boyfriend, two much older kids, and I were cruising out of a shopping mall parking lot in a freshly stolen car when red and blue lights began flashing. The car was surrounded, and everyone put their hands up in the air. And just like that, my world changed.

"Get out of the car!" police yelled over the megaphone. Hands raised up to the sky, we were shoved against a wall, patted down, then hand-cuffed and put in the back of police cars. It was my first and only time in handcuffs. Tears streamed down my face as I sat there shaking in the police car, not knowing what was coming next, but at the same time I felt a sense of belonging. This arrest gave me membership in an unspoken club that I knew my newfound friend group would find cool. It almost felt like an initiation to rebellious, street cred legitimacy, a badge of badassery. *This* was greatness to *them*, I thought. And then the fear quickly returned, cascading through me as I wondered if I had just derailed the glorious future in my daydreams. *Would Oprah have been given a show if she had gone to jail?* I wondered, hope waning by the second.

I was taken to the holding precinct and put alone in a room. Through the small window, I could see a giant table where police officers sat doing paperwork. It was a late Friday afternoon. Hours passed, and it wasn't until the evening when I heard familiar voices—my mom and Dennis. They had come to get me out of there. I dreaded seeing their faces, fearing the great disappointment that would be written all over them. My mother would be heartbroken. Then all of a sudden, from the tiny rectangle window, I could see that they were leaving. *What is happening*, I thought. *Where are they going, why are they leaving?*

Eventually, I learned that because it was late on a Friday evening, my parents couldn't get me out that night. Instead, I would be booked into a juvenile detention facility until Monday, when I could go before a judge who would determine the case and my fate. The others in the car were taken to separate facilities and the only other girl in the car, who was eighteen, had been taken to jail. I was alone. I was just fourteen, so I was taken to juvie. My mind quickly flooded with all the stories I'd heard and seen on TV about what happens inside juvie.

I was brought in a police van, handcuffed, to the detention center, where I was asked to put all my clothing and belongings into a bin for storage and given orange pants and a shirt. I was escorted to the shower area where I was strip-searched, then told to shower under supervision. I was anxious, embarrassed, and afraid. The shower water was cold. I followed the directions I'd been given and tried to put on a strong face while feeling helpless. I dressed in the orange clothes, socks, and plastic sandals. I was given a plastic comb for my hair and escorted to a crowded cell. The facility was overcrowded, and all the beds were full, so I was assigned a mattress on the floor.

The next two days felt like an out-of-body experience. I quickly figured out who to steer clear of and how to avoid a physical fight, while also on high alert that a fight could happen at any moment. The weight of knowing the despair my family had to be feeling quickly set in. I felt ashamed and regretful. Not only had I done something *bad*, but I couldn't shake the thought that maybe I *was* in fact *bad*.

Monday came, and I was ushered into the courtroom. I was assigned a legal representative, and, to this day, I don't remember speaking to that person beforehand. I worried about what I would say, if I would need to lie, if my friends would be in the same courtroom, if their stories would match up, or if I should simply tell the truth. I worried about what would happen if I was locked up for a long time. I worried that I'd be kicked out of school. I worried about what I had done to my life.

I didn't know I might have any rights and I was completely ignorant as to how the legal system worked, so I let whatever was going to happen, happen to me. As a little girl I had learned not to question or challenge authority, so I didn't. I stood before the judge feeling helpless and fearful. And within seconds, he decided that because I had no prior record, and because the facility was overcrowded, I would need to do a hefty load of community service hours but would be released that day. I held back tears and felt the deepest sense of relief. It felt like a moment of grace had touched my life, and I didn't fully feel I deserved it.

I WISH I could tell you that being released felt like a fresh start, but it didn't. I was drawn right back to that same friend group where I felt loved, seen, and important. I skipped school a lot, worked hard to save up enough money to buy a car, and used that car to drive everywhere but school. I was voted "Biggest Procrastinator" in the high school yearbook. It really hurt my feelings, but the truth is, it was accurate at the time. I was naturally smart enough to get away with doing a fraction of my schoolwork, and while I often turned assignments in late, my scores were strong enough to get the passing grades needed to hide my inner turmoil.

Between moving schools and homes, my friend group eventually dispersed. And after working multiple jobs, graduating high school, and getting a great paying job at a health club, I was living in my own apartment. The health club where I worked valued sales numbers over work experience, and the management quickly learned that if they had me give potential new members a tour of the club and then present them with membership options, my sales rate was much higher than even the seasoned sales team. I connected with the potential customers on a personal level and was quickly promoted from receptionist to sales associate. Then to sales manager. At eighteen I was in charge of managing the 8,000+ member club, along with leading a sales team of mostly men aged thirty-five to sixty-five. Not because my experience merited it, only because my sales numbers outperformed everyone else's. One of those men on the sales team, let's call him Brad, was thirty-seven and the most attractive guy who had ever given me attention. He looked like an A-list celebrity to me, and many of the women in the health club took notice of him too. He was always dating multiple women at once, but I didn't care. I silently swooned every time he walked by. Then one day he held eye contact with me just a bit longer than normal, and in an instant, I knew we were no longer just colleagues. Oh, and I was technically his boss, though he was nearly twice my age.

> *There's a charm about the forbidden that*
> *makes it unspeakably desirable.*
> — MARK TWAIN

Brad and I kept our romance secret because of our working relationship. And as my feelings grew stronger, watching him date multiple women became painful. I asked him to be exclusive, but he told me that wasn't his style. I was left with a decision: break up with him and abandon the relationship or stay in it and abandon myself. I decided to abandon myself.

When I was with him, I felt seen and adored and cherished. And when we were apart, I was consumed with the pain of knowing he was with someone else.

We will never attract or keep more in our life, or in our relationships, than what we believe we're worthy of. I just didn't know that or understand it yet. What I did know was that this situation didn't match the greatness I felt I had inside of me or that I was hoping to see come to light in my life.

I continued to make more and more money, but often wondered, *Is this really all there is? Will I do this forever?* And in the deepest quiet of the night, I would still think, *What about that talk show?* I started to have dreams of going to college. My mother wanted me to be the first in our family to go to college so badly, and now, with the money I was making at the health club, I figured I could at least afford a semester if I used all my savings. Maybe I could learn about the TV business.

> *We will never attract or keep more in our life, or in our relationships, than what we believe we're worthy of.*

When I spoke to my dad Mike about the idea of college, he freaked out and said, "Are you crazy? Look how much money you're making. You should definitely stay working in the health club job instead." At that moment, I was making more money than my dad, who had a union job on an assembly line working rotating shifts. He was decades into his career, and his daughter was making more money at age eighteen than he was in his fifties.

> *We must stop asking people for directions to places they've never been.*
>
> — GLENNON DOYLE

In the daily bustle at the health club, I felt celebrated and valued because I was outselling everyone else. And that validation can easily be confused with love. But in the quiet of my apartment, I couldn't shake the longing that more was assigned to my name in this lifetime. And I decided to trust myself. I applied for and enrolled in the summer semester of the state college. I quit my job, packed my bags, and decided I was going to walk full speed ahead into my greatness.

I quickly applied for jobs at the grocery store and the local restaurants in the college town. I got two part-time jobs, one slicing meat in the grocery store deli and the other waitressing at Denny's, where I worked after my classes during the week. But I missed an element of what I'd felt at the health club. At that point in my life, I still confused attention with love. And external validation with love. And significance with love. I got the idea to drive to the biggest city nearby, about an hour and a half outside of the college town. I passed by a large adult entertainment club, otherwise known as a strip club, and decided to stop in. At the time I didn't understand that because I didn't love myself, and didn't have strong self-worth, I was trying to find that love through the attention of other people in any form. No matter what the intention of their attention was.

When we don't believe we are enough as we are, attention starts looking like love, external significance starts looking like success, and validation starts looking like worthiness.

As I walked into the strip club, I saw a dozen or so dancers and about thirty customers sitting at tables, most all alone or with a dancer next to them. The room was dark and smokey. There was a bar and a few stages with lights and poles. *How fun would it be to perform?* I thought. *I could probably pay for college this way.* But as an introvert I couldn't quite imagine being brave enough to do it. Among the clubgoers, I noticed that there were waitresses, wearing black pants and white shirts, carrying trays of beverages. I stopped one to ask her how long she had worked there.

"A few years, the tips are really great. We get commission for every soda we sell. I make a few hundred bucks in a shift on a good day," the waitress said.

"Wow, and do you ever dance also?"

"No, not yet," the waitress replied, "but I think I might sometime." The waitress was encouraging, and I applied to work there that day. I was hired as a waitress, asked to show up each day in a white shirt and black pants, and charged with selling sodas for commission and encouraging the patrons to buy an extra soda for each dancer they talked with. The dancers got a kickback for each soda sold as well and were always expressing how thirsty they were to their patron of the moment. I quickly learned the game.

I SPENT MY first summer in college working after classes at the local grocery store and waitressing at Denny's, then spent my weekends driving up and back to the big city, waitressing at the strip club. I knew no one in my family would ever approve of this, so I kept it a secret. I developed a sense of community with my fellow waitresses and the dancers in the club. I got to know their stories and developed love and respect for many of them. As well as heartbreak and anguish for others.

Most said they were just stripping temporarily. And for many their *temporarily* never seemed to have an end date. Many were single moms or the breadwinners of blended families. Many were determined to break generational cycles of addiction or abuse in their families, and many had great hope of a better future for their own kids. A few were hardened and standoffish with walls up so large I wondered what kind of pain could have built them. But most were kind and vulnerable and just doing the best they could in life to get by and hold their family and bills and struggles all together. Many had dreams of becoming a nurse or a real estate agent or a social worker one day when they "got out of there."

While many might judge a strip club as shameful from the *outside*, I grew a deep sense of respect and appreciation for the hardworking, smart, strong women on the *inside*. Women just as strong, smart, and kind as those in any other place of work I had been exposed to.

I learned that women who society might judge as outcasts or shameful are really women with beautiful hearts and warrior spirits, who are often just doing the best they can, the best way they know how. Just like we all are. They have the same hopes for their babies and crave the same love we all do. They aspire to break generational cycles in their family and to make it in the world. And I saw that reaching those goals was made more difficult by the environment they found themselves in, whether by choice or necessity. I learned that the women at the strip club weren't any different from the women sitting next to me in my college classes, or the ones waitressing with me at Denny's or the ones shopping at the supermarket. **At our core, we are all trying to overcome feeling *not enough*; we are all striving for a sense of belonging and trying to learn to believe we're worthy of love.**

I WAS NINETEEN years old, feeling lost, and while I was growing in my empathy and respect for the new friends I was making in my classes and at work, I was still making mistakes and poor choices. My friendship with a handsome customer inside the strip club quickly turned to a romance outside of it. He let me know that he carried several firearms as a hobby, and on one date, he took me to a firing range to teach me how to shoot. The first time I fired a handgun, even with headphones on, it was so loud it sent shock waves through my body. I was more scared than I was interested.

The more I learned about my new beau, the more I realized we were two very different people, and one evening during a long drive back in his Jeep from the big city to my college apartment, I decided to end things.

"I don't think we're the right fit for each other. I think we should just be friends," I said to him. His face fell to a stoic gaze at the road ahead of him. The energy had shifted in the car. He became very quiet, and a feeling of fear took over me. In the back of his Jeep, within arm's reach, were several guns. I glanced back at them. And I realized I was all alone with a man I hadn't known for long on a dark, fairly desolate stretch of highway, with almost an hour left to go in the drive. *What's wrong with me?* I thought. *What am I doing with my life?* I started praying to God to make it home safe. At the time I didn't fully believe God existed, but I started praying anyway. Scared, I went into hyperalert mode, making sure my door was unlocked in case I had to open it and dive out. I was troubleshooting scenarios while praying they weren't about to happen. To my relief, my new ex-boyfriend dropped me off in front of my apartment, and I never saw him again.

In the quiet, do you feel the longing that more is assigned to your name?

Without the words, life experience, or knowledge to understand why, I found myself in a season of misalignment. Of incongruency with my soul. The life I was living didn't feel like the life I was created for. I was loving college so far but kept looking for love in all the wrong places, as the famous song goes. I was making *bad* choices and continued to think of myself as a bad, broken person. That didn't feel quite true if I allowed myself to think about it for too long. But if I dated guys that lied and stole and cheated and stayed with them in spite of that, then I thought I must be bad too. **If I needed other people to give me love, I must not be lovable on my own.**

HAVE YOU EVER felt this way or had similar experiences? Have you ever felt like you were learning the same lesson over and over again? Have you ever felt like you were looking for love everywhere except within yourself?

Two critical inflection points, two pivotal moments, were about to change the course of my decisions and my future. I was about to discover new ways of understanding love and worthiness, and from there I would embark on what would become a lifelong journey of understanding the true nature of both.

The two moments of grace that happened in my life began to open my eyes in new and transformative ways. First, a good friend of mine introduced me to faith and God, in a way that actually made sense to me. And I began to consider the verses of the Bible that say, "You are wonderfully made in His image," "You can do all things through Christ who strengthens you," "God is within her; she will not fall," "God is love," and the many more teachings that told me I was unconditionally loved and worthy. My friend took me to a church that embraced all types of people without judgment, and that day the sermon the pastor gave brought tears to my eyes. It was as if my soul recognized the truth that I was created in purpose and on purpose and from love. I still had more God-doubt than faith for a long time. It took many, many years for those words to penetrate and take root, but in this pivotal moment in my life, I decided to consider that maybe there was truth to them. My mind didn't believe them yet, but my soul did. And it started to change me.

The second moment of grace came in the form of something that felt much more like a Hollywood movie. I had seen a commercial on TV many times with a guy named Tony Robbins, who had coached everyone from US presidents to Olympic athletes. He was selling *Personal Power* cassette tapes about how to change your life. I ordered them and listened to them. Then I used the tip money I had saved from my multiple waitressing jobs to attend one of his live events. When I walked into the back of the giant room, there appeared to be about 10,000 people there. They were all jumping up and down and yelling and smiling. I worried I had walked into some kind of cult. I found a seat in the very last row of the room, close to the exit in case I needed to make a quick one. I decided to stick it out because I had worked really hard for that tip money.

That day, I learned what a limiting belief is and how to change it. I decided that my past and my past mistakes would no longer dictate how

I felt about my future potential. These concepts started to change my life. The inspirational seminar kick-started my passion and love for reading personal development, growth, and psychology books and my obsession with truly understanding how we each have the power to change the meaning we assign to our own stories. And as we acquire the tools to do it, we have the ability to transform our lives, our potential, and our future in the process.

WHEN THESE MOMENTS of grace come into our lives, like they did mine, they almost never change lifelong engrained patterns we're hoping to change overnight. In fact, for me, they were just the very first step. But it was a step in a new direction, onto a new path. I quit my job at the strip club. I never graduated from waitress to dancer during my summer there. My journey ended before I ever mustered up the courage, or the actual desire, to take the stage. I spent the next several years putting in the hard work of understanding why I equated and confused attention, achievement, and external validation with love and worthiness. I began to believe that I could heal my life and that I had the power inside of me to create the kind of future I dreamed of. Even though I wasn't sure how it was going to happen, I was determined to believe that it was going to happen. And that I was worthy of it happening.

I became the first in my family to graduate college. I was the class valedictorian that year at Washington State University, graduating with a 4.0 GPA, and I spoke at the commencement ceremony. No one knew then, or until this book, that their valedictorian had worked in a strip club. I continued to put in the hard work of believing my past didn't have to determine my future. And I continued to work on building my faith, both in myself

Each **setback** *is a divinely orchestrated* **setup** *for what we're* **destined to do next.**

and in God. It would be another decade before I started to believe that God might in fact exist. And it would become a lifelong journey that continues today of unlearning my limiting beliefs and gaining conviction that I am worthy of love exactly as I am.

I MADE ONE decision after another where I trusted myself. I took some detours and had some mishaps. On occasion, I found myself repeating old patterns, like dating an alcoholic boyfriend who didn't reciprocate my love—if I'd stayed with him I would have ended up repeating the cycle I was raised in with my father Mike. Or befriending hurt people who ended up hurting me. But each time I recognized the situation more quickly and did what felt most right for me. I later experienced a season of depression and anxiety. I became the first in my family to seek therapy as a regular practice in my life. I continued to ask God for grace in my life, even in all the years I doubted if He even existed. And Grace continued to show up. The darkness continued to tempt me, but I knew in my soul that I was born to be light.

After graduation, I took each job I landed very seriously and began to intentionally build my leadership skills. I explored different industries, including working at a tech company during the exciting dot-com boom, where I excelled in sales and worked my way up. I became the first in my family to get into graduate school, where I earned my MBA at Columbia University and started pursing my passion of sharing other people's stories through writing for the school paper.

I eventually went after my dream of hosting a show that shared other people's stories with the world, like my lifelong hero Oprah. The rest of the story might be familiar to you by now: midway through that dream of working in television with the goal of launching a talk show, I faced a setback, the problematic skin condition on my face that risked jeopardizing my TV career. I took a detour and launched a business in my living room, helping other women dealing with skin challenges feel seen and beautiful. I worked hard to trust that each setback was a divinely orchestrated setup for what I was destined to do next.

I'VE NEVER SHARED these stories about my past before, but they are a critical part of my own journey toward learning to believe I'm worthy and enough. A journey that continues unfolding each and every day. You can never judge a book by its cover, and we never know the shoes someone else is walking in, or the experiences they have walked through to get to where they're at in this moment. We often don't know the experiences they've journeyed through and might have never made it out of. Or the ones they're still suffering through in secret.

We Become What We Believe

As I share this story with you right now, so intimately, I can tell you with my whole heart and great conviction that we become what we believe. And that all things are possible. And that our steps are ordered. **Our setbacks are almost always setups for what we're called to do next in our lives.** Even when the setbacks and struggles don't make sense at the time.

Our past, even the parts we're embarrassed by or ashamed of, truly helps us become the person we're destined to become, with the unique skill sets we only developed because of what we went through. Many people have tried to analyze why IT Cosmetics was so successful, and it was never about the products, although of course I believe passionately in the ones we created. It was always about the connection with the customer, which led to loyalty and love for the brand. We tried to see every customer, to understand what they wanted, needed, and valued. We tried to make their lives better. And we didn't launch a product or a message unless it delivered on that. I believe that without the experiences I went through, the bad breaks, the unexpected mishaps, and the people of all walks of life that I've met along the way, I never could have built a successful business that truly connected to tens of millions of women. I've had the gift of being exposed to and getting to intimately know many different types of people, and that has shown me that my friend who works as an adult entertainer wants the same things as my friend who is a waitress at Denny's, who wants the same things as my professor with more degrees than I can count. And now that I've had the blessing of meeting some of the most iconic thought leaders in the world, I know that they all want the same things too. We all find fulfillment through growth in ourselves and contribution to others. We all want to feel enough and loved. And we're all on a lifelong quest toward believing we're worthy of both.

Our journey toward worthiness is always unfolding. It's a lifelong voyage that, if we let it, continues each day.

AFTER SELLING THE company Paulo and I started in our living room to L'Oréal, I gave them my word I would stay on as CEO and run it for three years. I did, and I continued to work incredibly hard, and we doubled the size of the business in the first two years after the acquisition. Being the first woman in their history to hold such a high title, and to be crushing numbers and contributing to the success of a publicly traded company, felt really badass. In my mind and in my ego. But then I had a feeling in my gut that told me it was time to step away. I was torn, because after the decade of the nonstop, often unglamorous work of building a business, I was finally getting to experience the extra-fancy stuff. I got to attend the big Oscars parties and walk red carpets and was invited to rooms I'd only seen before on TV and in movies. But when I'd work with a stylist and big fancy glam team, I found myself far more interested in their life stories and struggles and triumphs and dreams than I was in the gift of benefiting from their art on my face and body. I found myself sitting inside the walls of my huge, private, fancy office, larger than many of the apartments I'd lived in, feeling like it was my temporary home, but not where I was going to belong for long.

I started spending extra moments taking in each detail of my new life and celebrating it, as if I knew it would soon be a memory. It took me a while to process this feeling, but soon I had an overwhelming sense that I was supposed to leave and use everything I had learned so far in life to be of service to others. My mind wanted to stay and have fun and relish in the new, glamorous things that the world celebrates. Like award ceremonies, celebrity visits, and the fancy Chanel-like quilted sofa with pink pearl-encrusted pillows in my new fairy-tale office. But I had already learned this lesson in my life, that external validation doesn't equate to real love. I had to learn that lesson many, many, many times in my life, and sometimes still do, but every time my knowing always knows better. Because **external validation feels good but doesn't fill your soul.**

IN THE FALL of 2019, after I fulfilled my commitment to L'Oréal, I stepped away for good from IT Cosmetics, the company I'd given more than a decade of my life to, away from a team I loved with my soul. It was very hard. But I also knew it was right. My gut and my soul knew it was right. I had given everything I had to the mission of seeing women as beautiful and worthy, and helping them see themselves that way through the company I had built. I had an incredible team that poured their hearts and souls into this mission. And now that I no longer owned it and was no longer making the decisions only owners could make, it was time to trust it in the new owners' hands and step away fully. I decided to trust myself. **When we make the decision to trust ourselves, things unfold exactly as they're destined to.**

To not ask what can I do, but to ask what was I created for?
— ETHAN WILLIS

When I stepped away from IT Cosmetics, I wrote my first book, *Believe IT*, while binge eating Lucky Charms and sobbing my eyes out during most of the writing process. And just like I'm doing for *WORTHY*, I donated 100 percent of my author proceeds from the book, and to date, we've donated hundreds of thousands of dollars and millions of meals to the organizations Feeding America and Together Rising. I've had the honor of now funding leadership training in hundreds of prisons and women's shelters across the United States. And I truly feel like my calling to serve is just getting started.

I went from being arrested and booked into a juvenile detention cell to funding leadership training in more than a hundred prisons across the country. I went from being voted biggest procrastinator in my high school yearbook to being valedictorian and commencement speaker in college, and later, voted class speaker in grad school. From waitressing

External validation feels good but doesn't fill your soul.

and serving meals at Denny's—and yes, also strip club sodas—to donating millions of meals to those suffering from food insecurity. I went from saving my tip money to buy a ticket in the very back row of a Tony Robbins event to keynote speaking onstage alongside him for more than a dozen of his events and having him speak on my stage. I've hosted my own live event, focused on helping people feel less alone and more *enough*, with more than 200,000 people attending. I hosted all eleven and a half hours of the live event and put it on for free so it could impact the greatest number of people. I went from watching Oprah in my living room as a little girl to teaching alongside her as part of her "The Life You Want" class and calling her not just my mentor but my friend. I went from being told I didn't fit in the beauty industry to building one of the most successful companies in the beauty industry, in large part because I *didn't* fit in in the beauty industry. And because I was able to see people who the beauty industry had largely ignored, I went from the verge of bankruptcy to *Forbes*'s list of America's Richest Self-Made Women. I went from dating men who mistreated me and didn't reciprocate love to being blessed to be married to my husband, Paulo, a really good man and a generous, loving soul. It's been a lifelong journey that began with over three decades of feeling unworthy and not *enough*. It's only by continuing to do the work on feeling worthy of loving myself as I am that I'm able to attract, be attracted to, and feel worthy of others who love me well.

Where you come from, and even where you are right now, doesn't determine where you're going. **Where you are right now in your story matters less than the person you're becoming in it.** I have made, and still make, more mistakes than I can count. Often daily. But today I correct them sooner, forgive myself quicker, and catch myself before I attach my mistakes to my own self-worth or identity. I wake up passionate and determined to help every person I can reach feel seen and *enough*. Even if it's for the first time, or for the first time in a long time. It is my life's greatest mission. I am a work in progress, on this journey right alongside you. And I'm so beyond honored to be on it with you. For me, it's truly the privilege of a lifetime.

Grace Is All Around You

The more you acknowledge grace, the more grace appears.

— TONY ROBBINS

Grace is real and it's all over our lives. Yours and mine. And the more we notice it, the more of it there is to notice. Grace surrounds you, it goes before you, it's behind you and beside you and beneath you and above you. It's in the whisper that tells you to watch out, and in the moments you've felt unconditional love in your life. It's in the protection that didn't let you stray off course for long and kept you safe when you did. It's in the butterfly sharing its beauty with you and the warmth of the sun's rays on your skin. It's in the closed door you tried so hard to pry open, only now to be so thankful it didn't.

My story could have taken a very, very different path. In many more instances than I can fit in this book. When you think about the moments of grace in your life—the relationship that didn't work out (and even though it was painful, you're now SO grateful it didn't), the lucky break you got out of the blue, the

Where you are right now in your story matters less than the person you're becoming in it.

person who believed in you even when you didn't have the experience, the accident you survived, the addiction you're in a lifetime of recovery from, the heart that's beating for you right now in your chest—no matter how many times it's been broken, it's still showing up for you, the day your baby was born healthy, the room you were invited into even when you didn't feel qualified, the stranger who gave you a kind smile when there's no way they could have known you were having a bad day, the breath you're able to fill your lungs with right now that says you are alive—it can truly magnify the awe, wonder, and beauty of your journey.

Wherever you are in your life's story unfolding today, I believe your best days are ahead of you, if you want them to be. We all have a story, and we're all the author of it. **We can't always choose the characters or narratives that can come in and out of the pages, but we can always decide the meaning we attach to each of them.** We can decide if they, as my friend Robin Roberts says, were *our mess* or will become *our message*. We can decide if they were the *worst thing* that happened to us, or the *best thing* because of what we learned and the resilience we built. We can decide that what we fell *victim* to can be turned into a *victory* for ourselves and others in part by helping others *make it through* those same painful things that we've now *made it through*. **Maybe the things you've been feeling shame around aren't even shameful at all. And you have the power to decide if you want them to be.** We can decide if we turn our pain into purpose. And view our most challenging *setbacks* as *setups* in our lives, where we use what we went through, in the spirit of service and purpose, to now help others make it through too. To honor the grace given to us and pass that grace along to someone else who might need the grace that our experience can offer.

> *We can't all be famous but we can all be great.*
> *Because greatness is determined by service.*
>
> — MARTIN LUTHER KING, JR.

Celebrating the moments of grace in our lives reminds us of the ***greatness that's bigger than ourselves.*** We can look back at even our greatest moments of pain and realize that they're always happening *for* us, not *to* us. They're steering us on the path we're destined for and helping us build the resilience and strength to carry the calling on our lives, reminding us of the ***greatness within us.*** When we use all that we've been through to be of service in some way to others—*that* is the ***greatness that is us.***

PART TWO

UNLEARNING

*The Lies That Lead to Doubt, and
the Truths That Wake Up Worthiness*

CHAPTER 5

Don't Wait on Your Weight
The Lie: My Weight Impacts My Worth

People often say that "beauty is in the eye of the beholder,"
and I say that the most liberating thing about beauty is
realizing that you are the beholder.

— SALMA HAYEK

AS WE DIVE into this section of the book on the *lies* that lead to self-doubt and the *truths* that wake up worthiness, I want to start with one very specific lie, one that so many of us have believed for far too long: the lie that our weight impacts our worth, and that we should wait on our weight to fully live our best lives.

How many of us imagine that someday, when we finally hit whatever our goal weight looks like, our lives will be better? We'll go to the party or reunion. We'll swim in the ocean instead of hiding on the beach wearing a cover-up. We'll be willing to be photographed without hiding in the back of the group. What has the lie that you need to wait on your weight already cost you in your life? What has it cost you in your relationships? And in your ambitions, your precious time, and your potential joy? Has waiting on your weight caused you to miss out on making memories, to miss out on life? And if it isn't your judgment and beliefs around your physical weight, think about what *does* weigh you down in life that's causing you to wait on living it fully. Is there something you think needs to happen before you can embrace life to the fullest? Perhaps it's the weight of others' expectations or the weight of your own. Perhaps it's the weight of limiting beliefs or the thing you complain about and never accept or change.

This chapter isn't about weight. It's about how so many of us believe the lie that we need to wait on *anything* to live our lives to their fullest, and that we need to wait to believe we're worthy. This chapter is a battle cry for that waiting season to be over.

A LIMITING BELIEF is a thought that you believe to be true or a state of mind that limits you in some way. Limiting beliefs can be taught to us or learned over time, and sometimes we're not even aware we have them. These limiting beliefs make up the portion of our *belief system* (let's call it BS for short, as when it comes to limiting beliefs, they're often total BS) that can hold us back, keep us stuck, and fill our minds with fear and self-doubt. While we believe them to be true, they can often be completely made-up stories we tell ourselves, or have been taught, that are in fact not true at all.

The idea that we should wait on our weight to take the photo, to attend the reunion, to go out on the date, to wear the swimsuit, and to launch the business is a lie. A limiting belief. A part of our belief system that's complete BS.

An important step on your path of building rock-solid self-worth is gaining awareness of the limiting beliefs in your life and learning the tools, like the many we're exploring in this book, for how to overcome or reverse them. Identifying, overcoming, and replacing your limiting beliefs can be difficult work, and it can also be your life's greatest work. One of my favorite tools is simply to become aware of a limiting belief in your life that might be holding you back, then ask your soul, your knowing, your intuition, if that belief is actually true or not. See, I believe our mind can tell us things all day long, but when we get still and ask our own knowing, it knows a whole lot better than our mind. And I've learned to trust my soul and my own knowing over my mind. It's how I've made critical business decisions, and in this case, it's how I finally learned to stop waiting on my weight to live my life.

NoteWORTHY: For a guide on strengthening your intuition and tuning in to your knowing, go to WorthyBook.com/Resources

One study shows that when it comes to low body esteem, 89 percent of girls and women opt out of important activities when they don't feel good about how they look—like socializing, engaging with friends and family, and taking part in activities outside of the house. Have you ever done this? I have. In fact, my lifelong issues around body-doubt have cost me more time, energy depletion, and missed-out moments of joy in my life than I can bear to think about.

From my mid-twenties until my early forties, I didn't put on a swimsuit. I built a company that inspired millions of women to believe in themselves, and I had transformed my own beliefs about my skin condition to believing my flaws were in fact beautiful and empowering. Yet I couldn't get there when it came to my beliefs about my body. I declined invitations to events because of my weight. In group photos, I stood in the very back, behind everyone else, and even though my husband, Paulo, is completely indifferent about what size I am, I always made sure the lights were dim in our bedroom. I've had to do a lot of work overcoming my limiting beliefs to truly let new beliefs take root enough to stop WAITING on my WEIGHT to feel worthy.

What finally convinced me to change was the pain of imagining my future and what it would cost me if I didn't let go of these limiting beliefs around my body. I imagined the adventures I would decline, the precious time I'd lose worrying that nothing fit or looked quite right, and the memories I'd miss out on. I imagined the joy I'd lose, the deep connection with others I'd forego, and the pool time I'd miss out on with my kids. I considered what this limiting belief around my body had already cost me, and I knew in my soul that belief wasn't true. This knowing, along with the example of feeling unworthy that I'd be showing my daughter, Wonder, finally did it for me. When Wonder turned one, we took her into a swimming pool for the first time. We were at a crowded hotel. And despite the crowds, which included people I knew, I put on the swimsuit and did it. After a lot of hard work, through many of the tools in this book, when I'm now in a bathing suit, I literally will jiggle my cellulite with joy, knowing that if just one other woman sees it, she will hopefully feel less alone and more enough.

Each time a woman stands up for herself, without knowing it possibly, without claiming it, she stands up for all women.

— MAYA ANGELOU

There's a spot in the Arizona desert where Paulo and I love to vacation, and one day while spending time in the pool I focused on two oversized bronze turtle sculptures that spoke to my soul. Each turtle was about four feet long and two to three feet tall. One of the turtles was positioned outside the pool, a few yards away, standing with its front two feet perched up on a small rock, as if it were watching us swim. The second turtle was in the most joyous pose, sitting fully upright on its hind legs, resting all of its weight on its tail the way a human would sit up, leaning back slightly, basking in the sun. It was fully underbelly out, fully basking in the sunshine, fully body-confident.

I stared at these two turtles for the longest time, reflecting. For most of my life, my limiting beliefs about my weight had me living life like the turtle in the background. The one hiding. The one perched with its front two feet up on a rock, just close enough to see everyone else having fun and living life. The one waiting until later to get in on the fun. I've spent decades of life as that turtle. But no more.

> *Forgive yourself for believing that you're*
> *anything less than beautiful.*
>
> — IYANLA VANZANT

Now the second turtle, the one that's full underbelly out, basking in the sun, no longer hiding in plain sight, has my name on it. And yours too. Every time I go back to that spot in Arizona, I visit that turtle. I've even brought groups of friends there. Sometimes, it's a gift to see a visual reminder of what our limiting beliefs can cost us, and a visual reminder of who our intuition knows we're born to be. Even when it comes in the form of two turtles.

OUR THOUGHTS CAN get very loud telling us lies all day long in the form of limiting beliefs, but as I mentioned, this part of our belief system is total BS. Our knowing always knows the truth. One of my daily practices is when a BS limiting belief pops into my head, I instantly replace it with a better belief that I know to be true. I make the decision to trust my knowing over that old BS belief system that tries to resurface at any moment and hold me back. The more I implement this practice into my life, the more it takes root, and the fewer BS thoughts pop into my head. This has been a game changer for me in learning how to stop waiting on my weight to embrace life to its fullest.

> *Fashion Tip: Go with pants who accept you for who you are.*
>
> — LIA VALENCIA KEY

Here are some examples of how this practice plays out in my daily life, and perhaps if you have limiting belief system BS thoughts like these too, you'll find these replacement truths to be helpful.

Your belief system says: Don't put on a swimsuit.
Your knowing says: Enjoy the waves splashing on your skin. Be grateful you have the mobility to move in the water. You have strong legs and feet that feel the sand between your toes. You can feel the sunshine on your skin and the breeze hitting it.

Your belief system says: Everyone is staring at you and judging.
Your knowing says: Your confidence in your body is giving another woman a permission slip to have confidence in hers.

Your belief system says: Watch your weight.
Your knowing says: Watch your soul.

Your belief system says: This cellulite is awful.
Your knowing says: The genetic cell structure your Creator designed you with is perfectly made for you and has no meaning other than what we make up.

Your belief system says: I should feel embarrassed of my mom bod or dad bod.
Your knowing says: Be an example for your children of how they should feel about their bodies.

Your belief system says: When I get to my goal weight, I'll be more successful.
Your knowing says: A false belief will always leave you poor.

Your belief system says: When I fit into a certain size of jeans, then I'll have peace.
Your knowing says: If a belief costs you your peace, it's too expensive.

Your belief system says: My babies won't notice I'm sitting on the sidelines of the pool.
Your knowing says: I'm setting an example for them to one day also believe they're not worthy of swimming.

Your belief system says: You should wait until you're a different weight to have fun.
Your knowing says: Either have fun now, or be haunted by the regret for all the fun you missed out on.

Your belief system says: When you're slimmer, your family member will finally give you her approval.
Your knowing says: She never will approve of you until she learns to stop disapproving of herself.

Your belief system says: Replay that hurtful comment someone made about your body.
Your knowing says: Hurt people hurt people, and that comment has nothing to do with you.

Your belief system says: Judge the photo based on how your body looks in it.
Your knowing says: Feel the gift of that moment of life captured in the photo.

Your belief system says: You look terrible. Decline the video call so your friend doesn't judge you.
Your knowing says: Anyone who judges you isn't your friend.

Your belief system says: Measure your life based on the number on the scale.
Your knowing says: Measure a life well lived by the scale on which you've loved.

Your belief system says: Skip the day of fun, there will always be another party or reunion.
Your knowing says: You can never get this day back.

Your belief system says: Wear those painful heels so your legs look slimmer.
Your knowing says: It's time to go barefoot and run free.

Your belief system says: When you get to a certain size, then you'll be happy.
Your knowing says: Whatever you do, you take you with you.

Your belief system says: When I get thinner, he will love me more.
Your knowing says: Attraction comes from the exchange of emotional and chemical energy. And size doesn't biologically impact emotional and chemical energy.

Your belief system says: They told you you'd be so much happier when you lose the weight.
Your knowing says: That's just their belief system lying to them too.

Your belief system says: WAIT, WAIT, WAIT, you're not ready.
Your knowing says: Your WEIGHTING and your WAITING season is over!

Don't wait on your weight. To feel confident enough. To wear the swimsuit. To attend the party. To launch the business. To go out on the date. To share you want to be more than just friends. To take the risk. To learn ballroom dancing. To give yourself permission to be happy. To dye your hair your favorite color. To go back to school. To become a parent. To forgive. To change careers. To fall in love. To jiggle your cellulite with joy. To put yourself out there. To look in the mirror and celebrate the beauty that is YOU. To say I love you . . . to yourself and to them. And **don't ever wait on your weight to know you are WORTHY!**

CHAPTER 6

The Lie: I Should Only Be
Seen When I'm Happy

*Don't forget, while you're busy doubting yourself,
someone else is admiring your strength.*

— KRISTEN BUTLER

Person 1: "Why didn't you call me sooner?"

Person 2: "I just didn't want to bother you. Or bring you down with my problems. You've got too much going on to worry about my stuff. I like to call you when I have good news."

Does this sound familiar?

Right now in our culture we have a confusing mix of information coming at us from all angles. We have the unremitting reports of devastation, injustices, and tragedy in the news, and at the same time, we have best-selling signs and sweatshirts everywhere that say *Good Vibes Only*. Many of us are suffering silently. Many are wearing *Good Vibes Only* shirts.

These juxtaposed realities are also present on social media and the internet, where attention is being confused with love. Social media has fueled a collective wave of people getting attention for anything they possibly can. Apart from the value in using social media to bring attention to injustices and for advocacy, it's also become a modern-day method for individuals to present who they are to the world. And the temptation to confuse this new way of getting attention with feeling *enough* is taking a toll. In masses, people are starting to fall into one of two groups—either broadcasting their endless day-to-day mishaps and getting attention for them, or broadcasting how positive and strong and happy they are, while hiding anything that might not be as aspirational.

If you lose your keys, are late for work, burn the cake, have a cold, or someone was rude to you, do you share it with the world or text it to your friends? What we focus on we magnify, so when you're always reporting what's wrong—because you get attention for it and equate that attention with love—instead of feeling comforted and supported, you're much more likely to feel like your life is not going well.

And the more we're exposed to persistent negativity, the more we're desensitized to it. We also risk becoming hardened toward caring or taking action or helping someone who is truly the victim of a significant problem or important injustice.

On the flip side, there's a growing movement that says we always have the power to control our feelings, and therefore we should always choose to be happy. Good vibes only. As if more complex emotions, like anger and sadness, aren't equally valid and important. And while many advanced thought leaders do believe we can learn to choose our state of mind and therefore choose to be happy, the reality is the vast majority of the population doesn't have the privilege of time, training, or interest in actually understanding how to do so. So instead, we experience a growing pressure to present ourselves with constantly positive, *good vibes only* energy or a positive *mask*, depending on the circumstances.

If you're floating in the middle of the two scenarios above, as many of us are, then you likely hesitate to share your feelings or experiences or issues with others, even the ones you trust intimately, because you feel that if you can't show up happy, you shouldn't show up at all. Or you should show up wearing the "everything is good" mask. We start to believe that how we really feel isn't worth sharing. Or if we do share complex emotions, we'll bring others down, or worse, lose their respect, their approval, or their love. So we get in a routine where we wake up, make our coffee, put on our [insert your name] uniform, then play the role of *happy us* all day long. This false positivity infects us with the burden of living a lie, and infects those around us with the belief that they, too, should achieve this level of constant joy.

Toxic Positivity

We hide how we really feel so that we don't risk being alone, only to feel more alone than ever living behind a mask with a smile on it.

Psychologists refer to this as "toxic positivity," or the act of rejecting, suppressing, or avoiding negative emotions. Toxic positivity invalidates the authentic human emotional experience and can actually lead to its own trauma, isolation, and a whole variety of unhealthy coping mechanisms. And it's quite common. One recent study found that over 75 percent of people deliberately pretend to be happy, while ignoring their true emotions. As a little girl, I remember so many times when if I didn't happen to be smiling, some adult on the street or in the grocery store would order me to "smile!" Similarly, so many little boys are taught to hide how they're really feeling behind a mask of strength and stoicism. We're shamed for breaking the code of social conditioning, and we get the approval of our parents and our institutions when we master it. Then later, we perpetuate it by rewarding potential mates for replicating it. The better you know the code, the more attractive you are. The more you'll be loved. The more you'll be told you're worthy of love. No wonder so many of us are walking around hiding in plain sight.

I've been a lifelong student of personal development and human psychology. I believe that we are truly capable of making our life happier and more fulfilled in part through what we focus on and give our energy to, since what we focus on magnifies. Meaning if we focus on the negative parts of a situation, soon the entire situation will feel overwhelmingly negative. If we focus on the parts we can change or the parts that are an aha moment, lesson, or gift in a situation, our experience of the situation completely shifts. So, while I believe it's important to experience and express our full range of emotions, I also make it a point not to dwell in the emotions I don't want to magnify for too long. When we linger in a negative state of mind, it can turn into a habit and eventually become our default emotional go-to comfort zone. It's important to become aware that what we're feeling and experiencing in the moment is temporary, versus letting it become where we spend most of our time. And then we can make sure we spend the majority of our time where we most want to be.

As You Truly Are

I believe passionately that **we're responsible for the energy we bring into any room.** And I also believe we can allow ourselves to live in our full, true emotions, no matter how horrible they feel, and still show up with love at the same time. When our intentions are based in love, it doesn't mean we won't have the same wide range of emotions as anyone else. It just means we accept and process them and share them in a way that doesn't project pain and hurt onto others. I've been on a lifelong quest of learning to understand, heal from, and transform my own pain so that I don't transmit it to the people around me in an unhealthy way. But that doesn't mean I don't share it when I feel it. For me, there have been times when it would have been easier to keep hiding. **But you can't hide from yourself and heal at the same time.**

I love positivity and I believe that so much of life is the meaning we ourselves attach to things. The meaning we give to anything creates emotion in our body, and our emotions create the life we experience. There are so many situations in life that don't make sense or feel fair, but when you have a deep trust that your life is divinely orchestrated, you can recognize that everything is always happening for us, not to us. Even the things that feel unfair or don't make sense at the time. **Our lives are unfolding exactly as** they should. The most important part we need to play in our journey for that to happen is to show up as we truly are along the way.

We live in a society where we so often have no idea what someone else is *really* going through. And where others often have no idea what we're going through. A world where a highly curated social media feed can reassure others we're doing just fine, and signal to them there is no need to check in and see how we are, as if we're slowly unlearning the lesson that you can't judge a book by its cover. And it's so easy to forget that social media is often just the cover, and not the actual book of how someone is truly doing.

Anytime you connect with someone as you truly are, or share how you're feeling with someone else, even when it's not positive, you foster more intimacy in the relationship. It is a gift to both the sharer and the listener. Sometimes we don't want to call our friends for fear we'll bother them with our problems, or because we have nothing exciting or interesting to talk about, but when we do this, we just might be robbing them of the connection *they* might desperately need. Next time you feel like you don't want to bother a friend or loved one, try to see it as the potential gift of the connection you're offering to *them too* when you call! They just might need it at that exact moment!

You can't hide from yourself and heal at the same time.

I've had to work hard to improve this depth of connection, even inside my marriage. At one time, if my husband, Paulo, was grumpy and hoping to tell me all about it, I would tell him to come back later when he was in a better mood. We went on like this until one day I realized that it was fostering disconnection. Now when Paulo comes to me, I ask better questions. Okay, well, they may not be the most evolved questions, but I'll simply ask him, "Do you need to talk and connect? Or are you just hoping to vent?" Depending on the answer, I'll let him know if I have capacity in that moment or ask if perhaps we can reconvene later that day. And he does the same for me. We've also promised that when we're each playing the role of the listener, we'll proactively ask, "Do you need me to just listen, or would you like me to offer possible solutions?" It's been a game changer for both of us. Research shows that **listening is often depleting to the energy of the listener,** so it's important to have the capacity and desire to truly listen well, in order to connect. Listening is a superpower.

We've also implemented a tool in our marriage that I learned from my friend, creative entrepreneur and life coach Glo Atanmo. It's a tool I also use when I call or text my friends. Glo calls it a "capacity check." Before she asks for a friend's advice or asks them to be there for her, she asks them whether at that moment they have the capacity to have a deep conversation, or a lengthy one, or a thoughtful one, or one that requires the energy needed to give attention and presence.

Doesn't it just make so much sense? Now in my marriage and in my friendships, when I'm hoping to have a fully present or important conversation or connection, I do a capacity check and I've asked my friends and loved ones to do the same for me. It's important to know that it's okay to vent or dump or express it all, just first make sure you're aware of which it is that you need and make sure the other person does as well and has capacity for it. When I do a capacity check with my friends, if the answer is *yes*, we hop right on the call or dive right into the conversation. When the answer is *no*, then we agree to let the other know when our time or mental and emotional capacity frees up. An example of how to say no might be something like, "I value you so much, and today I'm running on empty. Can we set up a different time to chat so that I can give you my full attention, as I'd really like to be there for you fully?" This boundary tool protects you from sacrificing, betraying, or depleting yourself, while still fostering time and space to fuel connection with others. It also helps both people be even more intentional with valuing each other's time and energy.

Doing a capacity check, then hearing the other person confirm they have capacity, also helps create a feeling of safety. It's an invitation that gives space to bravely pour out your feelings and know you're truly being heard.

If you're a bit hesitant to ask your friends to check your capacity before having a conversation, and you're worried it might alienate them, a nice way to ease into it is to simply model the behavior yourself first before asking them to reciprocate. Begin to ask them if they have capacity to talk about something important or heavy before you share.

And if you're intentionally looking to grow and deepen your friendships and relationships in your life, it's important to prioritize making time for capacity for them as well. Offering your time and capacity with them is the most generous way to remind them they're worthy of it.

Living in Alignment

When you present yourself to others—whether online on social media, or in person—as feeling a way that's different from how you're truly feeling, you are out of congruence and alignment with your truth. And no matter how you justify it in your head, your heart will suffer, and so will your connection with others. It will feel incongruent and unfulfilling and empty and lonely and off. When you do this with the people you trust most, all these feelings multiply.

Living in alignment, or in congruence, with how you truly feel even when it's not *happy* might cost you some people in your life. But it's okay. **If they don't respond well to the real you, then they aren't for you anyway.** You couldn't have felt a true connection with them if they didn't know the real you to begin with. In order to foster worthiness, it's important to take actions that are congruent with believing you are worthy exactly as you are. Feelings, moods, needs, and all. Whether you're feeling sad vibes or positive ones. You are worthy of true authentic connection with others, and worthy of them showing up for the real you, the way you show up for the real them. **With congruency comes connection. With congruency comes intimacy. With congruency comes freedom.**

CHAPTER 7

The Lie: I Don't Deserve Better

*Are you not letting new people love you because
of how old people have hurt you?*

— STEVEN FURTICK

Y OU GUYS, I'M seriously burning *down there* right now." My girl-
friend Ella confessed her secret to our close group of friends sitting
around the table having lunch, and both compassion and silence swept
over the table.

Before I share the blazing truth of what happened here, let me first
reveal more about my incredible friend in the hot seat. (And, no, Ella
is not her real name, and yes, I got her blessing for every word in this
chapter. I'm letting you know up front as you'd be asking me both of
these questions by the end of what I'm about to share.)

When I think of the Alicia Keys song "Girl on Fire," I think of my
friend Ella. No, not in that way. In the *most victorious* ways. See, her
career success is off the charts, with awards, magazine articles, and a
bank account to prove it. She's an icon in her industry, and on the outside
and the inside she is, in so many ways, what the world would call the total
package. She's loved and celebrated by many people, both privately and
publicly. And at her core, she's a true love bug. You know, the kind of
person that can totally kick butt in her job, and yet does it in a way that

leads with love. She's a super thoughtful friend, always sending little gifts and loving texts to let you know you matter to her. Yet the part of Ella people don't see is that deep down inside, she feels unworthy of love. She feels *not enough*. In fact, she feels not even close to enough. She just hides it really, really well.

As I began to do the work of understanding the impact of trauma in my own life many years ago, I learned that virtually every single one of us has experienced trauma. And though each of our traumas may come in different forms and to different degrees, as Robin Roberts says, *you shouldn't ever compare despair.*

We've all felt pain in our lives. And without going into the trauma that's truly Trauma with a capital T of Ella's childhood, I'll just say her entire life has been a true hero's journey. One of identifying a mountain peak and then figuring out how to climb it, summiting it, and planting her victory flag right into the ground. She's proved she's deserving of being in the room, of being a boss, of developing loving, healthy friendships. She's the one her friends call for strength and her family calls for help. But her close circle of friends knows her truth: she turns to her addictions to both sugar and work to numb her feelings, and then hides in plain sight behind the real story she tells herself about herself—that she's not enough and is therefore unlovable. **Have you ever known someone, or been that someone, who can hear from the entire world that they're amazing, but just can't believe it about themselves?** That's Ella.

Have you ever known someone, or been that someone, who can hear from the entire world that they're amazing, but just can't believe it about themselves?

Ella often finds herself in romantic relationships where her love is unreciprocated. This isn't a conscious thing, of course. Ella wants with all of her knowing and might to be loved back. She was raised by her grandmother, and growing up, every time they drove over the railroad tracks her grandma would say to her, "Raise your feet up and make a wish."

Ella always, even back then, wished for a husband. Her greatest dream is to get married and have kids. Her greatest fear is being alone forever. Her greatest worry is that now, in her forties, she might be running out of time. So, she's developed a habit of opening her heart up to new men and ignoring red flags when they appear. She ignores the gut instinct that tells her when someone is being dishonest or when something just doesn't quite add up. Out of the fear of never finding anyone who treats her better or being alone forever, she stays in relationships far past the healthy point, just hoping they'll turn a corner for the better.

One relationship turned emotionally abusive, and Ella stayed in it for more than eight years, continually making excuses for her partner and hoping he would change. She started to believe him when he told her no one else would ever want her. She hid in plain sight by building her imaginary home and future inside of his. She could see it all—the wedding bells, the beautiful babies. The more she saw her home in him, the more she disappeared in her own soul. She has all of the professional, financial, and friend-group success she could dream of, but her biggest goal in life is to find romantic love. A true partner who loves her unconditionally. Her hero's mission isn't the one the press tells about her life, about a girl who overcame poverty to gain massive professional success. For a long time she believed her hero's mission would be finding the soul-filling, unconditional, lifelong love with a partner that fairy tales are made of.

"You guys, I'm seriously burning down there. He is such a liar, and my crotch is on fire." Okay, let's get to how this moment happened, and the fiery adventure Ella embarked on.

It might not surprise you to hear that it all started with a spark. His profile said *widower* and *father of two girls*. Ella liked his picture and instantly swiped right on the dating app. They exchanged messages and then scheduled a phone call, and like any good hopeless romantic, Ella couldn't help fantasizing about becoming a mother to two amazing motherless girls and a wife to this surely heroic man. Could all her hopes and dreams be delivered to her doorstep in one simple swipe?

Her cell phone rang, and as her screen lit up, her pulse raced. She answered *hello*, with all the confidence she could muster. He greeted her in a deep, tummy-turning-in-the-best-possible-way tone. He was charming, with an air of have-it-all-togetherness that gave her hope. He shared that his wife had passed from cancer, he had a past career in law enforcement, and he was now working hard on his own business while raising his twin daughters. Ella was a twin herself, so this felt like even more proof of her narrative—this was meant to be! The thought of raising his children and filling the hole in their lives felt like an amazing gift. What could be a higher purpose than to be a mom to two beautiful girls without one? The fantasy was taking root. The love story was writing itself.

Their phone calls led to meeting in neutral places, usually restaurants for dinner. And then they took a huge step forward—she invited him over to her place. Ella's living room is all white furniture and white carpet, and she's meticulous about having guests take their shoes off to keep it extra pristine. His appreciation for her décor and compliance with her rules made her heart flutter even more. As did his cologne. To her he smelled like . . . future husband. That first day in her home together, she sat down on her showroom-worthy couch, and he sat right next to her. Not in the chair across from her—right next to her. In his dapper jeans with rips in just the right places, polo shirt, and a confident smile, he reached one of his long muscular arms over and placed his hand on her knee as they talked. As he started gently rubbing her knee, Ella almost forgot what they were talking about. Words she doesn't recall were coming out of her mouth while the thoughts *please kiss me, please kiss me* went on repeat in her head. She didn't want to make the first move, she wanted to feel wanted. Then it happened. He leaned over and placed his lips onto hers, which led to a fully committed kiss. She felt her whole body surge with warmth and hope. Ella couldn't help it; she instantly fell in love. He didn't try anything more than a kiss that day. He was a gentleman, and his words of appreciation for her made her feel SO wanted. And being SO wanted feels SO good.

As Ella and her new friend grew closer, she learned his work schedule was atypical. He had developed an industrial cleaning product, and typically worked overnight with his team, cleaning business offices with the product. The more Ella asked about the company and his schedule, the more confused she got. You know when someone gives you an answer to a question, but you never feel like you fully understand the answer? She didn't want to press too hard since they were just getting to know each other. Then the red flags started flying.

When Ella called him in the evenings, he wouldn't answer. *If he is running his own company, why can't he answer the phone?* she wondered. He said it was too difficult to answer at work, and while her mind accepted that explanation, her intuition didn't. She hadn't yet been to his home, and she found that a bit odd too. The few times they had planned to go to his place, he changed the plans before they happened. Then one day they had plans and he didn't show up. In fact, he disappeared altogether. She couldn't get ahold of him for a few days. When she finally reached him, he said he had been in a motorcycle crash on the freeway and was in the hospital.

Learning this news, Ella immediately said, "What hospital? Where? I'll come see you right away!"

He quickly changed his story to say that he was in urgent care, not a hospital.

"Oh wow, did an ambulance take you to urgent care? Or who took you there if you got into a crash on the freeway?" Ella asked.

"A friend," he answered. He then texted Ella a photo of a motorcycle sitting on the side of the road. But Ella didn't see any signs of it having crashed. Her Spidey senses were now firing off warning signs all over the place.

Ella didn't know how to bridge the gaping canyon between her comfort zone of the past—which would be to ignore all the red flags and make excuses for them—and her new knowing and commitment to believing she was worthy of love. That wide-open canyon is a scary place. It can feel like we're walking a tight rope between what we fear most and what we want most. In Ella's case, between fearing being alone forever, and knowing she deserves honest, true love. Between what we know we can get in the moment and what we know we really deserve.

Ella wasn't quite ready to lose the potential future she had envisioned before their first date, so she ignored the voice of her own knowing. She knew he was lying to her. But that old part of her that was comfortable with people lying to her wanted to do what she did in the past, and pretend she believed him, ignoring her inner voice telling the unpleasant truth. She kept seeing him. She continued to be intimate with him when they were together. And let me not sell her story short here—according to Ella, the sex was OFF THE CHARTS amazing. Not just amazing like, okay, I'll-write-about-it-in-my-journal-tonight amazing. But earth-shattering, where-have-you-been-all-my-life, how-do-you-know-touching-this-does-that, you-should-open-up-a-How-To-Sex-school amazing!

Even as these mind-blowing intimate encounters were adding up, his stories weren't. Ella started digging a bit deeper into his past, hoping she'd find consistency that would prove she was wrong to worry. Because of her incredible professional career and connections, Ella knows how to find things out about people, and knows people who know how to find things out about people. She decided to presume innocence until she could prove otherwise, and so she carried on with him while she investigated.

Surviving on orgasms and hopeless romantic tendencies, after a few months, Ella made it official with him and they committed to being exclusive with each other. They removed their profiles from the dating apps, and then decided to take their trust and relationship a step further, and stopped using protection when they were intimate. Then came the straw that broke the camel's back, or I should say the match that burned the haystack down.

I love the way Oprah describes how your intuition is always talking to you. At first, it's often in the form of a whisper. And if you ignore it, then it will come to you in the form of a thump on your head. Then a brick. Then if you still ignore it, it will come in the form of an entire wall of bricks crashing down onto you all at once. That wall of bricks was about to hit Ella . . . all at once!

The day after their first unprotected encounter together, Ella started to feel an unremitting burning sensation down there. She thought maybe it was just temporary, but it wouldn't stop. Another day went by, and full-out fire.

Her precious heart hoped it was a yeast infection or UTI, but in her gut, she knew it was something she hadn't experienced before. Ella went to her doctor, who did an exam and took a culture. Then the phone call came—it wasn't a UTI, and it wasn't yeast. Her new friend had given her a full-blown sexually transmitted infection; he wasn't monogamous like he had promised her. *That's why he's so good at sex; he must be having A LOT of it*, she thought to herself.

Ella was so upset. She felt angry and betrayed about the STI, and it's important to note that she's far from alone. More than half of Americans will contract a sexually transmitted infection or sexually transmitted disease in their lifetime. In fact, studies show one in four teens contract one each year, and one out of every two people will have one by the age of twenty-five. For so many people it can be a source of suffering in silence. No one talks about it because it can feel too embarrassing. So, we often shun ourselves and bury it deep inside and let it take root in our identity of unworthiness. If this is you, I want you to hear me loud and clear right now: YOU ARE FULLY WORTHY EXACTLY AS YOU ARE. FULLY BEAUTIFUL. FULLY WHOLE. FULLY WORTHY OF LOVE. No matter what's happened to you that you wish you could reverse, no matter what experiences you've gone though that you wish you could undo, no matter what decisions you've made that you might feel were mistakes, and no matter what decisions someone else made that ended up hurting you unfairly. YOUR WORTH is not tied to any of these things. These are all parts of life's ups and downs, and I'm not for a moment diminishing the pain that some of life's ups and downs can cause, but it's so important to know with certainty that THEY DO NOT DEFINE YOU. ONLY YOU AND YOUR CREATOR CAN DEFINE YOU.

And what I know beyond a shadow of a doubt, and I pray that you take deep to heart right now, is that if this is you, then today the days of shaming yourself are over. Today the days of shunning yourself are over. Today the days of thinking you're less than are over. Today the days of thinking you're damaged are over. Today is a new day. A day where you get out of the lies and get into your truth. A day where you get out of your head and get into your soul. Because your soul knows and your Creator knows that you are whole and beautiful and valuable and fully redeemed and fully restored. That you are a living, breathing, unstoppable, powerful force of love. And that absolutely nothing—no person, no place, no thing, no past mistake, no celebratory success, no up, no down, no STI—can change the fact that you are fully and innately WORTHY!

We so easily think we're alone in these experiences because no one talks about them. If you know someone who's experienced a similar story and who these words could help, please share this passage with them, or share your book with them when you're done. No girl, no woman, no person left behind in knowing they're worthy!

Your self-worth is determined by you. You don't have to depend on someone telling you who you are.
— BEYONCÉ

The doctor prescribed Ella antibiotics, and in a couple days she was free of the burning, but now she felt an even greater pain as her fairy tale came crashing down. She learned through extensive investigating that while it was true he had two young daughters, there was no record of his wife, of his allegedly deceased wife, anywhere. *Could someone really stoop that low to lie about being a widower?* she thought. But even though she couldn't find proof his wife had died, she couldn't find proof she *hadn't*. Despite this, along with contracting an infection from him, Ella was

STILL tempted to think that maybe there was an excuse that made sense for all of this. From the outside it's so easy to see this unfold and yell NOOOOO, but it's also so easy to be the person craving love so badly that we decide to ignore our own knowing.

CUE the opening line of this chapter, and the importance of the circle around you. The circle to remind you of WHO you are, and what you're worth, on the days you're tempted to forget.

When Ella finished her story, we sat with our mouths open watching our beautiful, intelligent, strong, warrior, heart-of-gold friend doubt her own worthiness out loud. "I know I'm seriously burning down there right now, but I might give him one more chance to explain himself," she said.

"WHAT????? NOOOOOOOOOOOOOOOOOOOOOOOOO!!!!!!" the entire table blurted out. He was clearly a LIAR that had SET HER CROTCH ON FIRE! (And not the good kind of fire.)

"NOOOOOOOOOOOOOO!!!"

Her heart yearns for the deepest of loves and she was giving that love over and over to someone who was starving her of it in return. That was her old pattern, and we all knew she'd made great strides toward her new one. She had gotten off track. Until she made the decision to get back on. And she did. With a little nudge from her inner circle.

After a LOT of reminding her who she was, Ella concluded that she was going to end it. And she decided to tell him right away that it was over. "I just need to stay strong and not answer when he calls. Maybe I should change his name to add the word LIAR to it in my phone, so that I never forget," she said.

One of our friends at the table asked for her phone, went to her contacts, and promptly changed the title/company line below his name to LIAR LIAR CROTCH ON FIRE. Ella burst out laughing and we all joined in howling in laughter. Then, as we all passed the phone around to chuckle at his new title, we all saw his face for the first time. Silence.

"OOOOOH wow, he's SO HOT, okay . . ." one of our friends blurted out.

"Whoa, okay, how baaaaaadddddd was the infection?" another friend asked, only half joking, with tears of laughter streaming down her face. Yep, Liar Liar was HOT in more ways than just one. The silly puns continued, because sometimes the best medicine for your hurting friend is a really, really good laugh.

Ella called him to tell him that it was over. She told him she deserved so much more than someone lying to her, and that she hoped he considered what kind of example he was setting for his two daughters. And after that day, she never spoke to him again.

If you've ever allowed anyone to treat you as less than you deserve, you'll likely know that breaking it off cold turkey isn't always easy. And the deep reason you're committed to changing old patterns in your life, or your *why* for it, has to be so strong that you're willing to resist heading back to the old.

In the past, before she was clear about making the decision to love herself and to only keep people in her life worthy of her love, Ella would have stayed in it with Liar Liar, like she'd stayed in many toxic, unhealthy relationships, losing both years and hope. She would have stayed despite the lies, ignoring her intuition and telling herself she could change him. She had once believed the all-time favorite lie many of us have told ourselves: that he would change for her.

Through a lot of therapy and hard work, Ella had grown. She had come to see that the ultimate hero's journey, the fight of her life, would be giving that soul-filling unconditional love to herself first, before she could exchange that kind of love with someone else.

If you don't believe you're worthy of loving yourself
unconditionally, it's impossible to find, give, receive,
or believe you deserve unconditional love from someone else.
We cannot give what we do not have.

— MARIANNE WILLIAMSON

The beauty is in the revelation of this knowing. Like one of my fave quotes from the late Dr. Maya Angelou says, "Do the best you can until you know better, and when you know better, do better." Ella is done with the cage she'd built around herself. It had a giant sign that said *Enter if you're gonna hurt me, because that's what feels most comfortable to me. Warning: if you enter with good intentions, I might put you in the friend zone.* Now she is on the personal mission toward building and embracing her worth. Of identifying sooner when someone is treating her in a way that is less than she deserves. Of deciding she's worthy of the same standard of love *from* someone else that she gives *to* someone else. And not *less than*, just because she's believed in the past *she* was *less than*. She's deciding she's worthy of love exactly as she is. Not when her weight hits a certain number on the scale. Not when she becomes less ambitious. Not when she dims her light or her brain to carry a conversation. Not when she lowers her standards and gives hall passes to people who don't align with her choice of values. Not when she thinks, *Well, maybe friends with benefits is all I'll ever get*, even though her heart craves more. Ella has now crossed the threshold of knowing.

Your Emotional Comfort Zone

We all have a strong human desire for as much certainty as we can get in life. Certainty is comfort. I opened this chapter with the words of Steven Furtick: "Are you not letting new people love you because of how old people have hurt you?" I want to encourage you to consider this question in your life right now. Sometimes when we don't let new people love us, whether it's a potential healthy friendship or intimate relationship, the reason is that we've been hurt in the past and fear being hurt again. But the most prevalent reason is one that no one ever talks about. It's because our learned, conditioned default *emotional comfort zone* makes it more *comfortable* to stay in relationships, or keep seeking relationships from the type of people who are familiar to us, meaning new people who treat us just as poorly as people from our pasts. We're drawn to what's familiar. **As human beings, we're not wired to be happy, we're wired to be comfortable.** We're programmed to seek what we've known. **Even though we think we want to be happy, our subconscious drives us to do everything we can to get back to what's comfortable, a place that most accurately reflects our sense of worthiness.** We will even sabotage a potentially good relationship to get back to one that feels more comfortable to us, even if what's most familiar and comfortable is someone disappointing us or treating us poorly.

Ella was comfortable with partners who didn't treat her well. When being treated as *less than* matches our view of ourselves as *less than*, then we're drawn to those relationships. To bad boys we know will break our hearts. Clinical psychologist Suzanne Lachmann points out that "nothing interferes with the ability to have an authentic, reciprocal relationship like low self-esteem. If you can't believe you're good enough, how can you believe a loving partner could choose you?" And when we're stuck in that mode, even if we meet someone who adores us and treats us well, we don't find ourselves attracted to them, and automatically put them in the friend zone. When pain, rejection, and *not-enoughness* are familiar and comfortable to us, we can subconsciously be attracted to someone who will bring us that familiar comfort. When people have hurt your worth in the past, it can be most comfortable to seek out people that inevitably will foster feelings of unworthiness in you. Breaking out of the comfort zone can feel risky. Showing up exactly as we are and loudly proclaiming to ourselves *I am worthy of love exactly as I am* can feel so, so uncertain. Opening up to new people in our lives, who might look different from people in our pasts, comes with discomfort at first. Awareness, courage, and braving the uncertainty is how we start to break old patterns, redefine what feels familiar, and ultimately set ourselves free.

ELLA IS ON that new journey now. The true hero's journey of her life. She's also on a trek toward building her faith, and she prays daily that God "hurries up a little" in bringing her the partner she's destined to be with. As with all newly charted paths, it's almost never a straight line. It is filled with bumps and zigzags and setbacks and detours and wrong turns.

With an unwavering vision for the beautiful, true life she deserves, Ella continues to value herself more and more each day. Now when she sees red flags in a potential partner, she doesn't make excuses for them. Still, daily, she struggles with instinctively putting others' needs before her own, whether it's her employees, her clients, the press, her friends, or her family. But she now knows and believes that she deserves so much more, and she's focused on reinforcing her new story about what she deserves, until that new story becomes comfortable.

Ella now reminds herself that you can't change anyone else. She now makes a promise to herself to listen to her own intuition and be guided by it. And to no longer break that promise to herself. And now, today, she's loving herself every day a bit more than she did yesterday. Now, today, she's deciding to trust herself. And it's working. So now when I think of the Alicia Keys song "Girl on Fire," I think of my friend Ella. No, not in that way. In the *most victorious, unstoppable, summiting the mountain* kind of way.

> *The secret to getting what you want is to truly learn to believe you're worthy of it.*

As you do the work to build your own sense of worthiness, your default emotional comfort zone, and what you're attracted to and drawn to in friendships and relationships will evolve too. But the most important part of the evolution, the foundation of it all, is the worthiness part. This is how the journey, the knowing, the becoming, blossoms—one step at a time. One reminder at a time that you are worthy. One decision at a time to stop hiding in plain sight. **The secret to getting what you want is to truly learn to believe you're worthy of it.**

When I sat down with this same group of friends recently, I asked Ella if she still had his name in her phone under Liar Liar Crotch on Fire. She hadn't answered his calls, called him, or looked at his contact in a long time. She went to pull up his contact and immediately burst into laughter. Then showed all of us at the table. Not only was "Liar Liar Crotch on Fire" still his job title, but she had changed his first name to six words all in caps: DO NOT CALL LIAR INFECTION GUY. Cue the tears of laughter at the table, reinstate the silly jokes, cue the disappearance of all semblance of maturity. Listen, there's therapy and personal growth and self-love practices, and then also sometimes you gotta do what you gotta do—like change the contact on your phone to make sure you don't ever forget. Then we all noticed something else. She had even given him a special ringtone. She had downloaded a ringtone called "bark" so on top of his new name, the phone barked like a dog if he ever tried to call. It worked! She hasn't spoken to him since and hasn't been tempted to.

And in case you're wondering how Ella is now, she's dating and for the first time ever, she is whole. She's no longer abandoning herself and is no longer putting potential partners who treat her well in the friend zone. Ella's committed to not settling for anyone who doesn't love as hard and as pure as she does. And I believe she'll find them. My girl Ella is on fire!

CHAPTER 8

The Lie: I Don't Have Anything Special to Offer

Helping people face their own brokenness is easy.
The dilemma is to help them face their stunning beauty.

— UNKNOWN

ALL THE GOOD ideas are taken. Why should I bother to pursue mine? Someone's probably done it already."

"Why would he be interested in me? There's nothing about me that's particularly special. There are so many others way more attractive with less emotional baggage than me."

"I'm not pursuing my dreams because other people can do them better than me."

"I've got nothing truly brilliant or new or novel to offer the world."

BULLSH*T! Sorry for that language, Grandma, I just couldn't contain myself . . . but that's complete BS. And I hear these exact statements from countless people, especially girls and women, every day.

These are all lies, and I believed them for a long time too. Until I learned, time and time again, that they simply aren't true. Unless you believe them. Then they're still not true, but they become true for you. But they're still a lie! Okay, I'll calm down.

When I think about the incredible ideas, the love to be shared, the gifts and offerings that never make their way into the world because of these lies we believe, I feel both furious and fired up at the same time. Because the world needs your ideas, thoughts, voice, gifts, love, friendship, and offerings. Now more than ever. So let's tackle why one of the most common lies that keeps you doubting your willingness to go for it simply isn't true: that because someone else has already done it, or is somehow better or more appealing than you, you shouldn't do it or go for it.

If you offer your authentic self in your idea, gift, or contribution to the world, it is impossible for someone else to have done it already.

Remember, there is only one of you in the world. There is no one else who thinks or feels or creates the way you do. Therefore, **if you offer your authentic self in your idea, gift, or contribution to the world, it is impossible for someone else to have done it already**. If you put forth your idea, create your business, offer your love, write your book, share your thoughts, launch your product idea from a place of authenticity, then it has never been done before. It is novel. It is new. It is one of a kind. And no one else can do it the way you can. It's just not possible. Period.

Understanding and believing this fully is critical to no longer hiding in plain sight, and to fully embracing the worth of your ideas, talents, gifts, art, thoughts, voice, goals, and dreams and then deciding to fully express them. **Don't talk yourself out of the person you're born to be. You don't want to look back on your life and say,** *I should have, I could have,* **or** *I wish I would have.*

When I launched IT Cosmetics in my living room, it would have been easy to tell myself it would never work because there were already thousands of makeup companies out there selling makeup. The idea was already done. And that was true, there were thousands of makeup companies out there selling makeup, but if I hadn't launched my own, I never would have known if my ideas could succeed.

Or if a person seeking loving companionship decides not to sign up for the dating app, not to share with others that they're single, and not to leave the house to socialize or be around others, all because there are so many other far more [fill in the blank] people looking for love too, what's going to happen? The one certain outcome is that the person likely won't find the relationship they're hoping for. If, before we walk into a room or into a circle of friends, we hesitate, thinking we're not quite worthy enough to be there, then we walk into it with that energy and miss the chance to make real connections. Note: **We can only receive the kind of love and acceptance from others that we give to ourselves.** If a chef decides not to launch her dream restaurant because there are already other restaurants out there and it's already been done, she may miss being discovered by a neighborhood that would go wild for the recipes her grandmother passed down. It doesn't matter how granular you get; you'll almost always be able to find someone else who has done the exact same thing. So then, why do so many restaurants with the same cuisine thrive? Why do so many makeup companies succeed? Why do so many people who don't fit society's ultimate standard of x, y, or z still find loving relationships? Why do so many romantic comedies pull in big box-office numbers with the same storyline? Why are so many books on similar topics successful each year? Because there is always room for each person's unique way of doing it, there is always room for the secret ingredient that only your soul can add, and there is always room for quality.

I recently was in a fascinating debate with a book publisher's team where everyone was chiming in on the topic of whether or not there are any original thoughts in the world. Yes, people are coming up with stories and innovations that feel fresh and new. But when it comes to our minds and our souls and humanity, are there actually any original thoughts? Or are there just original messengers who convey those thoughts in their own unique ways? I have been blessed to have my life impacted greatly by many mentors, some of whom I've never met. Many thought leaders, researchers, self-help experts, spiritual guides, authors, pastors, and creators with an abundance of life lessons and wisdom under their belts. And when I read their books, get their advice, or hear their messages, almost all the concepts can be traced back to a religious, spiritual, or psychological text of the past. They're almost always rooted there. But that doesn't cause any of these thought leaders to be less effective or to have less impact on humanity and on the world.

If an idea is truly the first of its kind, that's amazing, although then you also have to worry if it's too early to catch on. I've been first to market in my company with truly novel ideas that didn't succeed because the market wasn't ready for them. Sometimes I've watched others have great success launching the exact same concept years later. But of course, there are plenty of times when being first to launch a novel idea is a huge win!

Of course, if you're able to launch an idea that's been done before but improve on its quality, your chances of it being embraced multiply! There is always room for improvement of an existing product, idea, or offering. **But neither of these—being first or doing it better—is an absolute requirement for an idea to succeed.** When you do it authentically, with your own take and emotions and vision and spin, it becomes a novel offering to the world. And you can never know how it will be received until you make the decision to stop hiding and offer it.

In the years I spent building IT Cosmetics, my intention was always to create products that were better than what was already available, and to position those products through marketing messages that helped our customers feel seen, worthy, and *enough*. Making a better product than what already exists in any space is hard. It often requires a lot of time, failed attempts in the development process, and a refusal to settle for a version that doesn't match your vision. No matter the pressure we received from retail partners asking for new product launches, we never launched anything new unless we truly believed it was better than what was out there. Because of this, for many years we didn't offer one of the most popular makeup items: blush. As you probably know, blush is often a peach, pink, or purple hue and is most commonly used to highlight the natural flush of color you already have on your cheeks. Thousands of companies sell blush, and no matter how hard my team of chemists and I tried, I just didn't feel like the formulas we created were in fact better than the many that were already out there. So I kept my promise to myself and to my team, and year after year, we didn't launch blush. Until one day, and one Cheeto, changed that. Yep, Cheeto, as in the bright orange cheesy treat. I'll explain.

The product development process at my company was pretty intense and very untraditional. I used to pray for novel ideas that would truly make my customers' lives better. And I would go to almost any measure to try and figure those products out. In addition to truly listening and learning from as many of our customers as I could, I also did many product development retreats with my team at a gathering space on top of energy vortexes in Arizona, where energy clearing and attracting crystals lined the hotel and boardrooms. It wasn't that I didn't trust God and my own knowing enough, but I figured since God also created energy vortexes and crystals, why not cover all my bases?

On one particular retreat, my team and I were in an incredible state of flow. Ideas for the coming two years of product launches were flowing out of us all week long, and on the last day of the gathering, we decided to focus on blush, one of the few products we still hadn't figured out how to improve. We threw out ideas from every corner of the room—but to no avail. By the time we packed up and headed to the airport, it seemed like our customers would

We can only receive the kind of love and acceptance from others that we give to ourselves.

officially have to wait another year for a way of feeling extra cheeky.

Back home, in the car with Paulo, I was snacking on a bag of Cheetos while explaining that we still hadn't come up with an innovative blush idea. I glanced down at my orange-stained fingers. Hoping he wasn't grossed out, I proceeded to stick each finger in my mouth one at a time to lick all the excess cheese off of them. He was driving, but I saw him glancing from the road to my hands, which were still stained orange. Just as I was about to tell him to stop judging, his face looked as if he was having a huge aha moment. And he was!

"What about a powder blush stain? That doesn't exist yet! And if Cheetos stain your skin, then a powder blush stain must be possible!" Instead of judging me for licking cheese residue off my fingers, he was busy connecting the dots on a brilliant concept. *Who knew Cheetos could spark a great beauty product idea?*

One huge problem with existing blush on the market is that it doesn't last. You apply the powder to your cheeks and after a few hours, it's faded. There are blush stains out there to solve the longevity problem, but they are all liquids or creams and are really complicated to apply, so they don't sell well. But I'd never heard of anyone making a powder stain. *If Cheetos have a powder-staining element to them, yet they're safe enough to eat, then Paulo is right,* I thought in that moment. *It must be possible to create a powder blush stain!*

This was a massive idea, and I told him so. And I said a prayer of thanks for the gift of it.

Then I rushed to share the news with our team, who were equally excited. We had it!

WE BEGAN THE product development process with two of our labs and the teams of chemists there. At this point in my company's growth, we were still relatively small compared to many of the more well-known brands out there. We spent over a year in development and rejected countless formulas until one day we did it! We made it, we manifested it, we created it—the first-ever powder blush stain!

Now came the fun part of launching it into the world. This process starts with sending early samples to all of the "long-lead" beauty press.

For a product to be featured in a traditional print magazine, which was like winning the lottery in those days, they needed to receive the sample four to five months before the day the feature or article would be published. We sent out samples to all of the magazines, and they were buzzing. We received word that our blush became a finalist for one of the biggest editorial awards in the industry. I couldn't believe it. And yet I could. It deserved it because it was truly innovative. Since we were a small company at the time, the thought of getting this huge honor and the press that came with it felt like a fairy-tale-like dream come true.

Months passed, and the marketing launch plans firmed up. We were approaching the sixty-day-out window from launch when I got a phone call. We hadn't received the coveted award.

"What, why?" I asked our PR team.

"The magazine's editor-in-chief said another brand is doing the same product. And theirs is launching sooner. Since you are both doing the same thing, they can't give the award to either of you."

I was devastated. Then I thought to myself, *How in the world is someone else doing the same idea at the exact same time? There's no way.*

Then I found out, there was a way.

One of our partner manufacturing labs had shared our idea and our formula with a much larger makeup brand. The lab made money off of every unit ordered, so if and when that much larger makeup brand released their (aka OUR) powder blush stain to their vast customer base and wide retail distribution, the lab stood to make a lot more money than they possibly could from our launch.

Was this okay? No. Was it completely wrong and totally messed up? Yes. Could I have sued them? Yes. Could I afford to sue them? No.

So, instead, I cried. And I feared that because someone else was doing OUR idea first, it meant it wouldn't work for us. Even worse, it could make me look like a copycat. Even though it was OUR idea! I was devastated. I felt completely betrayed by our manufacturer, and so deflated. I knew how rare and special truly novel ideas are, and it was so upsetting that ours had been given to someone else. If you've ever had someone steal your idea at work, or use the baby name you shared with them first, or the millions of other ways this can happen, at first it can feel like an unexpected blow or like you've been betrayed. It can even have you questioning if you should change or even cancel the idea that **you** originated.

We decided the best business move at the time was to still move ahead with the product. The manufacturer prioritized the larger brand's launch, and while we were still packaging it, the bigger brand introduced their powder blush stain into stores nationwide. It sold okay, but it didn't fly off the shelves. Then we launched ours. It sold incredibly well. I learned later that year through industry reports that my small company had sold considerably more units of product than the much larger company did. We marketed the product slightly differently, and our messaging about it was authentic to us. Even though the exact same product had already been launched, customers seemed to gravitate toward our messaging. So, at the end of the day, customers bought what they most connected to, not just what the product was. It was a huge lesson for me, and one I've seen play out many times since. It doesn't matter if someone else has already launched your idea, in this case literally. Because no one can do it like you.

I've experienced and seen countless other examples of this in life, in relationships, and in business. It's so easy to think we don't have anything special to offer. We reject ourselves before we let anyone else do it.

Next time you're tempted to doubt that you have anything special to offer in life, in business, in relationships, in love, and in offering your ideas, talents, heart, and gifts to the world, remember this: You in fact have the secret ingredient that no one else in the universe has access to, and can't add to the way they do it. You alone possess the most special thing possible to offer: YOU.

CHAPTER 9

The Lie: I Need to Please *Them* in Order to Love *Me*

If you live to please others, everyone
will love you except yourself.

— PAULO COELHO

*H*EY, CINNABON, STOP *staring at me. I don't see you.* I tried to
project a subliminal message to the gooey, frosting-melting-off-
the-top, fresh-out-of-the-oven Cinnabon cinnamon rolls sitting on my
kitchen island. I mean, not that I knew if the frosting was melting off
because I was absolutely *not* looking at them. If I made eye contact with
the frosting, or worse, the center swirl, they would take me down. And
that would be a major problem, because I wanted my mother-in-law
to approve of me. She was sitting about ten feet away, and I tried with
superheroic might to focus solely on the broccoli, salad, and berries that
were also spread out on the center kitchen counter. *Don't tempt me, Cinni
. . . I know you know I'll be thinking about you all day . . . I know you know
it's love at first sight, but I just can't be loyal to our romance right now. I've
committed to broccoli. And I don't even love him. In fact, I feel nothing at all
when I'm with him. But right now, I've gotta do what I've gotta do. I will
cherish our love affair that almost happened forever. It's better to have loved
and lost, than to never have loved at all.*

This was at Christmas, a time when I traditionally host my many families for several days. We all gather, share recipes passed down between generations, open presents, and cherish being together. Paulo's family always joins, along with a number of our friends, some without family, who have all become our chosen family. Our house is filled with all of the nostalgic holiday delights, an entire table dedicated to cookies and gingerbread houses with guests' names on them, several boxes of my mom's favorite See's candy, and bottomless drinks of any variety. My mother-in-law Vivi is a grandbaby magnet and fully commits to dressing herself in T-shirts that have whatever my daughter Wonder's and son Wilder's favorite cartoon character of the moment is. She also lives an incredibly disciplined, healthy lifestyle. I'm in awe of it. She eats mostly the same foods daily for her meals, like salmon and broccoli, and rarely ever consumes processed foods or sugar. She exercises daily and is in incredible shape. I . . . am not.

Overcoming body-doubt has been one of my greatest challenges, one that I've come such a long way on but will probably continue to be on for life. **My mission has changed greatly from one of wanting to *look* a certain way, to one of wanting to *feel* a certain way.** Through working hard to strengthen my self-worth, I'm finally to the point where I no longer let whatever size I'm at in the moment determine how I feel about myself. I truly feel worthy no matter my size. If you've experienced anything similar, you know what a hard-fought victory it is. It means I no longer worry if I want to enjoy delicious, and sometimes even unhealthy, foods. But that's not what this story is about. It's about people-pleasing. And in this case, I had a person to please: my mother-in-law.

Whenever my husband eats unhealthy foods in front of her, out of well-intended motherly concern she is very vocal about how he should abstain. What's beautiful for him is that he doesn't care. It doesn't bother him one bit. He just lets her advice go in one ear and out the other and proceeds to eat whatever he wants. When I eat something unhealthy in front of her, she never says anything, she just sits quietly. But obviously she sees me, and I can't help worrying about her likely disapproval. I crave her approval more than I crave the cinnamon rolls. So today it's broccoli. Today, I hide. I don't share what I want. I don't feel free to make my own choices. My deeply ingrained people pleaser takes over. In that moment, **I want to be loved more than I want to be me**.

The trait of people-pleasing is generally described as striving to please others in order to gain their approval, or avoid conflict or criticism, all while sacrificing your own wants and needs in the process. It can look like over-apologizing to others, being hyperaware of what others think, and struggling to set boundaries.

The many problems with people-pleasing include neglecting yourself; shouldering extra stress, tiredness, and resentment; welcoming the feeling of constant failure since it's impossible to please everyone; and living inauthentically, which impacts all aspects of your health, relationships, and life.

Research shows more than 50 percent of women and more than 40 percent of men describe themselves as people pleasers. And this compulsion to please plays out in many aspects of their lives. More than 70 percent of women say they go to extreme measures to avoid conflict, and close to 70 percent prioritize others' needs first, at the cost of meeting their own.

Learning to stop people-pleasing can start with small steps, including learning to listen to your inner voice, committing to speaking your truth, identifying your priorities, setting boundaries, practicing saying no, remembering you can't please everyone, spending time alone, making the commitment to yourself to prioritize your own needs, and strengthening your self-worth.

I really don't think I need buns of steel. I'd be
happy with buns of cinnamon.

— ELLEN DEGENERES

Okay, back to the cinnamon roll, still silently sending me sweet nothings across the kitchen island. As a half hour, then an hour passed on that Christmas Day in my kitchen, my thoughts drifted from how badly I wanted to eat a cinnamon roll to why I wasn't doing it. Why, as a grown woman who knows better, I still wasn't living according to what I knew. These deep beliefs that then create neural pathways in our brain are no joke, and if we're not intentional about our journey to rewiring them, it's so easy to fall back into old grooves. If love was what I craved from my mother-in-law, the only way for her to give it to me in a way where I could fully receive it would be if she gave it to me as who I truly am. If she gave it to my representative I was showing up as, I wouldn't be able to feel and receive it anyway. **If it was truly love I craved, I had no choice but to be all of me. Even if she didn't approve of all of me.**

I decided to eat the cinnamon roll.

As I made eye contact with that roll, inside I felt the intensity of two secret lovers meeting up behind closed doors and diving into each other's arms. But on the outside, I played it cool. I extended my arm out across the kitchen island, grabbed the spatula, and lifted the gift-from-above, right onto my pedestal—I mean plate. A warm river of gooey cinnamon-buttery-cream-cheesy frosting was strung across the plate, like a string on a kite. I confidently grabbed a fork, and . . . Took. A. Bite.

In that exact moment, my mother-in-law made eye contact with me. With a great big smile, she started talking about how excited she was to be there with the grandkids. I was confused. Did she not notice my disobedience? Where was the shaming silence I had anticipated? It never came. She continued to talk about how amazed she was with Wonder's reading comprehension and Wilder's keen sense of humor. I realized the last thing she actually cared about was if I was eating a cinnamon roll. I realized I had been projecting my insecurities onto her. All at the expense of us connecting more closely, all as the alluring warmth of the cinnamon roll dwindled.

I wondered how many other times I had misread the situation. There's a famous saying by Anaïs Nin: "We don't see things as *they* are, we see things as *we* are." In other words, we bring our own beliefs, experiences, traumas, insecurities, and biases into every situation, even though we might think we're seeing objectively. As a result, **we end up losing precious time worrying about things that never even existed and will never actually happen.** We waste so much life worrying what someone else thinks about us, though they might not even be thinking about us in the first place. Then we try to people-please based on thoughts we project onto others and assumptions we make about what would win their approval. Often that other person, unknowingly, is doing the same thing right back to us, doubling the wall of disconnection, all with the intention of connection and love. The only part of this that we can control is the part we bring to the table. And the only solution is to be more aware of it, mustering up the courage to drop the people-pleasing and show up as our full selves, even though that requires bravery and vulnerability.

In the case of the cinnamon roll, even if my mother-in-law had disapproved of my choice to eat it or judged me for it, it *still* would have brought us closer in one way or another. Because **even a negative reaction is better than the barrier of disconnection that comes with being inauthentic**. The energy exchange would have been real, and connected, even if it wouldn't have been positive.

Right now, the Cinnabon is who I am. I'm just not the broccoli. Sure, I want to be the broccoli. So bad. I've got big broccoli goals in life. Goals that include going vegan without defaulting to Oreos at every meal. (Yep, Oreos are vegan. Yep, you can become a very, very unhealthy vegan with enough dedication.) But right now, I'm just not the broccoli.

If you're a cinnamon-roller, eat the cinnamon roll. And if it's your time to become the broccoli, eat the broccoli. And if that's you, don't downplay or hide your broccoli victory in an effort to please the cinnamon-rollers. Be the broccoli, through and through.

NoteWORTHY: For a free bonus guide on how to stop people-pleasing, visit WorthyBook.com/Resources

CHAPTER 10

The Lie: If I Stand Out, I'll Get Kicked Out

Don't try to lessen yourself for the world;
let the world catch up to you.

— BEYONCÉ

WE'RE TAUGHT A girl code from an early age: if I stand out, I might get kicked out. I'm not talking about the kind of kicked out that my husband, Paulo, experienced at an over-the-top acting pro wrestling event where he thought it would be funny to join the actual pro wrestlers and throw his own chair from the audience right into the ring. Yep, that really happened. Yep, he got escorted out of the event. Yep, I still married him anyway. Sidenote: to this day he's proud of his showmanship and claims the chair throwing "made sense at the time."

As young girls we learn that if we're too independent or shine too brightly, we risk losing love and belonging. We learn to bond over problems and to make decisions based on group consensus, not on what our own intuition tells us. We're taught we can't be trusted alone. We learn that if a girl is too smart, she won't be popular or desired by boys. We learn we have to play the game of fitting in very carefully because **if we excel, we might repel. And if we're great, we might get hate.**

We could easily dismiss all of this as childhood silliness, except for the fact that these conditioned beliefs around gender norms often continue to be deeply ingrained patterns in adulthood. And if we don't recognize and unlearn them, they keep us shrinking and hiding. They keep us from trusting ourselves and we are left endlessly unfulfilled.

Growing up in London, my friend Danielle took pride in never missing a day of school no matter what. From age ten onward, year after year, she showed up even on the days she wasn't feeling her best. She once had food poisoning and literally refused to let it break her perfect attendance record, so she showed up for class, despite embarrassingly having to rush to the bathroom several times that day. As she entered her preteen and then teenage years, she started learning that the areas she excelled in weren't always celebrated by her peers. And she started feeling the social pressure to dim her own light in order to fit in. At the age of fourteen when she was about to win the award for her record of years of perfect attendance at her school, she sabotaged it all to avoid being teased. She actually pulled a sick day, despite not being sick, so that she wouldn't win the perfect attendance award despite her years of hard work to earn it. She threw it all away because she feared that by standing out for a great accomplishment, she'd be socially ostracized. Happily, things have changed for Danielle. Today she shows up daily for millions of women across the world through her online community with the mission of inspiring women to embrace their audacious ambitions.

Stuck in Societal Norms

Since as far back as it was an option, women have learned to sacrifice being successful for being liked.

What are the first things you think when I describe a woman to you as "really ambitious"? Do you think she's warm or cold? How do you think she dresses? What kind of mother do you think she is? Do you think you'd like her? Would she fit in with your friends?

And when I now describe a man to you as "really ambitious"? Same questions: Do you think he's warm or cold? How do you think he dresses? What kind of father do you think he is? Do you think you'd like him? Would he fit in with your friends?

Decades of studies, including recent social science research, find that if a man is successful, people like him more, and if a woman is successful, in general people like her less.

As human beings, no matter our gender, our deepest fears all link to us fearing we're not enough and fearing that because we're not enough, we won't be loved. So if we're perpetuating gender norms that the more successful a man is, the more we love him, and the more successful a woman is, the less we love her, what do you think is going to happen? And is happening? And has happened for generations? Women live their life hiding in plain sight, holding back the ideas, ambitions, and gifts they could offer the world, shrinking who they are. We do this because we crave love, except receiving love for being something we're not, or for being less than we are, is not satisfying. Only as our true self can we feel truly loved.

Men are often raised with soul-crushing societal judgment and pressure. They're made to feel like their professional success determines their worth. So they sacrifice their passions, ideas, talents, and gifts in order to hide behind a profession the world—and often their family—gives their stamp of approval. They're often taught they ARE their job, and if they don't have a good-enough, high-enough-earning one, then something is wrong with them. Men, just as easily as women, learn to hide in plain sight. To live incongruently with who they really are and what they really want.

These masks we learn to wear also affect how we see and often judge others. When two candidates run for office, any office, and one is a man and the other a woman, the press coverage is drastically different. And if you pay attention, even the comments around most family dinner tables are obviously coming from deep-rooted convictions of what box each gender should fit into. You'll often see and hear far more derogatory and appearance-focused comments made about the woman.

This carries over into the workplace too, especially when a woman is in a position of leadership or aims to be. When a woman makes a firm decision at work, takes an executive action, or makes a judgment call and gives direction to her team, she often gets called aggressive, cold, and unlikable. When a man does the same thing, he's referred to as confident and a visionary. A female leader often gets feedback either from her boss, from HR, or in her year-end review that she's "not a team player," is "political" or "too competitive." When feedback like this is given, it compels women to step back, lean out, and downsize their own potential. This type of feedback feels like criticism, that, because we've learned not to trust ourselves from the time we were little, can so easily be mistaken as truth. It leads to women thinking that in order to get ahead they need to take a less decisive approach. When in fact this can be poison to their potential.

Some studies show that in the workplace, men are often promoted based on future potential and women are often promoted based on past accomplishments. So, women often don't get promoted until we've proven 100 percent we can do it. Men get promoted if there is confidence that they will be able to do it.

In other areas of our lives, we often apply these exact same standards. As women, we don't promote *ourselves* based on our potential. If anything, we talk ourselves out of it. We focus on why we're not worthy of things, and what we focus on becomes our reality.

We are taught that women must be nurturing above all else, so when a woman is competent, she doesn't come across as nice enough. And if she's super nice, she's seen as more nice than competent. Which we subconsciously learn is okay. Because remember, intelligence and success cause women to be liked less. After contorting ourselves to fit these cultural norms, we end up liked, but not fulfilled. Liked but longing.

Liked but in agony. Liked but angry. Liked but empty. Liked but feeling unlovable. Liked but hiding. Liked but feeling unworthy.

And then it happens. At a certain age, **we've gotten so good at hiding that we achieve a goal we always dreaded but totally orchestrated ourselves—we disappear.** We go from hiding to feeling completely unseen. By those around us, by the world, and most devastatingly by ourselves. We go from hiding to feeling unseen, and feeling like we don't matter.

We tell ourselves the lie that we are feeling invisible because we are too old or too unattractive. Which is just the old lies evolved into slightly newer ones.

The truth is, **we've hidden from ourselves for so long that we finally become invisible.**

The good news is, it's not too late to change this.

From Invisible to Visible

> *Don't shrink who you are just to fit in spaces
> too small for your destiny.*
> — UNKNOWN

When was the last time you got still and asked yourself, *How do I really feel? What do I really want?* When was the last time you let someone else see the true, real you? When was the last time you truly saw yourself? When was the last time you spoke up, used your voice, and shared your opinion without second-guessing for a moment whether it's worthy of airing and sharing?

Sometimes we don't even realize what's happening, we just know we don't feel alive or connected or fulfilled. Becoming aware of how you're hiding and disconnecting from your true nature is transformative. Think back in your life to when you stopped raising your hand. When you started realizing that if you shrink who you are, everyone around you would feel more comfortable. When you started having trouble tuning in to your own intuition, knowing what you actually want and who you truly are.

The way to go from invisible to visible, from unseen to seen, is first to decide you want to. And second, to make the decision, step-by-step, to stop dimming your own light and playing it small. Start seeing yourself and letting others see you. Sharing how you truly feel and what you truly want. Believing you're worthy of all these things.

It's not too late. You're not too old. Your best days are ahead.

— MALLY RONCAL

If you're feeling like it's too late, I promise you it's not! And your timing is exactly right. It is never too late to build self-worth, step forward, speak up, learn to love who you truly are, and move toward what you want in your life. Change takes work. It comes with uncertainty, especially regarding how others might react. But squash that old lie and belief that shrinking who you are will bring you love and realize you can only foster true love and belonging by being exactly who—and all—you are! This can fundamentally shift all areas of your life and your fulfillment in it.

If you take a moment, can you think of one or more ways you've been hiding in plain sight, downplaying your talent, holding back, not sharing your gifts with the world? Is it because you fear they're not enough, or you worry you'll stand out and make others uncomfortable, or you worry they might even root against you?

You Are Worthy of Being Seen

Now, let's take some action together. What's one way, starting today, you're going to start living as more of who you truly are? What's one action you're committed to taking today to stop hiding in plain sight and to believe you're worthy? Are you going to write the first word of your book? Are you going to rest, and commit to knowing you are worthy of rest and restoration without guilt? Are you going to wear the boldly colored outfit? Are you going to speak your mind, set that boundary, or share your true feelings? Are you going to register the domain for your future company? Are you going to call the person and tell them you forgive them, not because what they did is right, but so that you feel free? Are you going to share that idea tomorrow at work? Are you going to wear the shorts, no matter how you might perceive your legs to look? Are you going to get back on the dating app? Are you going to start sharing your art with the world, or maybe on social media? What's one way, today, that you're going to take an action to stop hiding? Declare it! Proclaim it! Go ~~balls~~ ovaries to the wall. Take that next step. **You are worthy of living as and being all of who you are!**

Our deepest fear is not that we are inadequate. Our deepest fear is that we are powerful beyond measure. It is our light, not our darkness that most frightens us. We ask ourselves, "Who am I to be brilliant, gorgeous, talented, fabulous?" Actually, who are you not to be? You are a child of God. Your playing small does not serve the world. There is nothing enlightened about shrinking so that other people won't feel insecure around you. We are all meant to shine, as children do. We were born to make manifest the glory of God that is within us. It's not just in some of us; it's in everyone. And as we let our own light shine, we unconsciously give other people permission to do the same. As we are liberated from our own fear, our presence automatically liberates others.

— MARIANNE WILLIAMSON

When I first read this famous Marianne Williamson quote about being afraid of our own power and light, I was in my early twenties and didn't fully understand or connect to it. And now in my midforties I get it through and through. I've lived it. Maybe you have too.

And if you have, perhaps today will be the day that you decide you'll no longer shrink who you are to make others more comfortable. You'll no longer dim your light and avoid shining bright. **Maybe today is the day you'll decide—one thought, one step, one word, one action at a time—to liberate yourself from your own fears of seeing, acknowledging, and embracing just how powerful and beautiful and *worthy* you are to stand out as who you truly are.**

CHAPTER 11

The Lie: I'm an Imposter and Not Enough on My Own

Whatever you fear establishes the boundaries of your freedom.

— ERWIN RAPHAEL MCMANUS

I USED TO FANTASIZE that a guy would pull up beside me on the street and rescue me . . . you know, just like in the movie *Pretty Woman*," says my friend Lara, sheepishly. A group of us had gathered for lunch, and this was news to us.

"What? You? No," blurted out my friend Jenna.

"Oh, after seeing that movie I totally daydreamed about that too," I admitted, mainly to let Lara know she wasn't alone. "I wanted the guy to climb up the side of the building for me, umbrella and all, and I used to want to own one of those blue-and-white spandex outfits!"

My friend Julie chimed in, "I mean, I married a stay-at-home dad and wouldn't trade it for anything, but didn't we all imagine that whole scenario happening after that movie?" Everyone laughed and agreed.

"Listen, I'm not hating on no one, and if a dude's got that kind of car, and the skills to pay the bills, plus the motion in the ocean, he can pull up alongside me in that car and rescue me all day long," said my friend Hannah as everyone laughed.

Lara cut us off. "No, you guys, I actually seriously had this goal. Just like in the movie, I wanted an amazing guy to find me. I would fold neatly right into his world, and we would live happily ever after. It was a real goal for me that I pursued and tried to manifest."

"You're serious?" said Jenna, shocked since Lara, a rock in her family with a successful corporate job, is the last person you'd imagine wanting someone to rescue her. Listening to all the banter, I couldn't help but think of how different Lara's path would have been if any of her attempts to be "rescued" in order to live happily ever after had manifested.

AS LITTLE GIRLS, we learn through books and movies that we need someone else to rescue and complete us. Whether it's the fairy godmother transforming Cinderella and the prince then marrying her and her moving into his castle; the lumberjack rescuing Little Red Riding Hood from the wolf; the prince climbing Rapunzel's hair to rescue her from captivity in the tower; Snow White and Sleeping Beauty, both saved by "true love's" kiss; the prince's kiss restoring Ariel's voice in the animated version of *The Little Mermaid*; or the countless other examples, we learn that only when that other person arrives can we finally be whole and happy. We learn that we alone don't have what it takes, so we either sit and wait for them to arrive, or we pursue them feverishly. We learn as little girls that we can't trust ourselves simply with what we already have inside of us. Then we become grown women who don't. We learn from a young age to believe that even if we don't take action or make choices for ourselves, it will all work out because someone else who knows better than us will rescue us, then we will no longer live hidden. We learn at a young age to play sweet and meek, then give someone else the credit of our ultimate success when we come fully alive and blossom into our best future, thanks to them.

AS ADULTS, THIS narrative that we're not enough on our own can easily show up in the form of imposter syndrome, defined in the Oxford English Dictionary as the persistent inability to believe that our success is deserved or has been legitimately achieved as a result of our own efforts or skills. In fact, research shows 75 percent of women in executive roles have experienced imposter syndrome in their careers. Even in situations where our experience surpasses the necessary qualifications needed, we still often feel like an imposter, whether while stepping into a new job or stepping into our natural talent. We seek external confirmation we're enough, we look for someone we deem more qualified to validate our ideas, and we search for a romantic partner who affirms our value.

If we haven't found that person yet, or we haven't been rescued, we believe we're not whole. So we search tirelessly, looking for love, not realizing we ourselves are love. We never learn that before looking for a lifelong partner in love, we need to first learn to love ourselves.

We grieve and replay past loves we "lost" telling ourselves the story that we're incomplete and now don't have love in our lives, because we don't realize we are, already, love. We overanalyze a lost love, even when our intuition knows it wasn't healthy for us, and we tell ourselves stories like "he should have been" the one. Not realizing the truth that, as my friend Matthew Hussey, life coach and best-selling author, says, if it *should've been* then *it would have been.* It's completely normal and part of our nature to crave companionship, connection, and belonging. **Wanting companionship, connection, and belonging is different from feeling we need someone else to be whole or to have love in our lives.**

Trusting Yourself

In addition to the fantasy of needing a prince to save us, we also imagine we need a mentor to rescue us professionally. Ambitious women so often tell themselves the lie that if they just had a really great mentor in their lives, then they'd know what to do and how to do it. Sure, mentors can be amazing, just like I'm sure real-life princes are. But they're not where you find your power or your greatness.

I fully believe in the power of mentorship. I find so much joy and fulfillment in mentoring others, and I deeply value and cherish the mentors who have come into and are in my life, but it's important to realize that your magic is in YOU. With mentors and with lovers, you don't need to rely on anyone else to somehow be activated, valuable, or worthy. It took me many years to learn this lesson and fully embrace it. I mean, after all, I really was secretly hoping Richard Gere would pull up alongside me at any moment for most of my twenties. But in the end of that movie, it was Julia Robert's character who ended up rescuing herself and inspiring him to rescue himself as well. Instead of waiting for the answers to come along in the form of Prince Charming, a mentor, or anyone else, we can welcome them and their advice into our lives with open arms, but ultimately, we have to trust ourselves, our instincts, and our experience. **Once you learn to trust yourself and your own intuition, you'll no longer feel like an imposter, or like you need someone else's intuition to guide you.**

NoteWORTHY: For additional resources on building your intuition, go to WorthyBook.com/Resources

Mentorship, a great circle of trusted friends, family, or colleagues, and even relying on data and information, can all be helpful in making decisions, but when you lean on any or all of them exclusively, it can actually get in the way of learning to trust yourself. It can keep you stuck in the feeling of imposter syndrome, where you feel like someone else has a better idea of what to do and how to do it. And that you, on your own, are somehow unqualified to know.

Now, while I greatly value the advice I get from the mentors in my life, I actually make as many decisions in my life that go against their advice as I do that follow it. And they know that. And when I don't follow their advice, I let them know that my gut is telling me something else, and I'm gonna trust it instead. I put all advice I receive—from mentors or otherwise—through a filter of my own knowing, or intuition. I'll often pray about it. In this filtering process, I usually get a gut feeling that either says yes, that wisdom is right for you, or no, while that wisdom is great advice for some, it's not right for you to follow right now. My job is to get better and better at listening to and then trusting that knowing.

Developing intuition and learning to get still enough to hear your own knowing are skills we spend our entire lives building. Like muscles, these abilities get stronger and have more muscle memory with every use. There are inevitably times when we trust our intuition and it ends up seeming like we made the wrong decision, but I've come to believe that intuition is never wrong. It might result in an outcome we didn't want. That can feel very wrong. But I always trust that every disappointment comes with a lesson we needed to learn or relearn. To build the strength and resilience we have for where we're destined to go.

WHEN WE TRUST **our gut and it's "wrong," it's never actually wrong. It just results in an outcome we didn't want, and a lesson we needed to learn.**

DEVELOPING YOUR INTUITION and learning to trust yourself is so important, of course for every area in life, but especially if you are someone who likes to ask others for advice or if you are someone actively looking for mentors in your life. Remember, mentors can help support and *add value* to your experiences, but they don't *complete you,* as you have everything you need inside of you already! Optimize others' advice and experience for your own life by putting it through the filter of your own intuition. It's truly the only way to know if it's right for you.

Oh, a couple quick tips to share that I found super effective in finding mentors. In my years of growing my first company, I was so blessed to have many amazing mentors. None of them just happened to walk into my life. I pursued all of them. Many took years of me sending them notes, emails, and business updates before they gave me even a reply, let alone a fifteen-minute coffee together. But the one thing I did very intentionally as a hopeful mentee of theirs was to ask myself, *What is it I imagine they need* and *How can I be of service to them?* This is a game changer. When you're hoping for mentorship, it's easy to think you have nothing to offer that a potential mentor needs, and that's almost always not true.

In the many years when I barely had a spare penny, I would ask my mentors if I could bring them coffee or lunch. I let them know that whatever advice they gave me wouldn't stop with me—I planned to share it with as many other women as I could in the future. Everyone, including mentors, feels fulfilled when they impact and contribute to something bigger than themselves. I promised I would be the steward of their generosity with their time and use it to multiply their impact. That I would be there for them however I could, whether it was sending them an inspiring quote of the day or sending them a goofy dance or singing video to make them laugh if they're having a down day. I would literally offer all the ways I could add value to their lives (always free because I had no money, then later still free because I learned these are the only things potential mentors covet and don't get). They rarely took me up on any of these things, but they almost always ended up saying yes to mentoring me. Because they knew I understood this principle: **when you have empathy, and when you know the importance of adding value to *others*, not just asking for them to add value to you, you're far more likely to succeed in your pursuits.**

When we trust our gut and it's "wrong," it's never actually wrong. It just results in a lesson we needed to learn.

Also, when you're about to reach out to a mentor, do your homework before you ask for their time. If they have a book, read it. The mentor is the energy that's contagious to be around, but the real work you can do mostly for free online, by reading their writing or watching their videos, or researching.

You Are the VIP of Your Own Life

At a speaking event this year, I was standing on stage taking photos with some of the audience members after my hour-long keynote speech. The organizer of that particular event had arranged for everyone who had purchased a VIP ticket, which was about 10 percent of the audience, to get a photo with each of the speakers. The next day I received this message on Instagram from someone who was not in the VIP line that day, a woman named Abbey:

"Just a huge thank-you for your message at the event. My eighteen-year-old daughter Grace and I flew in from Iowa. I'm a single mom to her and her fifteen-year-old sister who were orphans from the Central African Republic until God brought us together five years ago. An answer to three souls' prayers. Grace wants to have her own business and is working on believing she's worthy. She has clarity and knows her why. Right now she is upstairs taking massive action creating videos. She wasn't allowed to meet you as we were not VIP at the event, and she was very disappointed. As she isn't ready to see rejection as God's protection just yet ☺ [a reference from my speech that day]. But I believe she will grow and achieve in the future so that she gets in the VIP line to thank you in person. Thank you for bringing God into your message as well, I couldn't ask for a better mentor for my girls. We see you, we truly see you . . . [heart emoji]"

Cue waterworks. As I sat reading this message in my Instagram DMs on my phone, I relished her strength and character. This single mom, Abbey, is the VIP of her own life. She didn't need a VIP ticket. Her belief in herself and her daughters was the best example of mentorship they could possibly see. In this single DM, without any ask attached, Abbey did the things above that I believe are so important. She didn't press the easy button or ask for anything. She simply shared how her daughter was upstairs working on her dream business right now, which happened to be crocheted earrings, clothing, handbags, bracelets, coasters, and more, and Abbey was encouraging her all the way. She also understood the importance of adding value to others, as in this single message she sent, letting me know that what I shared that day was seen, heard, and mattered to her and her daughter. Her sharing this with me, is her adding value to me. The most valuable kind of value. She has the confidence that she and her daughters will figure it out and trust in themselves and their faith. And she sent the message without asking for anything at all—she simply sent it with the intention of sharing her experience and saying thank you.

I sat in my living room with tears streaming down my face, imagining her daughter with hopes and dreams, upstairs in her bedroom filming videos to help get the word out about her business. I immediately went to Abbey's Instagram bio and looked for the link to her daughter's business. I found it! And my first course of action was of course—holiday gift shopping! Yep, I went on a small shopping spree getting some of the adorable crocheted sunflower coasters for my sister. Then I picked up the smiley face ones for myself. I marveled at the earrings and bags and got my own shopping high.

I then wrote Abbey back, and here's an excerpt from the message:

"Hi Abbey, thank you so much for your message! The only VIP line that ever truly matters is God's, and you and Grace and your other daughter are for sure in His!!! And Grace is in the second most powerful VIP line, her amazing mom's, who took the time to write a beautiful message to me! Thank you!!! I just spent a few minutes picking up a few Christmas presents from Grace's site this morning. Also, here is my email address, as I would like to make sure you and your girls get VIP tickets to my next live event as a gift from me. Sending you love today and thanks so much for your message! Jamie"

Her heartfelt reply shed light on a bit of her daughter's story, and theirs together. Abbey is the VIP and the hero of her own life. And through her example, she's showing her daughters how to be the VIP and the hero of theirs.

SOME PEOPLE LOOK for a partner or potential mate to save them. Some look for a mentor hoping they will. In both cases you're waiting on someone else to fulfill your dreams. Resist the urge to fall into the trap we learn in children's fairy tales, and then perpetuate later as adults, that alone, we're only capable of playing it small, and we need to wait until that one person comes into our lives to rescue us and give us what we need to play life full-out. Prince Charming, an incredible mentor, and a winning lotto ticket are all exciting to manifest and can be wonderful value-adds if they come into our lives . . . but wherever you go, there you are. Whatever relationship you enter, you still bring YOU with YOU. Whatever mentor gives you advice, you still bring YOU with YOU. **Your own knowing is more powerful than anyone else's advice.**

Take action now and trust yourself. **Being willing to get knocked down and get back up again, and fail, and learn, and grow, is more powerful than waiting for someone to come into your life telling you what step to take next.** You don't need to hold out for a hero. You have the power and everything you need inside of you right now to live the highest, truest expression of yourself. And when the princes and mentors and winning lotto tickets and happy surprises come into your life, they are gifts along the adventure. But they're not some VIP ticket that gets you into some magical room where all the answers are waiting for you.

Your knowing is the ticket. Cultivate it. Your hard work and resilience are the path. Brave it. Your soul is the magical room. Inhabit and trust it. You don't need a VIP ticket when you realize, you *are* the VIP. You don't need to hold out for a hero when you realize you *are* that hero.

CHAPTER 12

The Lie: If I'm Me, I Won't Be Loved

You either walk into your story and own your truth, or you live outside of your story, hustling for your worthiness.

— BRENÉ BROWN

Happy birthday to you, Haaaapppppyyyyyyy biiiirthday to YOUUuuuuuu . . . HAP-PAY birthday dear OPRAH . . . Happy Birthday to youuuuuuu," I sang fully committed from the depths and joy in my soul, as close to almost-on-key as I could muster. Then I hit a button on my phone.

"You didn't just send that to her, did you?" Paulo asked as if I must just be trying to get him to laugh.

"I just sent it in an audio text to her."

"You're kidding, right?" he said casually.

"No, I just sent it, for real!" I replied. His jaw dropped, as he tried to hide the look of concern and disapproval. My whole life, my family has made it a point to sing "Happy Birthday" full-out to whoever's birthday it is. Everyone fully commits, and almost everyone is completely off-key. It can end up sounding like a pack of howling hyenas mixed with an entire children's orchestra on their first day of using instruments. It's auditorily offensive, but it comes from a place of love. It's what we do. So I continue that tradition for the friends and family I love (lucky them, haha).

"You really sent it?" he asked again.

"Yes," I said confidently, though I was now starting to second-guess my decision.

"You know, Oprah just did the Adele interview and filmed live from her concert, right?"

Okay, he had a valid point, but I wasn't ready to give in. "If Oprah and I are gonna continue building an authentic friendship, I have to show up as the real me," I pointed out.

Without taking a beat, he quipped, "Yeah, but . . . so soon?"

WE TALKED EARLIER about the lie of feeling like we have to please other people in order to feel worthy. That means doing and being who and what we think they want us to do and be. But there's a twist on that lie that's important to discuss, and that's the fear that if we're ourselves, our unique, quirky, authentic selves, we might not be loved.

The fear that people won't love us if we reveal who we truly are is a very human fear. If you worry, whether it's around friends, romantic partners, colleagues, family, or even your own kids, that if they knew the real you they wouldn't love you as much, you're not alone.

Most research shows inauthentic and even perfectionistic behaviors develop in childhood, when we learn to disregard our own wants and needs and become devoted to meeting the expectations and needs of others, in order to gain the feeling of belonging. We learn to hide the parts of us that don't earn praise and turn up the power on the ones that do. We continue these patterns as adults. And the problem is, these patterns leave us feeling empty, disconnected, and ultimately unloved in the way we crave love most.

Merriam-Webster defines *authentic* as "true to one's own personality, spirit, or character; not false." Research shows when children feel seen and loved for their authentic selves, they feel joy and confidence. And when they don't feel loved and accepted for their authentic selves, they become depressed and insecure. One study shows 25 percent of girls say they don't think they look good enough without photo editing, and that they take on average up to fourteen selfies in an attempt to find the right "look" before choosing one to post. This is an ever-present challenge in the new high-tech world that's a growing part of our daily lives.

We have a deep human need to be loved for who we truly are, all parts of us, not for a version or false or partial idea of who we should be. And the act of showing up inauthentically to get love is actually a futile act. Because we can't ever get real true love that way. Yet we keep trying over and over, day in and day out, one gossipy coffee, one morphed PTA mom-to-mom smile-mask, and one filtered dating profile after the next.

Some of us do what psychologists call *homophily*, where we seek out the company of others who are like us. But many of us set our sights on a potential group of friends (remember the popular or cool kids in school) and then have to morph our own behavior in an attempt to fit in and be accepted. Most people who do this continue this pattern their whole lives, where it can morph into people-pleasing, perfectionism, being who we think our partner wants us to be, showing up as who our parents and teachers want us to be and who they will be proud of, performing the role we believe will have our children calling us a good parent, or gossiping about others to fit with a friend group over coffee. This craving for love and belonging is so deep that we will often go against our own values and personality just to gain the acceptance of others. But studies show that even when these tactics help us gain popularity, they actually decrease happiness, because we're living out of alignment with our integrity—in other words, we're being inauthentic.

Feeling true love and belonging can't be achieved by changing who you authentically are to try and get it.

We hide parts of ourselves, and show up in the world as an edited, repressed version. Sometimes this can be necessary for safety and protection in unhealthy situations. But when it comes to many of our most coveted goals in relationships, love, and life, our act of disguising our true selves isn't as subtle or successful as we imagine. We show up day after day holding a giant sign that says *Will Hide for Love*, and it's a sign that never works. It only attracts others holding the same sign. When you're part of a marriage or friendship where you or the other person are presenting a constructed version of the self, the relationship will almost always lack the depth of authentic emotional connection. And will feel unfulfilling and like something is missing.

Again, feeling true love and belonging can only come from being loved for who you truly are. It can't be achieved by changing who you are to get it. When love is bestowed on your inauthentic self, it doesn't register or compute as love inside of you.

Vogue and My Hiking Boots

I don't enjoy working out. In fact, I dread it. In recent years, I've tried to completely shift my mindset toward exercise. My path toward worthiness has included overcoming a whole lot of self-doubt and body-doubt. While I wish it was different, the truth is that for most of my life I've focused on working out primarily with the goal of weight loss, never for achieving physical and mental health, vitality, or simply feeling good.

A few years ago, after a year of spending more days in the hospital than out taking care of my mom, I realized what a gift it was that I still had mobility. I could walk or run or skip whenever I chose to, and my mom, no matter how much she longed to, just couldn't anymore. My mom Nina was my superhero my whole life. To see her in a hospital bed, knowing that despite how many doctors gave their opinions, they were all the same: she wouldn't get better—it was devastating. It also gave me a renewed appreciation for the gift of health and mobility. Every day when I did my morning walk, **I started saying to myself,** *I don't have to, I GET to*. **I decided to see my morning walks as a gift. This tip can apply to almost every area of life.**

In late 2022, I signed up for a weeklong trip to a hiking and wellness retreat with a few of my friends to focus on health and vitality. Of the two dozen or so attendees, about half were there for weight loss and the others for health resets or simply a challenge. We were given a very strict vegan diet and driven early each morning to a different hiking trail in the mountains, where we did four-hour hikes every day. In the afternoon, we had workout classes where our attendance was recorded.

When I first arrived at the facility, I noticed there was an entire "foot care" area outdoors where hiking guides helped you apply various goos and gel pads and bandages and wraps to your feet each morning before the hike. This seemed excessive, until I realized it wasn't. By the second day, everyone had blisters and skin tears all over our feet, heels, and toes. Hiking four hours a day when you're not normally a hiker is no joke. By day two, as our group of twenty sat around the single, long dining table, you could see the pain setting in as we all questioned what the heck we'd signed up for.

As the days went on, it didn't get any easier. On day three of the trip, my friend Lia and I were clustered with two men, lagging toward the back of the group, struggling up a hill. A few hours in, already covered in dirt, Lia, our two new friends, and I focused on not letting our ankles roll on the unsteady rocks and gripping onto our hiking poles like security blankets. The four of us stopped for water and to take in the view for a moment, and we all started talking, bonding, and laughing. I learned the two guys, Edward and Alec, were married. They were there to celebrate their wedding anniversary. Edward's shoes were hurting him so much that Alec swapped shoes with him. I was wearing a mix of hiking clothes I had bought from a serious hiking store, thinking I might somehow transform into a serious hiker in them, but they were totally mismatched, and each day by the two-hour mark, they were completely covered in dirt and drenched in sweat. Edward and Alec were dressed incredibly fashionably but not even their style could withstand the dirt and sweat that blanketed us all each day.

Lia and I may have been slower than most, but we owned it and even celebrated it. We decided that we were going to be slow *fully*, because it was the best we could do physically without risking an injury. Each day after hiking for four hours, Lia and I were so excited when it was over we'd jump for joy then start twerking in full celebration! (I'll explain how we got our best twerking moves later in this book . . . Grandma, skip that chapter.)

Despite the physical exhaustion, the scenery and crisp air were truly incredible. Nature is so healing and the gift of being in it wasn't lost on me.

Alec was a much more ambitious hiker than me, Edward, or Lia, so once he knew Edward had two new friends to keep him company, Alec joined the front of the hiking pack. It became a daily practice that Edward, Lia, and I brought up the rear, often at least half an hour slower than the front of the pack, but we gave it our all.

THE MOST SPECIAL part about this experience was that there was no cell reception in the mountains. So for four hours, it was just me, Edward, and Lia, fully present with each other. I loved that we didn't care, or even have any clue, what each other did for a living. We didn't make small or superficial talk. We first bonded over our physical pain and how completely off we must have been to sign up for something like this. Then our conversations turned to family and life experiences and hardships we'd overcome. It felt like a gift to spend focused, intimate time with my new friend Edward and close friend Lia. On the second-to-last day of my weeklong trip, I was so exhausted I almost didn't shower. I figured I couldn't possibly look any worse. It was a struggle to generate the energy needed to shower when all I wanted to do was collapse onto my bed. But I showered, watching the sweat and mountain dirt run down the drain for several minutes, mainly for my friends' sake.

That night, I dragged myself to dinner and took a chair next to Edward and Lia. My hiking soul mates. Someone across the dining table asked Edward, "What do you do for a living?" to which he replied, "I work in fashion."

Then she said, "What do you do exactly?"

I could tell he wasn't wanting to broadcast it, but I wasn't sure why. I figured he just wanted to be present, not thinking about work. After a beat he said, "I'm editor-in-chief of *British Vogue.*"

"Whoa! Are you serious?" she exclaimed, then said, "I totally know who you are! Oh my God, that's amazing. And you're sitting here with us!"

I looked at Lia, then looked at Edward. Then I looked at the clothes I was wearing. "I'm so glad I didn't know that until now," I said, laughing.

I've had people say, "Don't look at my makeup!" because they think I will have an opinion on it since I founded a makeup company, but I never notice anyone's makeup because for years it reminded me of work. It's the same way a dentist probably doesn't want to assess your teeth at a cocktail party. And in this case, I chose to maintain the belief—possibly out of self-preservation—that Edward didn't care what I was wearing. Because between my sweat and the dirt and the mismatched, anti-wicking, rugged-but-practical hiking attire, I was decidedly *un-Vogue.*

On our last day, Edward, Lia, and I were back to hiking in the back. Every day we would sing "reunited and it feels so good." Converging with them each morning started feeling like the comfort of home. We talked and talked and talked, and then I googled him in front of him and started yelling "EDWARD!" when his cover of *Time* magazine popped up and when I saw all of the photos of him in the front row of every single global fashion show. He asked what I did for a living, and I shared my story of IT Cosmetics. And Lia talked about building her jewelry and handbag company Valencia Key™. I learned about his entire odyssey from modeling to editorial to how he ended up as editor in chief of the world's top fashion magazine. I learned that his first book, *A Visible Man*, would be launching later that month.

AFTER THE RETREAT ended, we stayed in touch, and Edward invited Lia, me, and our friend Jacquie (who had also been at the retreat but hiked far ahead of us in her matching FITKITTY CULTURE™ outfit without breaking a sweat), to his book launch in Hollywood. When I walked in, I saw countless fashionable celebrities and supermodels clamoring around him. Edward was dressed impeccably, and even though the party was dark inside, he never removed his sunglasses. It was a glamorous sight to behold, and so very different from just a few short days before when we were all covered in dirt, sweat, and victory. Many of the world's top supermodels were at the event. Supermodel Cindy Crawford and her daughter, supermodel Kaia Gerber, and I all bonded over building businesses; and Lia, Jacquie, and I had the best time watching Edward be celebrated, and felt so much true joy for him because we'd had the gift of truly getting to know him at a soul level. Several times after ending a conversation with another party attendee, he passed by us and stopped for a great big hug, the way I do if Paulo or my close friends and family are in the audience of an event where I'm speaking. The depth of connection felt fulfilling.

Edward, Alec, Lia, and I have stayed close friends, and sometimes I wonder, had I known he was the head of *British Vogue* when I met him, would we have developed such a close friendship? Would the temptation to try to be more "cool" or more fashionable or more "on" have been too hard for me to resist? Or would I have told myself that since everyone wants something from him all the time, I should give him space and not strike up a conversation. Then I wouldn't have shown up 100 percent as my true authentic self. And had Edward known I was in the beauty industry, or perhaps that we had mutual friends, he likely wouldn't have been able to be so vulnerable, exhausted, sweaty, and tired, and fully share his true self either. I'd like to think we both would have resisted all of these and truly connected deeply anyway. But what I know for certain is that because we had no pretenses, no fears, no striving for some kind of acceptance, and we bonded as our true selves, we created a deep, lasting friendship.

Reveal the Real

Do people know you for what you do, or know you for who you are? Do you let what you do for a living cloud how you show up? Does your perception about what others do for a living influence how worthy you feel of making a bid toward connection with them? Does the story you tell yourself about how you're "just" a [fill in the blank]—stay-at-home parent, or high school graduate, or at a certain place in your career—lead you to showing up differently and more timidly around others? Does the narrative you believe around how you're too young or too old, too tall or too short, how you didn't come from the right area or family or didn't go to the right school, or don't have the right experience or background end up interfering with how you present yourself and allow yourself to connect with others? It's so easy to think that we're protecting ourselves or leading others to like us more, when we're actually preventing them from truly knowing us, and preventing ourselves from feeling connected and seen.

You stifle human connection when you show up as only part of or completely different from who you authentically are. Hiding part or all of who you truly are creates a barrier of disconnection, which can leave you feeling lonely. We're now in a place in society where loneliness is at an all-time high. Feelings of disconnection are at an all-time high. Technology and rapidly evolving artificial intelligence will only further alienate us.

We think we need to show up as an edited version of ourselves to be worthy of love, when in fact it's the opposite. If you're not the real you, it's impossible to have the deepest, truest love. For me, unlearning this old lie and mustering up the courage to show up as who I really am, even in the moments I feel I'm not enough, is a daily practice and lifelong quest. One risk, one real moment, and even one fully committed belted-out song to a friend at a time.

As for Oprah, the singing didn't scare her off, thank goodness. I'm hoping she found the realness refreshing. Because she knows better than anyone, **the path to love and connection is to reveal the real.** Even when it comes in the form of singing an off-key, fully committed rendition of the "Happy Birthday" song.

CHAPTER 13

The Lie: Labels Are Permanent

If speaking kindly to plants helps them grow,
imagine what speaking kindly to humans can do.

— ANONYMOUS

WE HIDE BEHIND labels and hide because of labels. Labels someone gave us once and we let stick, labels we've given ourselves, and now, with technology, even the labels of ratings that strangers give us online. From the time we were teased or bullied and told why we were inadequate as little kids, to that label a relative once gave us, to a name someone once called us that never stopped replaying in our mind, to the time our ex gaslit us into believing a label and our desire for love tricked us into letting it take root inside of us. From the words we tell ourselves about ourselves every time we look in the mirror, to the labels we replay over and over like a soundtrack every time things don't go our way. From our ride-share driver rating us as a passenger, to if we have a checkmark on various social media platforms indicating someone else has deemed us valid, to emoji labels in the comments of our posts indicating how others are labeling our thoughts or art, to how many followers we have and how many likes our posts have, publicly quantifying our *popular* label. **It has become so easy to earn the label SUCCESSFUL or HAPPY in our online personas, all while knowing we're feeling the label of FAILURE or LONELY in our real lives.** It's so easy to confuse fake labels with real identities, and if we're not careful, we let the fake labels impact our sense of identity. The labels you've let stick to you and that you believe about yourself impact your entire life. **Deciding to remove those labels and choose new ones that match your worthiness is transformative.**

How Labels Take Root

Everything in life is simply the meaning we attach to it, the story we tell ourselves about it, and often the label we give it. And with enough repetition or reinforcement, we begin to believe that meaning, or label, is in fact the truth. For example, if someone tells me "Jamie, you're not very smart," and I let that comment take root in me, and think about it over and over, what happens next is that I'll start to notice every time something happens that reinforces the belief that I'm not smart. The meaning we give to something can turn into what we believe with certainty about it. Or about ourselves. The reticular activating system in our brain, or our RAS, multiplies the speed at which this happens.

Our RAS is like a giant filter in our brain filtering out over 99 percent of all stimuli around us to help us focus on what's important to us. Right now, for example, there are millions of stimuli all around you: how the air smells, what it feels like touching any part of your body, the texture and color of the walls, the tone of the light in the room—every single sight, smell, and sound that surrounds you right now. But your RAS is blocking most of it out so you can zone in on what matters to you, or what you've deemed important. So right now you might only be noticing the page of this book or how much you'd like to be eating a chocolate chip cookie. But you're not paying attention to the millions of other possibilities around you because your RAS is filtering out everything but what you deem important. It does this to help us survive.

The classic example often used to describe the RAS is in the car-buying process. If you buy a blue Honda and drive it off the lot, all of a sudden for the next several months, you see blue Hondas everywhere. They were always there before, but you never noticed them because they weren't important to you. Now that you own a blue Honda, your RAS brings them to your attention every time you pass one on the road.

The same thing works for labels, once you let a label take root and believe it. Take my example of the "I'm not smart" label. My RAS would reinforce that belief by finding proof all around me that I'm not smart and highlighting it for me. Every time I make a mistake, my RAS will bring it to my attention, reminding me "You're not smart." Every time I don't know the answer to something, or someone disagrees with me in a comment online, or I question whether I should share an idea, my RAS will remind me "You're not smart enough." If I say something particularly clever, I won't register it as much. But those mistakes? My RAS will magnify them intensely. Before we know it, these negative labels become deep-rooted beliefs, and with enough repetition, those deep-rooted beliefs, or labels, become part of our identity. What you focus on multiplies. Your RAS makes sure of it.

Similarly, if you decide to put an empowering label on yourself, or someone else does, then with enough repetition it takes root, and it can also become a belief. And attached to your identity. Both of these scenarios are so important because, remember, we become what we believe.

The Power of Labels

Labels are powerful, and when we believe the empowering ones, they can help us positively shape our identity and self-worth. A great example of this is with my dear friend Ed, who I mentioned earlier. When he was a little boy, there was a defining moment with labels placed on him that changed his life. Ed was struggling at home with an alcoholic father, and at school he was getting picked on for being small. His classmates would tease him, calling him "Eddy spaghetti." His first-grade teacher, Mrs. Smith, knew that he had low self-worth, and Ed believes she orchestrated something that changed his life forever. One day in class, they were doing testing to pass the grade and a man walked into the classroom and up to the back of the class where Mrs. Smith was. He said, "Mrs. Smith, we need to know who your smartest student is, and we want to use their test to represent the class."

Ed heard Mrs. Smith say, "That would be Eddy Mylett. See him over there? I would pick Eddy; he's my smartest one." She said it knowing that little Eddy could hear her. And when he did, his eyes lit up and he got a great big smile on his face. He remembers thinking to himself, *She picked me, I'm the smart one.*

The man then announced, "Okay, Eddy Mylett, we need you to come with us," and he proceeded to take Ed to a special room where gifted students were being tested. Ed struggled with feeling worthy, and on that day, his teacher who believed in him made him feel not only smart, but special and valued. And she was willing to highlight him out of an entire group of kids and declare him as her most gifted one. And Ed let that label take root. Some days those words his teacher said about him were all he had to lean on. He wore them in his mind proudly. Ed grew up determined to break generational cycles of addiction in his family, and to believe he belonged in rooms filled with others who were exceptionally smart and gifted. He went on to have tremendous business success, and today through his podcast *The Ed Mylett Show*, his social platforms, and his books, he inspires millions of people daily to believe in themselves too. Ed has thought about Mrs. Smith thousands of times in his life, and to this day he believes she arranged for the man to come into the classroom in order to plant those powerful seeds in Ed. And now he spends his life helping others believe in themselves too.

In *Let Me Tell You about You*, a book he was working on at the same time I was writing this one, Ed shares a profound tool when it comes to labels and identity. One inspired by the gift his elementary school teacher taught him decades ago. Each and every day of his children's lives, he's said to them, "Let me tell you about you . . ." and then proceeds to tell them empowering words and labels about who they are so that they take root in the form of deep self-worth. For example, each day he says to his daughter Bella things like, "Bella-boo, let me tell you about you. You are smart, you are kind, you are generous, you have your daddy's eyes. I believe in you, I love you."

Ed recently visited his daughter at her freshman dorm in college. When he was leaving her dorm room that day, her group of friends were there. As he went to say goodbye, one of her friends shouted out, "Aren't you going to tell her about her first?" Ed started crying. He realized that doing this daily for Bella, even on the days she rolled her eyes or didn't acknowledge how much it meant to her, had taken root. She appreciated it so much she had told her friends about it. Ed grabbed Bella's hands and said, "Bella, let me tell you about you . . ." and poured into her true words about the beauty and power of who she was. Ed's story has inspired me to do this with my daughter, Wonder, and my son, Wilder, each day.

Disempowering Labels

The opposite is also true and, unfortunately, common. When the people around us give us disempowering labels, we often let them stick for decades.

When well-meaning family and friends give us teasing labels, they have no idea how easy it is for those labels to take root. Before we know it, we've internalized the disempowering labels we've heard from others, and, more commonly, the disempowering labels we've placed on ourselves. We think these labels define us. We think everyone else sees them too. These labels are only words, and at best usually outdated and at worst complete lies, but they have the power to make us disappear and feel unworthy.

The lie: *I am my labels.* The truth: *Your labels aren't permanent. They are temporary and you can remove the disempowering false ones and replace them with true, empowering labels that serve you!*

I WAS CONCEIVED during a onetime encounter between two people who were never together again. I was kept a secret before I was placed into adoption the day I was born. I could be tempted to see my own story with labels like UNWANTED or SECRET or MISTAKE or ABAN-DONED . . . but what I know to be true is that God never left me. What I choose to believe, what I know in every ounce of my being, is that God has stamped me with the biggest, most special, and beautiful of labels. Labels that say WANTED, MORE THAN ENOUGH, MY PRECIOUS LITTLE GIRL, WONDERFULLY MADE, CALLED, QUALIFIED, WORTHY, and I imagine a giant stamp right across my forehead that says CHOSEN. I know that He has stamped every single one of us with these same words too. And that these labels are true.

But this belief about myself hasn't come overnight. It's been an ongoing effort to learn how to replace old labels with new ones that I say and believe about myself. New labels I knew I needed to believe in order to feel like I belonged, as a daughter, as a friend, as a mom, in a loving relationship, as a CEO, and even inside the shape and size of my own body.

What labels have you given yourself, that you're still carrying around, that just aren't true? Maybe they're labels like NOT ENOUGH, UNQUALIFIED, BAD MOM, MADE TOO MANY MISTAKES, OUTCAST, FAILURE, INSUFFICIENT. Today I have news for you: Not only are those labels a lie, they're also not permanent. They're not fixed. Any label you put on yourself, or someone from your childhood or your family or a hurtful person put on you, is made like a Post-it note. It looks like it might be stuck, but it's only got that light adhesive on it—it's removable. And maybe today is the day you're going to decide to peel off those old labels that are holding you back and keeping you hiding from living life as the fullest, highest expression of who you truly are.

New Labels

What labels have you let stick to you and take root? What labels are you hiding behind? I would like to invite you to do an exercise on labels that is intended to help bring awareness and then empowerment. The only thing it requires is for you to be really honest with yourself. This is an exercise of truth and reflection, between you and you. Below, you'll see three columns. If you want more space, you can re-create this in your own journal, on paper, or on your computer at home.

Disempowering Label	What has believing this label cost you? What impact has it had on every area of your life?	New Empowering Replacement Label/Belief

Disempowering Label	What has believing this label cost you? What impact has it had on every area of your life?	New Empowering Replacement Label/Belief

NoteWORTHY: You can also grab the free Worthy Worksheet on Labels at WorthyBook.com/Resources and print it out.

In the first column I want you to write down the disempowering labels you've given yourself. The false ones that maybe you never let anyone know you believe, but you do. The painful labels that you or someone else placed on you, which are lies that you're tempted to believe. Maybe they're labels like FAILURE, UNLOVABLE, UNQUALIFIED, NOT FUNNY, COWARD, UNATTRACTIVE, TOO OLD, TOO YOUNG, UNWORTHY, DAMAGED, REJECTED, HESITANT, NOT SMART ENOUGH. It can be helpful to think about labels as they pertain to certain parts of your life such as your personality, level of achievement, age, abilities, body, potential, and past.

Now for the middle column. This might be the hardest thing you do today, but perhaps the most important. Next to each label, I want you to write what believing that label has cost you in your life. What has it cost you in your relationships? What has believing that label cost you in your job or ambitions? What has it cost you in your joy? Then go deeper. For example, did the label not only cost you the thing, but then also the confidence to go for the thing after it? Or if a label cost you your voice in a relationship, did that then snowball into you not speaking up in friendships? What has each label cost you on the surface level, and what has it cost you beyond that, like perhaps how you show up to or set examples for the people you care most about in your life? You can spend several minutes or several hours or even several days on this.

When I first did this exercise, it changed my life. I realized that some of the labels I put on myself, or someone else said about me and I chose to believe, had caused me to *feel* less than and to eventually believe I *was* less than. And I found that the most hurtful labels are the ones I put on myself.

It's very eye-opening when we consider what each of our disempowering labels has cost us in our lives. Have they gotten in the way of you going after your dreams? Have you stayed in an unhealthy relationship because of them? Have you let a friend mistreat you because of them? Have you not spoken up because of them? Have you stopped looking in the mirror because of them? Have you lost your joy and zest for life because of them? Do you withhold sharing your ideas with others because of them? Do you not wear a swimsuit in public because of them? Do you stand around the outside of a party and never dance on the dance floor because of them? If you've labeled yourself UNWORTHY, what has that already cost you in your life?

Finally, in the third, right-hand column across from each disempowering label, I want you to write a replacement belief for it. Something you *know* is true about the core and essence of who you are. Something that *your Creator* would say about you. Or your best friend would say. Something that you know in your soul to be true about yourself. A new label or new belief that you want to replace that old one with. Maybe if your old label is UNATTRACTIVE, your new label is WONDERFULLY MADE IN HIS IMAGE or BEAUTIFUL. If your old label is UNLOVABLE, maybe your new label is WORTHY OF LOVE or UNCONDITIONALLY LOVABLE or MADE FROM LOVE OF LOVE. If your old label is DEFICIENT or DEFECTIVE, maybe your new label is VICTORIOUS or RESILIENT. If your old label is BAD MOM, maybe your new label is LOVING MOM. Your new label is the truth of who you are. It's the real you, the YOU you were born as, before the world and people-pleasing and hate and hurt and judgment and self-doubt taught you who to be.

WE CAN'T JUST ignore and bury the deep stories we tell ourselves about our identity around worthiness, because they'll just keep showing up louder and louder forever. When we acknowledge them, they start to lose their power, and we start to realize they aren't true because our soul knows they aren't. When we do the work to disbelieve them, they continue to shrink. Their volume of authority in our lives, our thoughts, and our identity continues to decrease.

A few tips on *thought reframing*, or replacing old disempowering labels with new, true ones. One theory says you have seventeen seconds to intercept a negative thought and replace it with a positive one before it takes root. In your daily life, when that old label comes to mind, instantly catch and intercept that thought, and replace it with your new, true label in your mind. Make sure to feel the truth of that new, true label. Do this as often as you can, until you don't need the reminder anymore. Until it becomes second nature and habit.

Another helpful exercise is to write out all of the old labels on Post-it notes or pieces of paper. Then make a ritual of burning them or tearing them up into pieces and throwing them out or flushing them down the toilet to disappear forever.

Write your new empowering labels in your gratitude journal, or on notes you stick to the places you see most during the day, like on your computer monitor, closet, phone, or car. Write them on your bathroom mirror in erasable marker or makeup so you see them every morning when you brush your teeth. Write them as if they're absolutely true. Example: I AM WORTHY. I AM A LOVING MOM. I AM SMART. I AM FUNNY. I AM BEAUTIFUL.

Reinforce these new labels in creative ways until they take root. Make one of them your word of the year. Set one or two of the new labels as daily reminders on your cell phone so when the alarm sounds off and you glance at your phone, it reminds you of your new, true label. Write them in permanent marker on the inside of your favorite clothing tags. You'll be the only one who sees them every time you get dressed. Leave a list of them on your desk. If you want to go to more extreme measures, get a bracelet or tattoo with your most important empowering new label on it. You'll notice the more you reinforce your positive words, the more you'll see these words everywhere because your RAS will make sure you do. And if you post a photo of how you remind yourself of your new words and labels on social media, whether it's through a Post-It note on your mirror or even a tattoo, be sure to tag me. I'll repost it to inspire others to remove their old labels and decide to believe their new ones too! Visual reminders are powerful tools; you can use your *WORTHY* book as one too. When you finish reading it, place your *WORTHY* book in a spot where you'll see it every day and be reminded of your favorite lessons, tools, takeaways, and most importantly, your worth. Whether you place your book on your living room coffee table, bathroom counter, or office desk, studies show visible reminders can make a powerful difference in achieving your goals.

DISEMPOWERING LABELS FEEL heavy, like you're wearing badges of lies all over you. Removing these labels permanently feels like truth and freedom. Embracing empowering and true labels feels like energy, an uplifting wind beneath your wings.

Labels are made up. And they can be unmade up. They can be removed.

You are the author of your own identity. You are the main character in the story of your life, and the character description is up to you and no one else. I believe one of the most important skills of your lifetime is mastering the art of communicating with yourself. When you change your story, and you change your labels, you change your life.

Part Three

TRANSFORMING

The Journey of You: Building Unshakable
Self-Worth and Unconditional Self-Love

CHAPTER 14

The Secret to Fulfillment: Self-Worth Is the Multiplier

Sometimes your next level of life isn't achievement, it's alignment.

— BRENDON BURCHARD

RIGHT NOW IN your life, would you say you're truly fulfilled? Or do you feel like something is missing? Perhaps you're not quite sure what it is, but you find yourself asking questions like *Is this all there is?* Or saying to yourself, *I thought by now, and with all I've accomplished, I would feel happy, but I just don't.* Or *I have so much to be grateful for, so I'm going to tell the world I've got it all, but I just can't shake this longing I feel inside for something more. And yet no matter how much more I get or build, it doesn't satisfy the longing.* Or *I must be ungrateful and selfish if I still feel unfulfilled given everything I have.* When it comes to the true, honest answer to how you're feeling right now, deep down inside, about your level of fulfillment in life, this chapter just might crack the code for you on why you feel the way you do, and what to do about it.

The tool we're about to discuss has fundamentally changed my entire life, and I am so excited to share it with you. It's helped me understand why I felt empty despite accomplishing so many of my goals, and it has helped me forge full speed ahead on the path to true fulfillment. Buckle up, because it's gonna feel like we're back in the classroom for a minute. But don't worry, I've got you! This chapter might feel a bit serious, but we didn't come here to play small, we came to build true self-worth. Plus I promise there's a lot more fun coming up after it. So we'll be in class for a few pages, but I'll be sitting in the seat right next you. I'll even share my notes if you need them, and I'll save your seat if you have to run to the restroom or grab a snack and come back. The teacher in the front of the class is your knowing, your soul, and it's the best teacher alive. And when the bell rings at the end of class, we can be study partners afterward, on this one beautiful lifelong journey. You in?

The Four Keys to Fulfillment

While **self-worth** is an absolute requirement for true fulfillment, a strong sense of self-worth alone isn't enough for the highest feelings of success and happiness in life. There are a few other components required. For ultimate fulfillment you also need **self-confidence, growth**, and **contribution**. We've covered a lot of ground on **self-worth** and **self-confidence**, and for ultimate fulfillment, **growth** and **contribution** are also key.

The need for **growth** can come in many forms: taking up a new hobby, picking up a book, doing work in therapy, taking on a new challenge, or continually working to grow an existing passion. There is a joy and aliveness you feel when you're growing, and most growth in life comes from pursuits, both internal and external, that build your skills, competencies, and traits, and inevitably your self-confidence.

For ultimate success, happiness, and fulfillment, you also need the feeling of **contribution**. To be contributing to others, a cause, or something bigger and beyond yourself. Research shows people who volunteer are more satisfied with their life and report better mental and overall health. The need to contribute can be met in many forms in your life, from simply letting someone else know they're seen and they matter, to helping serve others through donating your time, your money, or your ideas.

Self-confidence, growth, and contribution are fundamental human needs for ultimate happiness, fulfillment, meaning, and joy. I could write a whole separate book each on confidence, growth, and contribution, but the key and focus here is how they relate to self-worth.

Cracking the Code: The True Fulfillment Equation

Building on the mountain of studies on self-worth, self-confidence, growth, and contribution, through real-world research in the form of countless shared interactions, stories, and experiences with the millions of women who've become part of my IT Cosmetics journey, and through mentorship with a group of incredible advisers, I've derived this equation as a breakthrough recipe for true fulfillment in life.

First, estimate your level of these three things in your life right now: self-confidence, growth, and contribution. Then multiply the total sum of those by your level of self-worth. This will give you your current level of fulfillment. (Note to all of you who don't love math: I promise you don't need to speak *math* to apply this to your life right now!)

In the beginning of this book I shared these words: **in life, you don't rise to what you believe is possible, you fall to what you believe you're worthy of**. Countless studies and science-backed research show the importance of self-worth, self-confidence, growth, and contribution to overall fulfillment in life, but the most critical of these components to true fulfillment is self-worth. It is the multiplier. When you take the sum of your self-confidence, growth, and contribution, and then multiply that sum by your level of self-worth, you have your level of true fulfillment. And even if you have high self-confidence, you're growing, and you're making a meaningful contribution to society, if you have zero self-worth you won't feel fulfilled. Because **self-worth is the multiplier and zero times anything is zero**. You simply cannot ever achieve true fulfillment in life without it. You can have varying levels of any or all of these three: self-confidence, growth, and contribution. But you can't ever feel truly fulfilled without feeling worthy.

TRUE FULFILLMENT EQUATION

©Jamie Kern Lima

(Self-Confidence + Growth + Contribution) x Self-Worth = Fulfillment Level

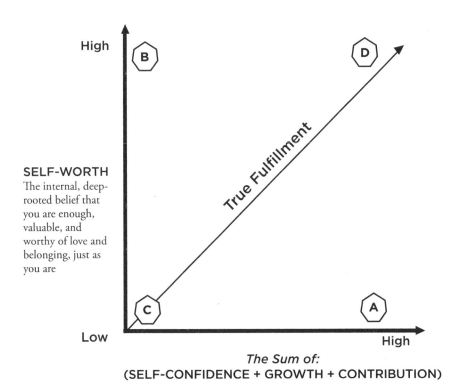

SELF-WORTH
The internal, deep-rooted belief that you are enough, valuable, and worthy of love and belonging, just as you are

The Sum of:
(SELF-CONFIDENCE + GROWTH + CONTRIBUTION)

Your level of self-confidence + the amount you're growing and evolving in your life and as a person + your focus on service and contribution to others

LET'S TAKE A look at four examples on the TRUE FULFILLMENT EQUATION chart and talk about where you are in your life right now. And then go on an exploration of where you'd like to be! For each of the following four examples, reference the TRUE FULFILLMENT EQUATION chart to see a visual of where they land.

Person A is incredibly successful on the outside. They are challenging themselves to learn and grow, and they are doing things to help serve others. Despite looking successful and appearing as if they have the ideal life on the outside, they feel perpetually unfulfilled. So many perfectionists and high-achieving people sit in this spot and can't figure out why they feel like something's missing and that they're not enough. No matter how much they accomplish, it's never enough and they don't feel truly happy or fulfilled.

Person B feels a deep sense of peace, worth, and love, but does not feel competent or confident in their own skills and abilities. And while they might be content, they lack the joy of true fulfillment that comes from building confidence, growing, and contributing to others beyond themselves.

Person C has low self-worth and low self-confidence. They're likely not challenging themselves to grow and likely only thinking about themselves, without regard for how to help others, even in the smallest of ways. Person C is deeply unsatisfied with life.

Person D is truly fulfilled. They have a strong inherent self-worth and believe themselves to have high levels of skills and traits. They're likely always growing, learning, or challenging themselves to try new things. And they're not only focused on their own happiness and fulfillment, but on things beyond themselves. They likely are empathetic to others and try to help and serve others in life, whether through kind words, a helping hand, or through contributions big and small.

Okay, time for a fun, potentially life-changing math class! Let's put this equation into practice in your life right now to see where you fall on the chart. I've simplified it to get a visual representation of your current fulfillment level.

Below, simply score yourself from 1 to 10 based on your honest assessment in your life right now in the four key areas, and write your score next to each of the four categories in the blank space to the left of it.

____ **Self-Confidence** (How you evaluate and assess yourself based on external qualities, competencies, and traits. How strongly you believe in your abilities to meet life's challenges, your willingness to try and go for it, and to succeed.)

____ **Growth** (Pursuits, both internal and external, that build your skills, competencies, traits, and passion.)

____ **Contribution** (Giving your time, talents, energy, or resources to others, a cause, or something bigger and beyond yourself.)

____ **Self-Worth** (The internal, deep-rooted belief that you are enough and innately worthy of love and belonging, **just as you are.**)

Now we just plug in the numbers to see where you are on the chart.

Step 1: Write your self-confidence, growth, and contribution scores in the spaces below and add up their total sum. Your total should be somewhere between 0 and 30:

_____ +	_____ +	_____ =	_____
Self-Confidence Score	**Growth Score**	**Contribution Score**	**TOTAL**

Step 2: Mark your **total** sum number from step 1 on the chart below in the horizontal axis.

Step 3: Write in your self-worth score from above here. _____

Step 4: Mark this number from 1 to 10 on the chart below in the vertical Self-Worth axis.

TRUE FULFILLMENT EQUATION
©Jamie Kern Lima

(Self-Confidence + Growth + Contribution) x Self-Worth = Fulfillment Level

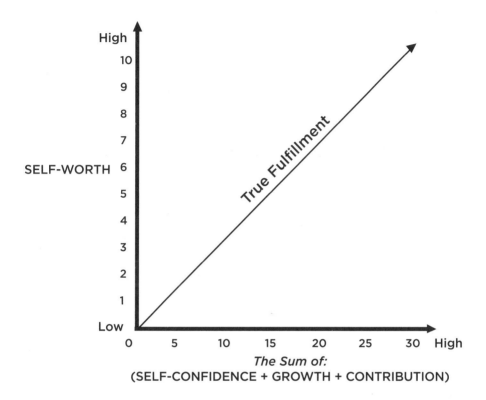

Seeing where you fall on this chart right now gives you a quick, simplified visual representation of your current TRUE FULFILLMENT EQUATION fulfillment level. Your score will likely fall above or below the arrow line and that's totally fine, but the closer it is to the upper, right half of the graph, the stronger your level of fulfillment.

NoteWORTHY: While we're using a quick, easy-to-grasp visual of where you fall on the chart, for a more in-depth exploration of this equation go to WorthyBook.com/Resources

Does seeing where you fall on this chart today surprise you? Or does it feel just about right? If you feel like you scored lower than you hoped, don't be afraid, be empowered. This is simply a tool to gain awareness of where you are now and how you have an exciting opportunity to venture toward an even more fulfilling life if you choose. We are all works in progress, and our path to building strong self-worth is a lifelong one.

Remember: self-worth is the multiplier. Notice that if you can give yourself very high scores in self-confidence, growth, and contribution, but if your self-worth is sitting at a 1 or 2, then your overall fulfillment in life will feel very low. Having everything else without self-worth isn't enough for true fulfillment. You can feel fulfilled in a job but not in who you are. You can feel fulfilled in the public eye or in how you show up for your family and everyone else, but if you don't have deep, internal, innate self-worth, you'll always feel like something is missing, and you won't have the ultimate feeling of true fulfillment in life. It will likely always feel like what you're doing and what you've accomplished is never enough, or like you're not enough. **If your self-worth feels like a zero, then your fulfillment score is 0.** The point is that without self-worth, you will feel a deep void. Low self-worth means you'll feel it minimally, and high self-worth multiplies your sense of fulfillment.

This chart is a great tool to revisit often as you implement the tools in this book and journey toward building unshakable self-worth. I find that each time I revisit it, I'm a different person from before, and slowly but surely, by focusing on all four of these elements in my life, especially on the foundation of self-worth, I'm inching my way up the path to true fulfillment.

HERE'S THE MOST important key, without which you'll never experience ultimate fulfillment in life: you, right now, are truly worthy, exactly as you are. Believing this doesn't mean you don't continue to passionately pursue all the things you want in life; it means that when you actually get them, you're able to enjoy them, and if you don't get them, you still feel fulfilled and unshakably worthy. Have you accomplished goals, had huge milestones come to pass, gotten that thing you've always hoped for (the relationship or the kids or the house or the goal weight or the job), had the dream finally happen, poured your time and gifts into helping others, but then still felt a sense of emptiness or like it didn't bring you the kind of ultimate fulfillment you'd hoped it would? If so, it's likely due to getting the high that a boost of self-confidence brings, the satisfaction that growth brings, or the joy that contribution brings, but still having a lack of self-worth underneath it all. Self-worth is the multiplier and the single most important factor in achieving **truly fulfilling** personal success, business success, financial success, spiritual success, success in love, and success in life.

CHAPTER 15

Do You See You?

*Being loved feels warm. Loving yourself
feels like the entire sun inside of you.*

— BILLY CHAPATA

T'S A FIRE. Evacuate now. The fire alarm is real." The hotel worker
sounded frantic. The fire alarm had been going off for quite a while
without stopping, and this was the second time I had called down to the
front desk.

"What? Earlier you said it wasn't . . ." I quickly realized now wasn't
the time to ask why a few minutes prior they had assured me it was a false
alarm and there was no need to worry. Now I had only seconds to decide
what to do. Was this something I should be worried about, or was it just
a minor issue causing the alarm to go off? Still holding my curling iron in
my hair, I opened the door of my room on the seventh floor of a London
hotel. I was getting ready for the UK launch of my company and already
at risk of being late. People were running through the hallway. I took a
couple of steps down the hall and saw a scene I'll never forget.

Around the corner and all the way down the hall to the four elevator
banks, the entire floor was filling with smoke. It seemed to be coming
out through the bottoms of the four elevator doors as well. I instantly
went into survival mode. I felt both completely in shock and intently
focused. My mind raced through possible options, some of which I had

to instantly eliminate: we couldn't jump from the seventh floor as it was too high; we obviously couldn't take the elevators. I glanced up and down the hallway in both directions looking for the stairs. I couldn't see a sign. *They must be somewhere*, I thought. I rushed back to my room and yelled to my friend Lia, who was getting ready in my room, "Let's go! We've gotta get out now!"

I grabbed my laptop, which in hindsight makes no sense as there were other more immediately useful things I could have grabbed—like perhaps my shoes! Without a plan, Lia and I rushed out of the room. My assistant, Zega, who was on the same floor, joined us in the hall. Paulo had left the hotel about twenty minutes earlier to pick up breakfast at a bakery, so I mentally marked him as safe. We hurried down the hallway. "I'm going to find us an exit," I declared. "Let's knock on everyone else's doors quickly and yell fire!" I'll never forget the look on Lia's face when she saw the hall and elevator banks filling with smoke. It billowed like cloud cover, but instead of being in the sky, it was about a foot above the floor. The scene truly looked like something from a movie. Lia's jaw dropped and she froze. And when I say froze, I mean she stopped moving. I looked in all directions but couldn't see a sign for stairs anywhere.

A woman came screaming down the hallway asking us how to get out. I saw a large window at the end of the hall and knew we had to get to it. I saw no other option. The four of us rushed forward. Lia held my hand, silently running right behind me. Normally I am someone who is attuned to everyone's energy around me, but in this case, I was completely numb despite the people screaming around me, almost as if I were in some type of heightened survival mode and my body was prioritizing my focus over everything else. I had never experienced anything like it. I completely blocked out everything around me that didn't seem like it could help me survive.

When we got to the window, there was a large handle on it. I reached down and opened it. There was metal scaffolding outside the window. Barefoot, we climbed through the window and onto the fire escape, which was a set of metal stairs that were welded to the outside of the building. In complete silence we started down. Others followed. Seven flights down, the stairs ended in construction rubble. When my bare feet touched the sharp rocks and piles of metal and debris on the ground, I grabbed Lia's hand again. Arm in arm, we navigated our way through it and onto a street where hundreds of onlookers were gathering. I looked back up at the building and saw that the entire top of the hotel was on fire. Above the top floor, thick black smoke billowed and flames blazed ten to twenty feet into the sky. In that moment, as Lia and I stood there barefoot in the street clinging to each other, we made eye contact and both started sobbing.

Survival Mode

When I look back on that experience, I think of the very different reactions we all had. Some people in the hotel were panicking, some were screaming, Lia and others froze. And I'm not sure how many others experienced what I did, going straight into an almost mechanical survival mode, silent and laser-focused on solving the problem because our lives felt at stake.

I disassociated to survive. I completely blocked out how scary the floor of smoke was, and while normally an empath, I also blocked out the panic and fear of the people around me and disconnected from my own.

This form of survival mode clearly helped me in the hotel fire. But imagine if I spent my day-to-day life in that mode. It would not be ideal. And yet, for most of my life, that is exactly what I have done. I've defaulted to only doing and being what and who I needed to in order to survive the situation. To win the approval. To hear "good girl" and later "good job." Being in survival mode meant I sacrificed vital parts of myself. I hid parts of me I thought were less than, in hopes that others thought I was more than. In burying the parts of me and how I feel that made me vulnerable, I ended up hiding from true connection, intimacy, and the highest, fullest experience of life, for most of my entire life.

Survival mode can so easily become the way we live day-to-day. It can become our default emotional state and our default comfort zone. It leads us to being who we think we need to be to survive or optimize our lives in that moment. Who we think we need to be to optimize our relationship in that moment. Who we think we need to be to protect our hearts, our sense of belonging, our pride, our job, our approval, and where we derive love from. When we maintain a constant state of being who we think we need to be, then we live our lives disconnected from who we truly are. And if we do this for long enough, we may start to lose touch with who we actually are.

There are many ways we choose to disconnect or live in a constant state of survival mode because we don't feel worthy. We immerse ourselves in busyness; we live in a constant state of being overwhelmed; we disassociate and numb out; we live inauthentically or without integrity, distanced from who we truly are and what we want. We can put on a smile or even entertain the entire room, all while retaining an imaginary wall between ourselves and another person, the environment around us, and even between our head and our heart. We can disconnect from a group or crowd just as easily as we can disconnect from a one-on-one conversation that appears on the outside, or even to the other person, to be deeply intimate.

Do you truly connect with yourself and know yourself? Do you see you?

This barrier of disconnection can feel protective, like a survival tactic, and of course it can serve us in a healthy way in many situations, including when we feel uneasy, unsafe, or a sense of mistrust around another person or place. However, when we bring along a barrier of disconnection as a default, separating us from the places and people we crave true connection with, including ourselves, it can take a significant toll on us, on both our emotional and our physical well-being.

While it's a common topic to consider connection with others, what's not as common to consider is connection with ourselves. So let's turn our attention from outward to inward. Are you showing up as the real you, to you? Do you truly connect with yourself and know yourself? Do you see you?

The Costly Toll of Disconnection

Think about all the lies we've talked about so far in this book. When we live those lies, we end up presenting a false story of who we are or how we feel, whether it's to make someone else happy, because we believe we need to perform to be loved, because we think if they see the real us they'll no longer like or love us, because we believe we're either too much or not enough, because we fear we'll be rejected or found out, because we want to impress, or many other reasons. They all create disconnection from others and disconnection from ourselves, and the toll of disconnection is severe.

Most of the behaviors that lead to disconnection make sense in our minds, and when we couple these beliefs with our body's wiring to survive and protect itself, these behaviors all can easily feel like justified strategies. We all crave love and belonging and fear not having them. What we often don't realize is that when we're not who we truly are, we don't actually have true love and belonging anyway. It's not possible. We can have the façade of it, but it's not true, full, authentic connection when you're not participating in it authentically.

The same can be said for the connection you have with yourself. **The only way to have a true, intimate connection with yourself is to fully see, acknowledge, and embrace who you authentically are.** And to believe you're worthy of it. When you are out of alignment with or disconnected from who you truly are, you can easily feel lonely and isolated, even in a room full of people. Even in a car ride with your family. Even at coffee with a close friend. Even in your bed with your partner. Even when staring at yourself in the mirror. And it's that disconnection, even when it's from yourself, that takes the costly toll.

THERE'S A POPULAR video online, perhaps you've seen it, of how a baby reacts when their caretaker stops making eye contact with them. In the video, a caretaker intentionally starts to ignore a sweet little baby. Initially, the precious baby looks bewildered. Then the baby starts to show facial expressions of sadness. After a bit of time passes, with the caretaker still refusing to look the baby in the eye, you can visibly see the baby start to feel pain, fear, and deep sadness. The baby's eyes well up with tears of desperation and fear of abandonment. As a longer window of time passes with the caretaker refusing to make eye contact, the baby begins to show more signs of emotional distress. Finally, the baby starts crying and becomes distraught. The video cuts you to the core and makes you want to jump through the screen to soothe and hug the baby in your arms. It's hard not to tear up watching it.

We all need what this baby needs. To be seen. To be valued. To be loved. Can you imagine yourself refusing to acknowledge the existence of this baby right in front of you? What feelings would it stir up in you to ignore this sweet, precious soul? You could probably never imagine doing something like this intentionally. It's also painful to imagine yourself in the baby's position, longing to be seen, loved, and reassured of their existence and safety, and the fear that emerges when that attention is denied.

Yet, are you treating your own soul this way every single day? Are you going about your life, ignoring your deep needs to be seen, loved, worthy of acknowledgment, and reassured that you're safe in your own arms? That you've got you? And that your Creator is in you and has got you and sees you and loves you? Are your needs and my needs, right now, any different from that baby's when it comes to needing connection? No. We need love and connection just as much as that baby. We've just learned to numb, disconnect, disassociate, and survive without them. Because most of us, and generations before us, have never been taught to fulfill these needs ourselves. We've been taught to grow up, put our big girl panties on, be selfless, suck it up, buck up, be strong, get to work, take care of everyone else.

We've learned to categorize needs, especially emotional or soul-level needs, as weakness. We've often learned to equate not having any emotional needs with strength. We've learned to regard external accomplishments, whether in family, appearance, or career, as success. But those external accomplishments don't fill the need for connection that only comes with sharing our authentic self and being seen and loved. Most importantly, we need to receive these needs from ourself to ourself. And we need to receive and give them in order to foster true connection with others as well.

THIS LEADS TO the question: What is happening to you, if you aren't looking yourself in the eyes? If you're not seeing you? If you're living in a constant state of busyness or survival mode? If you're ignoring or hiding yourself from yourself and from others? Are you treating your own soul like a caretaker not making eye contact with it? Are you feeling on the inside the way the baby felt, but disguising it from the world and even from yourself, perhaps with a shirt that says LOVE and a smile to prove it?

Disconnection is a disease.

— DR. BRUCE D. PERRY

Disconnection is a form of trauma. And when you're living disconnected from yourself and others, you can be around people yet still feel lonely and isolated and unseen. In his book *What Happened to You?*, psychiatrist and neuroscientist Dr. Bruce D. Perry says, "Lack of connectedness is an adversity, putting you at risk for physical and mental health problems." He shares how "isolation and loneliness can create sensitization of the stress response systems, and in that way can be traumatic."

Living disconnected can protect us at times, but if it causes us to forego true human connection and community, it can also cause this kind of trauma.

With the growing role of technology, smartphones, and computers in our daily lives, we're exposed to more information—including bad news and tragedy—than ever before. Dr. Perry notes that this kind of stress in our lives is our modern form of trauma. One way to regulate stress is through human connection and community. When we discuss and share negative events with others, it helps us soothe and regulate and process it. When we can't do this, when the stress becomes unremitting in our lives, it can turn to distress . . . and trauma.

Social media and technology make this disconnection and disassociation easier and more common. We replace in-person conversations with emails and texts. We replace phone calls with audio messages. And our words never actually connect with the other person's in real time.

Instead of checking in on people, we see their latest post on social media and mistakenly assume they're doing great and don't need us to check in. We post our best representative version of ourselves on a dating app and swipe, wondering if what our prospects' profiles say is even true. Or if they actually look like their photos. We silence our real feedback on the experience, whether from an inappropriate rideshare driver, or a food delivery gone bad, because we want to get a good rating from them on our account. We post a highlight of our day on social media instead of how we're actually feeling. We scroll and often feel less-than when we compare our real lives behind the scenes, to everyone else's curated highlight reel posts. **We slowly evolve toward feeling less and less *enough*, and more and more *alone*.** And many of us have gotten in the habit of addressing that loneliness by posting a happy photo to falsely reassure the world and ourselves that we're not. The disconnection broadens.

SO MANY OF us live in hiding, show up inauthentically, or feel like we're in survival mode, disassociated from our feelings or who we truly are. We numb out by filling up our calendars, diving into work, or wallowing in ours, our kids', or other people's agendas and problems of the day.

Our self-prescribed means of surviving are often through our favorite flavors of numbing: busyness, food, substances, technology, shopping, gaming, and hiding in plain sight, whether alone or with others, and more. These activities simultaneously bury our feelings, talents, dreams, and needs. When we walk through life inauthentically, hiding, or numb, we might feel less immediate pain, but that's only in the short term. We might protect ourselves from some of the negative, but we also prevent ourselves from tapping into our purpose, our joy, our creativity, our aliveness. The long-term pain of looking back on our life and wondering if we actually truly enjoyed it, is arguably a much greater pain. **We make it through but don't make it count.**

When it comes to your life, are you living to make it through, or are you living to make it count?

Five Powerful Shortcuts to Self-Worth

Now let's dive into five powerful tools that are shortcuts to building self-worth. As with all parts of this book, you'll know in your soul if any or all of them speak to you, and if not, please skip them. I've found all five powerful and effective in my quest to believing I'm worthy, and toward living a more fulfilled and connected life.

Shortcut #1: Seeing Outward and Seeing Inward

If you struggle to love yourself, and if you find yourself defaulting to focusing on your self-perceived flaws, here's a powerful shortcut to reverse that: start loving and appreciating the beauty and positives in the things around you. When you start to see the good in everything around you intentionally, it becomes a mindset. A way of being. A habit. A reframe of how you program your mind to see things that will eventually

When it comes to your life, are you living to make it through, or are you living to make it count?

trickle over into you starting to see the positives, strengths, good, and beauty in yourself.

One powerful recent study found that 91 percent of people and 93 percent of teens say negative self-talk is a key obstacle that interferes with their ability to experience joy. The Joy Study, commissioned by Ulta Beauty, also found that in spite of how common negative self-talk was in the more than 5,000 people surveyed, 67 percent said it's so much a part of how they function that they don't even notice that they're doing it. The majority also said they lacked the tools and resources to overcome negative self-talk and bounce back from difficult situations. If you know someone who struggles with negative self-talk, please share these self-worth shortcuts or your copy of *WORTHY* with them. When we realize how so many of the things we thought were just us are actually the majority of us, it can help us feel less alone and then take the next step of learning how to truly feel more *enough*.

It's so critical to gain awareness over your thoughts and the words you say to yourself about yourself, as self-love can't grow and flourish in an environment filled with shame and put-downs. There are even studies that show plants can't grow when surrounded by people speaking negativity over them. There are experiments that show how containers of cooked rice will either ferment beautifully or start to mold and rot based on if someone is speaking to the rice positively or negatively or ignoring it altogether. When we're constantly speaking or thinking negative words about ourselves, it lowers our vibrational energy and destroys our hope, optimism, and joy. Yet so many of us have been beating ourselves up emotionally for so long that it's a difficult habit to break. Intentionally focusing on the good and positive attributes of the people, places, and things around you can be a powerful tool to combat this.

When you build self-worth and begin to love who you are, it's the quickest way to change any problem in life, because the vibrations you send out and the way you react to things completely changes. Let me explain the reverse of this as well, for an important perspective. There is a famous saying, *You don't see things as they are, you see things as you are*. Another is *Hurt people hurt people*. Both draw the same conclusion: people who don't love themselves and who aren't happy inside often see things that way outside. If someone doesn't love themselves and isn't happy inside, they're far less likely to truly love or be happy for others. If someone is always beating themselves up on the inside, they're far more likely to look around them and see everything wrong on the outside. **They don't see the rose on the stem, they see the thorns on it and then complain how many thorns there are in the world.** They watch the news and complain or go online and troll and stick thorns in everyone else. This is so often a reflection of their lack of self-love. This state of mind, over time, has caused deep neural pathways to form in their minds to the point where self-hatred is their comfort zone.

Well, if you're someone who wants to figure out how to love yourself more on the inside, but you struggle with seeing the best in yourself and loving yourself, here's an INCREDIBLE hack. Take everything I said above and reverse it! Here's what I mean.

While it's true you don't see things as they are, you see things as YOU are, the reverse is also true and just as effective. Instead of seeing you as you are, you can see YOU as THINGS are. I know, read that again. But here's what I'm saying. The first step is to start seeing the things around you in a positive light. Instead of seeing the thorns on the stem, see and love the rose and its beauty. You're seeing the truth, just focusing on a different part of it. When you start intentionally focusing on the GOOD of things around you, you start to carve new neural pathways in your brain, and you eventually and inevitably start seeing and focusing on the GOOD things about you. And what you focus on becomes your reality. It's contagious. So when you wake up in the morning, instead of thinking, *Ugh, I'm tired*, focus on thoughts like, *Wow, I'm so blessed to feel these warm dry sheets, and to lay my head on a soft pillow, and to wake up in a safe space able to stand up. How beautiful!* Instead of focusing on that dent in your car door that annoys you every time you go to open the door, focus on how blessed you are to have the privilege and freedom to own and drive a car. Instead of seeing the annoying thing your kid is doing, look at their precious little lips and cheeks and relish in the moment that they'll never be this young again. This might sound ridiculous, but instead of being annoyed doing dishes, marvel at the creation of the sponge and the ease at which dish soap lathers. It's all beautiful, if we decide to see it that way.

And this isn't about just thinking positive things, although that's a great approach. This is about a science-backed tool that will change your life and the way you love yourself. If you intentionally practice seeing the love and beauty in the things around you, you stop beating yourself up internally and you inevitably start to see the love and beauty in yourself. It becomes your pattern, your habit, and eventually your default way of experiencing life. What you focus on gets bigger, what you appreciate appreciates, so when you learn to appreciate things around you, and then the things within you, it changes everything. When you recognize and appreciate the worth of the things around you, you begin to magnify the worth within you. **The more you acknowledge the beauty around you, the more you'll see the beauty within you.**

Shortcut #2: Writing and Worthiness

If you practice journaling or plan to start, there's one specific tool I've found to be especially impactful as a great self-worth shortcut. When you journal about events or experiences in your life, whether positive or negative, write the date next to them in your journal, then revisit them six months later. When you do this, in particular with the difficult or negative experiences, take some time to intentionally reflect and write about something you've learned from the event or situation and at least one good thing that's come from it—whether it was a lesson learned or a way in which you grew from it. Or perhaps simply the strength you've built or knowledge you've acquired having gone through it. You can do this again at the one-year mark as well. This not only helps reframe the past experience into one that's more positive, but also helps solidify your knowing that you can make it through hard things, that they don't define you or impact your deep internal identity.

Shortcut #3: Higher Intentions, Higher Self-Worth

So often we speak and act without considering the intentions behind what we say or do. Taking the time to truly consider, and perhaps refocus, our own intentions can be a powerful self-worth shortcut, and when your intentions for what you say and do are good, and you acknowledge your own good intentions, your self-worth gets stronger. Because at our core, we generally believe that good people deserve good things. We believe that good people are worthy. And we often judge whether someone is a generally good person or not based on what we believe their intentions are. If they're positive or negative, if they're to help or to harm. If they're caring or not. This is also how we judge ourselves. So when you build the muscle of focusing on the good intentions behind the things you do and say, in big ways and small, you get an instant shortcut to stronger self-worth. Paying attention and acknowledging yourself is key. Give yourself an imaginary (or real) pat on the back every time you recognize your own good intentions, and slowly but surely your positive self-talk will grow louder and truer than the negative self-talk that often tells us lies all day long.

Shortcut #4: You Are Worthy of Being Seen, Heard, and Understood

In her twenty-five years of hosting the *Oprah Winfrey Show*, Oprah interviewed thousands of guests, including multiple US presidents and the most famous superstars in the world, and they all had one thing in common. No matter who they were, no matter how publicly esteemed, at the end of their interviews they would all lean over to her and ask her the same thing . . . a version of "How was it?" They needed confirmation of, as Oprah puts it, *"Did you see me, did you hear me, did what I say matter to you?"*

Our need to feel worthy of being seen, heard, and understood is at the core of who we are. And it all begins with seeing, hearing, and understanding ourselves.

If seeing yourself is something you struggle with, one hack to solve that is to truly *see* someone else. If you struggle to look into the mirror and see into your own eyes, if you struggle to acknowledge your own beauty and value, and to acknowledge your own worth, let someone else know that you see them. You hear them. And what they have to say matters to you.

I've discovered that one of the quickest tools to getting what we need in life, especially when we're struggling to get it, is to first give it. Yep, this might seem counterintuitive at first, and you might be thinking, *How can I give something when I'm the one who needs it?* But it's a powerful tool that works.

It's just like Newton's third law of motion: for every action, or force in nature, there is an equal and opposite reaction. When you see someone else, truly see them, you are seen right back.

You can do this with a stranger in the coffee shop, or perhaps another person in the grocery check-out line. An easy way to do this is to make eye contact and simply say hello. Or ask them how their day is going. Or give them a sincerely honest compliment on something you notice.

In fact, we are suffering from such a loneliness epidemic in our world, that when you take a moment to truly see and acknowledge another person, in many cases you might just be the only person she sees in her entire day who makes eye contact with her. You might be the only person in her entire day who reminds her that she exists, that she matters, that she's seen, and that she's worthy. And when you see someone else, you begin to feel seen as well. First by that person, in a beautiful, powerful way. And eventually and more easily by yourself.

Shortcut #5: Windows and Mirrors to Your Soul

When was the last time you looked in the mirror, right into your own eyes and truly saw yourself? When was the last time you made eye contact with your partner, or loved one, and actually held it? So that you saw them and they saw you? Something happens in our soul when someone looks deep into our eyes and truly sees us. Especially when we ourselves look into our own eyes. When you do this long enough, you don't notice seeing anything physical, you begin to connect much deeper than that.

Take a moment and recall a time in your life when, perhaps, you've had a crush on a potential romantic partner, and you can look at their face or body, no problem. But when they make eye contact with you, and their eyes meet your eyes and hold that contact, you get a completely different intensity of feelings and emotions. It can be overwhelming to the point where you even look away. This is because when you truly see into your own eyes, or when someone else truly sees into yours, it surpasses surface-level visibility and can penetrate soul-level connection.

And while the excitement of eye contact from a blossoming crush can be a rush, it's truly seeing yourself, and the beauty that is you, that's an even more powerful love.

How you love yourself is how you teach others to love you.

— RUPI KAUR

To fuel the real practice of connection, it's so important to first learn to TRULY connect with yourself. The real you! It's time to truly SEE you. In all of your miraculous worthiness.

Mirror Work

One way to foster true connection with yourself is the practice of mirror work, originally created more than four decades ago by the late, iconic transformational teacher, author, and self-love expert Louise Hay. Mirror work is the practice of gazing at yourself in the mirror while saying positive affirmations to yourself. You can say them aloud or quietly, for long periods of time or even just short moments. Hay calls doing mirror work "one of the most loving gifts you can give yourself," and the practice aims to help you strengthen your connection with yourself, **overcome your inner critic**, learn to love yourself, and to believe the positive affirmations you're saying about yourself. If this is the first time you're hearing about mirror work, it might seem a little out there, or perhaps even silly, but in the decades since it was created by Hay, science has caught up and is now backing it up. In addition to the countless studies that show how powerful your thoughts are, as well as the words you say to yourself about yourself, a 2017 study published in the *Journal of Positive Psychology* found that doing mirror work enhanced the efficacy of compassionate self-talk and heart rate variability. In other words, mirror work can help heal your heart and soul.

If you often experience loneliness in your life, learning to connect deeply with yourself through mirror work can be the transformative and foundational step toward combatting it. **Our depth of connection with others can only be as deep as our depth of connection with ourselves.**

So what is mirror work, and how does it, well, work?

To start, find a mirror. A cell phone camera won't work since when you look into the camera lens, or at your face on the screen, you're not actually able to make direct eye contact. You'll need a true mirror where you can make direct eye contact with yourself. It can be a small or large mirror, even one in your bathroom or car. In Hay's teachings she advises you start by looking yourself in the eye, and taking a look at what you see. Do you see you? Just notice . . . do you really see you? Not just in physical form, but at a soul level? Then, just breathe. Next, as you hold eye contact with yourself, say your name followed by *I love you. I really, really love you.* So, "[Your name], I love you. I really, really love you."

This might be the first time you're ever doing this, and perhaps in the past, you've seen looking in the mirror as something you'd rather avoid. Or something that tempts you to find things you've determined as flaws and faults. True mirror work is a practice that changes all of this. When you say "[Your name], I love you. I really, really love you," Hay's teachings say the aim is for you to connect with your inner child, who has likely been neglected. And when you start connecting with your inner child who wants so much to be loved, and perhaps hasn't been for years and years, you begin to take care of yourself on a deeper level than you've done before. Hay advises that if these words are too hard to say, you can start by saying, "[Your name], I'm willing to learn to like you." And then progress from there.

One study found that 70 percent of women and 80 percent of girls feel more confident and positive when they invest time in caring for themselves. Mirror work can be a powerful way to do that.

If you look in the mirror and immediately hear negative self-talk, it's just your old way of thinking passing through. Acknowledge these thoughts, then let them go, and then look into your eyes again and say, "I love you. I really, really love you." You can also say, "[Your name,] I love you and I accept you." When you love and accept yourself, the floodgates of connection can burst open.

To be beautiful means to be yourself. You don't need to be accepted by others. You need to accept yourself.
— THICH NHAT HANH

When you say, "[Your name], I love you. I really, really love you," it might not feel true at first or even might feel odd. But it's so powerful. As you begin incorporating this practice into your life, you can add it to your morning routine by saying each morning in the mirror, "I love you, what can I do for you today?" Then listen to what you feel.

You can practice forgiveness in the mirror as well. To begin, look into your own eyes and say, "I forgive you." You may even want to be specific, such as "I forgive you for holding on to old unhealthy patterns," "I forgive you for saying hurtful things to yourself," or "I forgive you for your past mistakes." Then at the end, say to yourself, "I forgive you and I am forgiven." At the end of any mirror work you do, you want to reinforce love and approval of yourself.

You can do affirmations in the mirror, such as *I see you. I believe in you. I love you. You are worthy.* You can even write those affirmations on your mirror. If you have a large mirror, you can sit down in front of it, so you're more likely to stay a bit longer. Try asking yourself questions like, *What can I do to make you happy today?*

Research supports the idea that we benefit from specific praise for meaningful effort, and we can offer that praise to ourselves. Saying something specific, such as, "It was amazing how you spoke up in that meeting today, even though you were nervous." Or "You really researched that presentation so thoroughly, I'm so proud of you!" Or "Great job taking that two-minute time-out earlier today rather than losing your cool with the kids." This kind of self-feedback can help us develop greater self-awareness and shore up our sense of self-worth.

THE SCIENCE OF understanding the power of mirror work, in many forms, is expanding by the day. In her book *The High 5 Habit*, my friend Mel Robbins teaches how the simple act of looking at yourself in the mirror each day and giving yourself a high five releases dopamine in your brain and boosts happiness. This simple habit has garnered millions of fans around the world now incorporating this daily practice into their lives.

As science catches up to the positive impact of affirmations and mirror work, parents across the country are beginning to teach these practices at a young age. In a quick search on TikTok or Instagram, you'll see videos everywhere of little ones staring in the mirror and repeating words of encouragement and affirmation passionately to themselves. While the cuteness of these causes them to go viral, they're also building important tools to self-worth along the way.

Most adults haven't even heard of mirror work, let alone been raised around it, and if this is you, it's not too late to begin incorporating the power of it into your life right now. Even as it pertains to your inner child that always remains inside of you.

Here's an inner-child mantra I wrote that's helped me heal unworthiness in my life. And I'm honored to share it with you as well. To begin, look at yourself deep into your eyes, and perhaps you'll begin to see your inner child. Next, consider this idea: when we think of babies and children, we often innately believe that they are automatically worthy of love, that they don't have to earn it. But why do we change the rules on ourselves? When did we decide that we now somehow need to earn love, often conditionally? In your life, when did the world around change and start telling you that you had to earn it? Was it in the guise of well-intentioned parents just trying to replicate what it meant to be a good parent by passing on the expectations of what it means to be a good son or daughter? Was it through books or cultural pressures or when comparison took over?

Go back to the time when you were a baby. Imagine holding yourself, like a baby, as a baby. If it helps, you can even tape a photo of you as a baby or small child onto your mirror. Then if it feels right, maybe wrap your arms around yourself in a big self-hug while you look into your own eyes, in the photo or in the mirror. Say, "I love you. You are so worthy of love. You have been worthy of love since the day you were born, and you are just as fully worthy of love right now. There's nothing you've done or could ever do that makes you unworthy of love. You are made worthy, fully whole, fully deserving. I love you. I see you. You matter so much to me. You are so valuable. You are enough. You are worthy, exactly as you are. I love you. You are so loved. You are worthy of receiving love. Of giving love. You are love. I love you."

If you're a person who practices a specific faith, you can incorporate prayer into mirror work as well. One of my favorite ways to do this is to stare into my eyes and imagine seeing myself the way God sees me. Knowing I am made in His image. Fully worthy.

TO BEGIN INCORPORATING the practice of connecting deeper to yourself through mirror work in any of its forms, you can start slowly, even if it's just for thirty seconds at a time. Then gradually increase, working your way up to five or ten minutes per session. There are no hard rules, and no right or wrong ways to do it, just trust what feels right for you. You can use your mirror work time to do daily affirmations, or to put on a playlist of relaxing music in the background and simply make eye contact with yourself and see yourself. You can expand your practice to include some of the elements mentioned above including focusing on forgiveness or acceptance. You can also speak words of encouragement over yourself and your day ahead, such as, "You got this. God's got you. Life is always happening *for* you. You're born fully capable and totally worthy." You can also take your mirror work beyond eye contact, and stare at and celebrate your body in the mirror. Make sure that when an old soundtrack of criticism might start playing, silence it right away and revert back to kind, loving, TRUE affirmations.

When we learn to see, hear, understand, connect with, and love ourselves, it changes every aspect of life.

If you get up every morning and decide to love yourself just a tiny bit more than you did yesterday, those tiny bits add up.

— LOUISE HAY

NoteWORTHY: For additional resources on mirror work, a WORTHY playlist, and daily affirmations visit WorthyBook.com/Resources

CHAPTER 16

Know Your Why, Then Fly, Girl, Fly

If you don't see a clear path for what you want,
sometimes you have to make it yourself.

— MINDY KALING

Y OU'RE NOT THE right fit for us or for our customers. It's a no." That painful rejection was a pivotal one. It came on the heels of hundreds of other rejections over the previous two years trying to get my company IT Cosmetics off the ground, but this time, I had been so hopeful that it wasn't going to be another no. I was teetering on bankruptcy, and I was in a space where daily I was mustering up all the strength I had not to let my self-doubt take over. I wanted some type of sign, someone to believe in me and the vision for my company, some type of positive momentum, some indication somewhere that I should keep going.

Leading up to the call, I had repeatedly envisioned getting a "yes" in my body. I so badly wanted to get my products onto the live TV shopping channel QVC. I just knew in my gut if I could get a shot on live TV,

I could demonstrate and prove how good my product was and that it actually really worked. So to hear "You're not the right fit for us or for our customers. It's a no," felt like an excruciating punch in the gut.

Have you ever felt like you're supposed to be doing something, you just know you are, but no one else seems to agree with you, or no matter how hard you try to manifest it, it's just not happening? Maybe you're craving partnership and bravely putting yourself out there on the dating app, and maybe you're even going out on lots of first or second dates, but nothing seems to work out beyond that? Maybe you courageously put your gifts, talents, product, or ideas out into the world, and they were not embraced. It felt like no one "got it" or "got you." When this happens, especially over and over, it becomes so easy to quit. To decide that it's proof we don't have what it takes. Our gut must be wrong. And if we're not careful, that can quickly turn into "we're not worthy of it" as a core belief and eventually an identity.

AFTER THIS PAINFUL rejection from QVC, I lay under my covers, unable to hold back the tears for the third day in a row. I just couldn't make sense of it. *Why does my gut feel like I'm supposed to be doing this? When I get still and meditate or pray, I feel peace in the idea that I am supposed to be doing this. Yet everything and everyone around me is saying the opposite.*

That morning I wrote these words in my journal that just flowed through me, from my pen to the paper, in a way that felt like a divine download: *Know Your Why, Then Fly, Girl, Fly.* I read these words every day until I didn't need the reminder.

My *why* for my dream at the time was so much bigger than myself. See, my whole life I grew up loving those images in the beauty ads and on television, but deep down inside they always made me feel like I wasn't enough. When I launched my company, I had a much bigger vision, one that no one seemed to believe in at the time. I wanted to have real women of every age, shape, skin tone, size, and skin challenge as models. I wanted to call them beautiful and mean it. This *why* was profoundly personal for me, because I wanted to end the perpetuating pain of *not-enoughness* that comes from seeing such false, photoshopped representations of what's considered beautiful. I wanted to change the definition of beauty in the beauty industry for every little girl out there who would otherwise be exposed to it and learn to start doubting herself, and every grown woman who still does. This *why* was deep and meaningful for me. And after receiving that hard-to-swallow rejection from QVC, I found myself tempted to give up on my dream. In that moment, I wrote those words in my journal, because I needed the reminder that what I was doing was so much bigger than myself. Those words: *Know Your Why, Then Fly, Girl, Fly* literally helped me get back up out of bed and keep going. Because **why** I was doing it mattered so much more to me than how hard and how much work it was to do.

Your Why

I believe in attaching a deep, powerful *why* to every goal and dream, big and small. Because when you do, you're a lot more likely to achieve it. This is true whether the goal is tangible, like *I want to lower my cholesterol by twenty points*, or the goal is more qualitative, like *I want to feel happier and more present every day.*

On your path of learning to believe you're enough and you're truly WORTHY, it's so important to carve out time and truly understand your deeply personal WHY for wanting to believe it.

Trying to spread our wings and fly toward worthiness requires determination. Our entire lives we've learned messages that keep our flight toward worthiness grounded. **Carrying the weight of our conditioned belief system can feel like trying to fly while having lead balloons attached to our wings. Knowing your why becomes wind beneath your wings.**

When you have a big goal or dream or vision for your life, it's almost never enough to just know with clarity what it is, or even to take action going after it. Identifying your *why* is an important secret ingredient that makes the dream much more likely to actually happen. Your *why* is your deeply personal reason for doing what you're doing. Your reason for wanting what you're wanting. Your *why* gives you the meaning and purpose that act like fuel.

I've leaned on my *why* for so many goals and dreams in all areas of my life. The pursuit of going after your goals and dreams, for anyone brave enough to embark on it, is almost always hard. Without a clear vision of where we're going and *why*, it's just so much easier to quit along the way, or never embark on it at all. I think about this ultra-painful time I was rejected again by QVC, and how discouraged I was. And then I think about how we ended up building the biggest beauty brand in QVC history. How I ended up going live on TV myself for more than 1,000 shows. I can't help but think about how easily it all could have *not* happened.

> *We need vision to maintain hope. And your why acts as your vision.*

This is a step most people either aren't aware of or skip because they don't realize how important it can be. They think just knowing how to do something is enough, but it rarely is. Which is one reason so many people easily give up on their goals. They haven't identified a meaningful enough reason for *why* they must happen. Not *should* happen, but absolutely *must*. **When you have a strong *why* for your goal, it becomes something you can lean on when you're feeling discouraged. It can be the fuel that keeps you motivated and inspired. It's the reason you've identified *why* you *must* keep doing what you're doing.**

Find out who you are and do it on purpose.
— DOLLY PARTON

RIGHT NOW, I want to help you identify a *why* for your personal pursuit of believing you're WORTHY.

In my example above, while crying under my bedsheets after a significant rejection, knowing *why* I was doing what I was doing helped me decide to keep going. **We need vision to maintain hope. And your *why* acts as your vision.** When I think back to that moment crying in bed, had I not leaned on my why, and instead just decided that QVC telling me "It's a no" was the final straw, my entire life would have changed. I would have let someone else's doubt about me turn into doubt in my own head, and eventually I would have **doubted myself out of my own destiny.** Because I knew why I was doing what I was doing, even when it wasn't going my way, I had that as one of my tools to lean on to get back up and keep going. Even through the years of rejection, I would wake up each morning and remind myself of it. I woke up believing I could change the beauty industry and thinking thoughts to myself like *Girls and women everywhere need me to keep going today.*

THINK ABOUT YOUR own journey toward believing you're enough. And believing you're worthy of your greatest hopes and wildest dreams, I want you to consider *why* you want to. What is your true, deep *why*?

Perhaps it's to decide that the generational cycle of learning to please everyone else, while betraying yourself, is going to stop with you, and you want better for your kids. Perhaps it's with a goal of eventually helping others believe that they are worthy. Maybe it's to one day help others who have experienced similar trauma or setbacks that you have. Maybe it's to be a living example of learning to do hard things, so that other people see what's possible and start to believe it's possible for them too. Maybe it's to learn to love yourself unconditionally, so that you can attract, then give and receive that kind of love in an intimate relationship or friendship. Maybe it's because you want to build the confidence and resilience of putting your art or ideas or story out into the world, to help your kids believe they're worthy of doing that too. Maybe it's to learn to speak your voice and decide that it's worthy of being heard, so that you can speak for those who don't have the same opportunities. Maybe it's starting your own Worthy Circle to connect with and uplift others. And maybe it's as simple as knowing that you are confident enough and feel worthy enough to be who you truly are, you'll automatically inspire others to do the same.

EVERY MORNING I write in a gratitude journal, and I frequently also write out my goals. And while writing your actual goals on paper is powerful, I make two additions to a traditional goal-writing practice. First, I write out my goals as if they're already true and have already happened. For example, instead of saying, "I want to wake up early, meditate, and walk for at least thirty minutes each morning," I write, "I wake up early, meditate, and walk for thirty minutes each morning." Or instead of "One day I will be a *New York Times* best-selling author," I write, "I am a *New York Times* best-selling author." Or instead of "I am going to learn to prioritize rest," I write, "I prioritize rest well." Writing them as if they've already happened helps wire your brain and body to believe they will happen, and you can more easily act accordingly. The second addition I make to a traditional goal-setting practice is that next to each goal I list my specific and meaningful *why* for it next to it.

When you write your *why* behind the reason you absolutely must accomplish each goal, your deep-rooted authentic *why*, it takes things to a whole new level and makes your dream more likely to happen. It's like goal-setting on steroids. Because when you attach meaning and emotion to something you want, it's now no longer just a thought in your head, it's something you feel and connect with in your body.

When you attach enough meaning and emotion to a goal, you exponentially multiply its chances of happening.

Your *why* is the meaning and emotion. It's not enough to know *how*. Many of us know how to eat healthy, but we don't. We know how to go do exercise, but we don't. You also need to marry the *how* with the *why*. A *why* that is so deeply personal to you, that nothing is going to stand in your way, even when the uphill battles get hard.

So, why is it, in your one beautiful life, you absolutely must learn to truly believe you're worthy? Spend as much time as you can considering and getting clarity on this. You might know the answer instantly. Or you might need some time to write, pray, or meditate on it. And once you have your why identified, revisit it often. You might find it evolves over time as well. And once you know it, it becomes an invaluable tool to lean on during setbacks, and to use as fuel during the mission forward.

Know your why, then fly, girl, fly.

NoteWORTHY: You can download a FREE *Why* and goal-setting worksheet at WorthyBook.com/Resources

CHAPTER 17

Circle or Cage

*Be careful telling your dreams to
people who aren't dreamers.*

— TRENT SHELTON

LET'S RIP THE Band-Aid right off: Are the people around you most, including your friends and loved ones, your circle or your cage?

Here are some ways to tell which feels true for you.

Think about how your inner circle makes you feel. Take a moment, maybe even close your eyes, and ask yourself, *Are they empowering? Do they truly want the best for me, not just what they think is best for me?* **Do they lead with love?**

Or are they disempowering? Do they want me to conform to their expectations for me? **Do they lead with fear?**

Do you share all of who you are, knowing they love you for all of who you are? Or do you hide parts of yourself from them so that they don't judge you, shame you, or love you less?

Do you have varying beliefs about political or social issues, and support each other anyway? Or do they pressure you to believe theirs?

Do they feel like a supportive, uplifting circle, forming a giant hug around you, and lifting you up higher with supportive hands and shoulders you can stand on? Or do they feel more like a cage of expectations, weighing you down and keeping you confined, with a misleading sign on the cage door that says *Belonging*? You'll know the true answer because you'll feel it in your body.

> *Just as we can know the ocean because it*
> *always tastes of salt, we can recognize enlightenment*
> *because it always tastes of freedom.*
>
> — BUDDHA

Your inner circle should feel like a hug and taste like freedom. It should be a place you can exhale. Where you can mess up, get it wrong, cry it out—all with the unshakable certainty that love won't be withheld from you if you do.

A strong supportive circle reinforces worthiness by loving and accepting and reminding you that you are valuable and enough exactly as you are. A cage is the opposite and makes you want to change or hide who you are in hopes of belonging, understanding, approval, and love.

Your Current Circle

When it comes to your closest circle, most of us never intentionally choose the group we surround ourselves with. We so often let the environments we're around or raised in determine the people we're around. And then we become a product of our environment. The group in our environment becomes our default circle, be it family, peer group, classmates, or work colleagues.

When you think about the people you most frequently talk with, ask advice from, or spend your free time with, do you respect and admire them? Have they gone where you want to go? Are they inspiring, are they emotionally evolved, and do they have the attributes you aspire to in life? Do they take care of their body and health the way you want to take care of yours? Do they love others and themselves unconditionally?

If you're sitting there right now thinking your current circle, whether made up of family or friends or both, is a bit like a cage, but you love them and don't want to abandon them, don't worry. That's not the only option. In fact, most of us are surrounded by people who are often good, but were given to us by default, and who could actually stunt our growth if we don't transform the relationship dynamics going forward. If you feel like your current circle is more of a cage, and you want differently for your life, part of growing into the person you were truly born to be is becoming aware of this, finding healthy ways for these relationships to evolve, and forming new relationships in your life so you grow a healthy, empowering inner circle.

Your inner circle should be a place you can exhale. Where you can mess up, get it wrong, cry it out—all while knowing that love won't be withheld from you if you do.

Differences Can Unite or Divide

Given the political landscape and the evolution of technology, including social media and how we now receive information, many of us are faced with a whole new level of divisiveness at family dinner tables, friend-group texts, and holiday gatherings. The days of healthy debates among loved ones on hot topics have commonly been replaced with division and intolerance for differing views. This is a new type of cage being created, one with a sign on it that says *Conform and agree or be excluded.*

This cage goes beyond close family and friends, and now involves social pressure to only spend time around people who believe what you believe. And in some circles if you don't, you risk being canceled, ostracized, or excluded. In the modern-day cancel culture, we often see people get shamed and judged for spending time with people who believe differently than they do. We're pressured to only surround ourselves with **like-minded people**. When what matters is that we surround ourselves with **like-hearted people**. Some of the people with the biggest hearts might feel very differently than you do on controversial issues. Similarly, some people who might agree with you on issues might also be bankrupt in their mindset, morals, or capacity to love beyond themselves. When you spend time with people who have completely different views than you on politics, faith, or social issues, it doesn't mean you agree with them, and it certainly doesn't mean that you're bad. It means you'll have a greater and deeper understanding of humanity, and how, in this one precious life you have, you might be able to actually help heal humanity through love.

Spend time with people who are like-hearted, not necessarily like-minded.

I make it a point to spend time around people who vote, live, and love differently than I do. Who disagree with me on many of the most hotly debated topics. And they all sharpen me, even if I might not agree at all with them, and in fact, because we don't agree.

You can never understand humanity, and therefore can't impact it, if you don't understand the humans that form it. And you can never bring more people to your version of the light if you only spend time with people who are already in it.

We are at a moment in time where having the courage to be *first* is more important than ever. **You can be first in your family or peer group to love more and judge less. The first to take a stand and intentionally celebrate differences instead of canceling people because of them. The first to realize that the fastest way to dull yourself down is to *only* spend time with people who agree with you.**

BEFORE YOU THINK less of your family or peer group if they don't handle differences well, take a huge step back and acknowledge that most people are simply unaware of the impact the new ways they're getting their information are having on them. We've rapidly transitioned from vetted journalism to a no-barriers-to-entry, online free-for-all of information. Google any popular quote, and you'll immediately see thousands of graphics of that quote attributing credit to several different people. No one can actually prove who said it first. The explosive growth of the internet combined with zero barriers to entry has created a smorgasbord of varying credibility.

People who spent decades trusting the news are now also trusting unverified sources of online information and not knowing the difference. To add fuel to the dumpster fire of information flow, you have social media algorithms feeding you more articles and ads and products and people that reinforce your beliefs without ever displaying opposing views. We're only shown "facts" that support our views, and these "facts" make their way into our social media feeds, news feeds, email inboxes, and phones. This leads people to have a hyper-skewed view of information and events.

While movies like *The Social Network* are helping to shed light on these issues, new challenges are accumulating faster than anyone can keep up. Artificial intelligence is rapidly infiltrating all parts of our lives. Some online influencers are now using bots to get fake likes, comments, and engagement; videos now edit the appearance of someone's face and body shape however they want in ways undetectable to our eyes; what we're seeing holistically is not even real anymore. And yet this space is also the future of commerce and community.

Spend time with people who are like-hearted, not necessarily like-minded.

So if you're feeling like your family, peer group, and colleagues are more divided than ever, and if time spent around them feels more like a cage than ever, don't be surprised. And know that you're not alone in this. Being aware of it is important in deciding the role you want to play in it all, so that you don't risk getting . . . well, caged.

When There's Nothing Wrong with Your Circle Except They're Not Right for You

Sometimes even a loving, kind family or peer group can stand in the way of your dreams. It can be almost as hard to distance yourself from people with good intentions as it is to abandon people who are clearly bad for you. What I mean by that is we all crave love and belonging. Being included feels good. Having other people need and want us feels good. But it shouldn't come at the price of dimming our light, or embracing and becoming all of who we are.

So many people miss out on their calling of being first in exchange for fitting in. The temptation to play life small, dim our light, or change who we are to fit in happens just as easily when we're in unhealthy circles as when we're surrounded by people who want the best for us, but we know that what they believe is best for us isn't what's best for us. If you feel like you're showing up as only part of who you are or are holding back from your dreams and ideas and opinions and ambitions so that you can belong in a circle, it's the same cage, and it can be harder to leave. Maybe you know you need acceptance, or rest, or joy, and your family is only sort-of good at those things, so you stay right there in that comfort zone only sort-of resting, sort-of feeling joy, sort-of being accepted, feeling sort-of worthy, and that's sort-of good enough. But it's also only sort of what you need and what is possible. An example of this is the story I shared about how my dad wanted me to stay working at the health club because I was making good money, when my soul knew I was supposed to pursue my dreams.

Do you talk yourself out of living as the truest, highest expression of yourself, because where you are is good enough? And comfortable enough? And safe? And pain-free? Do you feel that all you're worthy of is "good enough"?

If staying in your current circle feels like you're shrinking who you truly are, at the price of talking yourself out of your own truth and calling, then it's time to reevaluate.

Keeping the peace around you should never come at the price of keeping the peace within you.

Loving from a Big-Picture Perspective

It's tempting to build resentment toward our families or friends when we feel like they don't love or accept us for who we fully are, like we have to conform to their expectations in order to be loved. Resentment is the bitterness and indignation we feel at how we've been treated by another person. Yet holding on to resentment only hurts the person holding it. It is a tempting but low vibration choice. Forgiveness is a better one. Forgiveness doesn't say that what they did, how they spoke to us, or how they treated us is okay. It simply says we're not going to give it our attention or let it consume energy anymore and we're going to set ourselves free. **People are so often just doing the best they can with the resources and capacity they have.** This understanding has freed me from resentment and helped me gain empathy.

Once you're on your path to seeing the people in your environment with nonjudgmental eyes, you realize that all the power lies within you, not them. You get to decide the kind of relationship, or not, that you have with the people in your current circle. And you get to decide how you want to grow and evolve going forward.

HERE'S AN IMPORTANT lesson to soak up right away. Just because you're growing and changing and improving and healing, it doesn't mean anyone else in your circle/cage will want to do that themselves. And you can't make anyone else change who doesn't want to. **Part of the path to freedom is releasing your own expectations of how you think they should be, and simply loving them for who they are.** And then deciding the best, healthiest boundaries and relationship you want to have with them going forward. Do you want them in your inner circle, your outer circle, or neither?

Remember, when you're the first in your family to want more for your life, or challenge the status quo, or take a risk, or bet on yourself and your ideas and talents, or break a generational cycle, or think, or vote, or love differently, you're a trailblazer. And being a trailblazer can feel lonely. So much so that many people will choose to conform to everyone else so that they keep that sense of belonging. But when you change or conform who you are to belong, you actually don't belong at all, because it's not the real you who's belonging. You won't feel the true love and fulfillment of belonging unless you are your authentic self.

Inner Circle and Outer Circle

Imagine two circles. One inner, one outer. Both important.

Your **inner circle** is the people you choose to be closest to. The ones who are the wind beneath your wings. Who inspire you to fly to greater heights. Who you share your secrets with. Who don't project their own fears onto you. Who truly want the best for you, not just the best for themselves. Who care *about* you and care *for* you. Who see you and your opinions, hopes, ambitions, challenges, and quirks—all through the lens of love.

Your **outer circle** is also people you care about and love. But their belief systems, habits, and emotional evolvement can create the feeling of a cage in your life depending on the circumstances. They might be the family who raised you, friends you had growing up, or a colleague you sit next to at work. They might be people who you really like, but only want to spend time around in certain situations. They might be people you love working out with every day but would never trust with your secrets. Or people who you want to see on holidays but notice that whenever you do spend time around them, your energy feels lower, and you hide parts of who you are to make them comfortable. They might be people you love and care about deeply, and they might be really kind and loving, but they are only able to see your opinions, hopes, ambitions, challenges, and quirks through the lens of judgment, fear, or limited capacity.

Both of these circles surround you, giving you a sense of belonging. But you can give the people in them very different levels of access to you, prioritization, trust, vulnerability, and time. Both circles, and the people in them, should feel like circles and not like cages. Sometimes a person feels like a circle, but when you bring them closer it turns into a cage, so they need to stay in your outer circle in order for you to have a healthy, loving relationship with them. And if there is a certain person who brings toxic energy to your life consistently, they shouldn't hold a place in either circle. They belong on the outside of the outer circle, and you can love them from a healthy distance when possible.

If carrying the people around you costs you your capacity, then they're *too* heavy.

> *Anything is possible when you have the*
> *right people there to support you.*
> — MISTY COPELAND

Take a huge step back and look at the people around you, including the people who raised you. Observe without judgment; just see what feels true for you. Some might feel like examples you aspire to emulate, and others might feel like warnings. Some might feel like they deplete all of your joy when you're around them. Others might feel like they fill your joy tank up when you see them. Just start to observe and feel the impact on you. As you start the process of designing and rearranging your inner and outer circles, observation and awareness are so important. **You can't fly to the heights of your calling with lead balloons attached to your wings.**

Blue Slurpees, Cheetos, and Emotional Residue

Blue Slurpee drinks leave blue residue on your tongue. Cheetos leave orange residue on your fingers. (And of course IT Cosmetics' original powder blush stain leaves a flattering pink stain on your cheeks ☺.) The theory of "emotional residue" explains that people's emotions leave traces in their physical environment, which can impact, influence, and be sensed by others.

In other words, the energy and vibes of the people you spend time around stick to you like residue. Unlike blue or orange residue that you can physically see, emotional residue is invisible to the eye, but you can definitely feel it. And unlike blue or orange residue that can wash off in an hour or two, emotional residue can last much longer. It can even last forever if you're not aware of it and don't intentionally avoid it.

Would you rather keep the peace around you or keep the peace within you?

Have you ever walked into a room with one or more people in it and just felt your own vibration change? And then when you left that room, you had a hard time shaking it off? That's emotional residue.

Similarly, have you ever been around someone, and you just feel so much more vibrant and joyful and alive because of them? Or someone who perhaps just leaves you feeling seen, heard, understood, and emotionally held? These are all types of emotional residue you feel after being around different people.

Sometimes these are just small things that you take note of how they make you feel over time. When my husband, Paulo, and I started dating, we were walking through a parking garage once, and as we hugged and kissed each other goodbye, in the very moment our lips touched, there was a visible electric spark. While my mind knew it was probably due to some type of static electricity, I also believe in signs, and I got so excited. He and I couldn't believe it and instantly became giddy like schoolkids with the joy of blossoming love. We later described the exciting moment to a family member who had absolutely no reaction. I remember how their lack of energy immediately brought ours down. To this day, I love that family member dearly, but they're not part of the inner circle who I call when exciting or silly things happen. **It doesn't mean I love that person any less, it just means I am intentionally protecting the gift and vibration of joyful energy when I feel it buzzing.**

Being aware of emotional residue is important, because if energy is contagious, curating the kind of energy you're around and the frequency of your exposure can impact all aspects of your life. Awareness of the emotional residue you feel can be a great tool to use when deciding who you want in your inner circle, your outer circle, or nowhere near your circles.

Boundaries

Setting healthy boundaries, intentionally deciding who has what levels of access to you and deciding the amount of time and attention you give to them, can feel scary, especially if you have people-pleasing tendencies and just want everyone to be happy. But you need to take a huge step back and prioritize what matters most, to both your health and your joy. **Would you rather keep the peace around you or keep the peace within you?**

> *You've healed too much to not raise the*
> *bar on who has access to you.*
> — CATHY HELLER

Brené Brown once shared the story of how she taught her kids to never surround themselves with what she calls candle-blower-outers. She uses the analogy of how we each have a flame inside of us, and how this is our spirit, our soul, our light, and it's important to surround ourselves with people who celebrate our flame shining brightly. And protect it.

People who have room in their lives for our light that comes with us. She advises her kids and others to make sure they don't surround themselves with the opposite kind of people, the candle-blower-outers. Or worse, those who convince you your light isn't worthy of shining or try to tell you that your flame blew out on its own.

SETTING A BOUNDARY is like blocking the wind or breath coming your way that's about to blow out your flame.

A boundary might be in the form of starting to say how you really feel, even when you're tempted to people-please yourself into a lie. It can mean saying *no* because that's how you feel, when you're tempted to say a *yes* that you don't mean. It might mean telling your parents you appreciate all they've done, but you're choosing to parent your own kids differently. It might mean being the first in your family to forgive, even if others still hold a grudge. It can mean only sharing parts of your life with the people who you trust as stewards of the information. It might mean protecting your peace by sharing your ambitions with the people who will celebrate them, versus those who will criticize them. It might mean intentionally carving out larger amounts of time with members and potential members of your inner circle, and reducing the time spent with your outer circle.

Some people might have a problem with you setting boundaries, but the real problem is that they haven't done the work yet to heal and realize that.

The only people who get upset about you setting boundaries are those who are benefiting from you having none.

— BRIAN WEINER

The need for healthy boundaries will almost always have to be recognized, determined, and implemented by you. And don't be surprised if maintaining them is a lifelong challenge. Especially when most of our lives we've defaulted to seeking love and belonging from the people in our environment that we were raised in, as they're the ones we've asked for advice from even when they have no idea or understanding of our situation. They're the ones we've sought comfort and belonging from, even when they might not have the capacity to meet our needs. And the relationships are likely reciprocal in varying extents, so don't be surprised if the new boundaries you implement are met with resistance as well. As human beings, one of our deepest fears is that we're not enough, and if we're not enough we won't be loved. When you grow and change and branch out, it can leave your friends or family feeling like they're not enough or they're no longer worthy of your love. So understanding this as you work to build new, healthy boundaries can help you meet their potential resistance with grace.

Setting boundaries can feel like a betrayal to others. But not learning to is almost always a betrayal of yourself.

You might notice that when you go back home, perhaps for the holidays, or when you immerse yourself into outer circle peer groups, you slip from keeping your boundaries in place. Often when we go back home or back to old friends or old places or environments that didn't see our greatness, it becomes extra tough to not feel imposter syndrome or fall into feeling unworthy again. This is the danger zone—the times you have to stay hyperaware of others' projections and limiting thinking and limited capacity. Otherwise, you'll start falling into old actions, old behaviors, old patterns, and worst of all, an old identity and belief of what you're worthy of. You might start to feel like you're stuffing yourself back into an old snakeskin or sausage casing that you've already outgrown and shed.

You can start implementing healthy boundaries by saying how you truly feel without apologizing, saying no when you mean no, and only saying yes when you mean yes, valuing your own time and asking others to do the same, and sharing your needs with others. Be firm and kind without overexplaining.

"No" is a complete sentence.

— ANONYMOUS

It's likely going to be an imperfect process. There might be stumbles, roadblocks, and setbacks along the way, but keep going. And remember: **Implementing boundaries can often feel like a betrayal to others. But not learning to is almost always a betrayal of yourself.**

Curate Your Circles and Chosen Family

As you grow and evolve, you might decide that your current inner circle is more beautiful than you could have imagined. Or you might decide to make a few adjustments, set a few new boundaries, and curate a revised inner circle and outer circle. The family, peer group, and colleagues that you've ventured through life with so far might play a big or small part in both.

Your circle might be two people or five people, just make sure they're the right people.

Often, when people begin a quest toward healing and toward personal growth, they adopt the idea of chosen family. This means that the people you consider your closest family might not be the same people you were raised with. They might not be related to you by blood. They might simply be people in your life who you have the depth and closeness and intimacy with, which you'd consider family-like. You might hear terms of endearment used to describe great affection for friends who are considered chosen family, including terms like "sister from another mister" or "brother from another mother." Chosen family might be the people you spend holidays and important gatherings with, and chosen family can also include all or part of the family you were raised with or born into. Chosen family is exactly who you choose as family.

Your circle might be two people or five people, just make sure they're the right people.

You can cultivate your friendships this way as well. The closest friends you grew up with might not feel aligned with who you've become, and you may have grown apart. That's okay. As an adult, it's totally possible to cultivate new, close friendships. **True friends want what's best for you based on your hopes and dreams, not what they think is best for you based on their own hopes and dreams.**

One of the many reasons a great inner circle is so important to living your best life is that the people in it remind you of your greatness. Of your gifts. Of the beauty and power that is YOU. Because all of us, even the most famous, publicly praised people, need reminding.

I actually keep a list of some of the kindest words and affirmations people in my inner circle have said to me about me, and I pull it out and read it privately every time I'm tempted to forget and tempted to feel *not enough*.

> *Spend time around people who pull you*
> *into your future, not your past.*
> — UNKNOWN

Elephants and Your Inner Circle

I love the story author and thought leader Jen Hatmaker shares to illustrate how an inner circle shows up for you.

Jen was going through a very hard season in her life when a close friend of hers sent her a photo of elephants, all female, standing in a circle formation. The elephants all faced outward, looking out from the center of the circle with their backsides and tails facing into the center of the circle. At first, Jen was confused why her friend would send her a photo of elephants. Her friend went on to describe to her how in the wild, when either a mama elephant is giving birth or when an elephant is hurt, all the other female elephants in the herd back around her, enclosing her into the center of the circle formation. They gather in tightly together and close ranks so that the mama elephant or the hurt elephant in the middle can't be seen, protecting the most vulnerable of their group from the view of predators and more harm. The elephants then stomp and kick up soil and dirt to mask any scent and throw off any attackers. They send a clear signal that if anyone tries to attack their loved one while she's vulnerable, they'll have to get through her inner circle first.

Jen describes how when the baby elephant is delivered, the sister elephants kick dirt all over the newborn to protect its skin, and then they start trumpeting glorious music in celebration of new life, and sisterhood, and something beautiful being born in a harsh world as Jen says, "filled with enemies and odds." The visual of elephants taking this formation as they do is such a great allegory of the power of a beautiful inner circle. A circle has our back and protects us when we're weak or vulnerable. They trumpet loudly in celebration when we birth new ideas and embark on new victories. Sometimes we're in the middle of the circle being protected, and sometimes we are part of the circle that fiercely protects our vulnerable beloveds. The first time I heard Jen Hatmaker speak and share this analogy, I cried. Because it felt like truth. When we have the gift of this type of friend, family member, or loved one as part of our inner circle, and when we show up for them in the same way, it's the most beautiful feeling.

True friends want what's best for you based on your hopes and dreams, not what they think is best for you based on their own hopes and dreams.

And when we can't count on the people in our circle to show up for us, have our back, or cheer us on to our greatest potential, it can leave us feeling empty and disconnected. Curating empowering inner and outer circles, who love and value you for exactly who you are innately, reinforces worthiness.

THE BEAUTY IS that your story is always unfolding, and you can build and continue to curate your circles. For the rest of your one, heroic, beautiful life. And you can decide how you want to show up in them.

Are the people you choose to spend time with, including your friends and loved ones, more of a circle or a cage?

I lost a friend of mine while I was writing this book. On his arm he had a tattoo of a famous quote by John Shedd that said, "A ship is safe in harbor, but that's not what ships are built for." I've always loved that quote. It reminds me how we are all born with a beautiful mind and soul, filled with wild, imaginative thoughts and ideas that the world needs desperately.

You might be safe in silent harbor, or in a circle that's more like a cage, but that's not what you were built for. You were built to brave the ocean, and feel the salt water splash on your skin, and the winds fill your sails. You were built with every part it takes to put in the hard work that accomplishes the dreams on your heart. You were built to endure the waves. You were built to soak in the sun. You were built to navigate uncharted waters and celebrate the wonder of the glorious adventures ahead that have your name on them. You are worthy of speaking your opinions, taking risks, and shifting culture. You are worthy of standing up to bullies, tapping into your courage, and standing up for others who can't afford to tap into theirs. Don't stay stuck in a cage that calls itself a circle. Don't cancel yourself out of your calling. Your soul and the world need what only you can give.

It takes intentionality and conviction to decide you're worthy of all circles and no cages. It takes bravery to trust yourself, even when others tell you to dim your light. And it takes a whole heck of a lot of courage to live as the real you, when there's no one else like you. A cage that traps you might feel comfortable to your mind, but your soul knows you were born to fly free and that you deserve a supportive and celebratory circle—a circle that acts as the wind beneath your wings on your journey.

NoteWORTHY: Learn more about joining a Worthy Circle or creating your own at WorthyBook.com/Resources

CHAPTER 18

Overexposed and Underdeveloped

Nothing will work unless you do.

— MAYA ANGELOU

I SKIPPED THE EXPECTED business power suit, slipped into a comfy pink knit dress that felt like pajamas, and delighted in how its casual joy was disguised by a sprinkling of rhinestones. I decided to be me even if it meant I didn't visually look the part of the room and the conversations I was about to walk into. What I didn't know was that this would be the one and only time I met one of the most famous rappers in the world. I was at the Forbes 400 event, where *Forbes* magazine celebrates the 400 most influential people in philanthropy. The event is incredible, and I feel so sharpened every time I've had the blessing of being invited. The ideas and brilliant minds in the room, coupled with the commitment to help humanity, are awe-inspiring.

This particular year the event was hosted in New York City, and we had spent the day discussing innovative ideas and initiatives and were wrapping it up with a cocktail party and live entertainment. A friend of mine happened to have worked with this rapper previously and wanted to introduce us. I figured it would be a two-second hello and was absolutely sure he'd have no clue who I was, but as soon as I shook his hand, he said to me, "I love your infomercial." *WHAT?*

"You do? You've seen it?" I said with surprise. *What was he doing watching my television infomercial where I show makeup on real women with real skin concerns?* I tried to stay present and listen as he explained that he had studied the infomercial and congratulated me on the infomercial's success. "Yeah, it's brilliant how you positioned the product and then removed your makeup to connect with customers," he said. I thanked him, we talked for a brief while longer, then parted ways.

The very first thing I thought to myself as I walked away from meeting him was that **it's almost never an accident when someone is successful.** Success in all forms almost always leaves clues. And one of those clues is best put in the words of the late Dr. Maya Angelou, "Nothing will work unless you do."

Even though I was surprised that this world-famous rapper with a multi-decade career had seen my TV infomercial, I remembered how I study all types of people who are successful across all kinds of industries because I love to try and recognize patterns and learn why they've been successful. He was likely so successful in his career, not just because he was talented, but because he was a lifelong student and a hard worker committed to development. Committed to studying excellence wherever he sees it, in case it can make him sharper. He has a long-lasting career, likely in part because his development has paralleled his exposure.

WE ARE IN a culture that glorifies instant gratification. There is a whole generation expecting to be promoted with a fancy job title before they complete their first internship. And while I am all for ambition, it's so critical to understand that you are the steward of your potential, growth, possibilities, and dreams.

I've read so many books that are all rah-rah and filled with what feels like generic positivity, but they skip the *keeping it really real* part.

But the *really real* part is how you'll get *really real* results, and that's what this book is about. My purpose in this chapter is not to deflate you. I promise you have everything you need inside of you right now to accomplish your greatest hopes and wildest dreams. I promise you that you are worthy of them. But there is one critical ingredient in the success formula that most people are tempted to skip over. In order to truly achieve your ultimate goals, including how to build lasting self-worth and self-confidence, you have to build and fine-tune the skill of generating your own momentum along the way. I promised you I'd be right along with you in these pages, and I have your back, so I've gotta talk about the *really real* stuff. Okay, let's go.

Experts in Exposure

Have you ever followed someone on social media who is super popular or knowledgeable or inspiring, only to realize one day that they've never actually done the thing they talk about? They're just really good at talking about it.

As the world of technology evolves at hyperspeed, there are no barriers to entry anymore and no qualifications required to becoming an "expert" or a "guru." Among the benefits of this is that entrepreneurs, creators, product inventors, and artists can get their works out to the world directly, without relying on a middleman to say "YES" or "NO" to reach their audience or customers. They don't have to rely on a company to decide if they want to distribute or promote their product or invention or art. There are many more benefits. But there are also some major downsides.

People with nothing but popularity or the ability to cultivate it are now able to share their expertise on whatever topic they choose. In the past, a popular person was hired to endorse a product or service, but that product or service was often an established company that had to follow all regulatory and safety regulations for their product or service.

Now popular personalities are selling their own products or services often without any of the knowledge, experience, infrastructure, or safety and regulatory compliance understanding. Consider this: Have you recently purchased products promoted on social media without considering if they're coming from a safe, vetted, and reputable source?

Remember the days when a critic's review in the newspaper or on TV had so much power? People trusted that critics had in-depth knowledge of the industry. So if a critic gave a restaurant, a movie, or a book a five-star review, people trusted it and bought the product. And the critic's reputation, often based on decades of building trust, was on the line. Well, now people are watching TV less, reading the paper less, and getting information online more, and just about everyone, whether they have any experience or qualifications, is now a vocal critic.

In my years working as a journalist in television news, every word I wrote in every story had to be fact-checked. If you made an error and it went out over the airways to viewers as a truth, you could be fired for the error. The station would immediately issue an on-camera retraction and apology to the viewers. Similarly, as journalists we were prohibited from sharing our opinions on anything. Our job was to report the facts. An opinion of any kind was also grounds for being fired. Working at television stations, I was a firsthand witness to how my colleagues—often with decades of experience—prided themselves and found their purpose in delivering factual stories to help make viewers better informed. Today, there are endless articles online and countless websites putting out articles as news, when they're rarely ever fact-checked and are filled with unvetted sources. It's now nearly impossible to verify who said a quote first, with the countless websites attributing any and every quote to multiple "original" sources.

The "experts" online that we and our children follow are now, often in so many ways, **overexposed and underdeveloped**. When experts or products or businesses gain popularity, their follower count, and subsequent product sales, flourish. Online personalities deem themselves experts, then give out advice that impacts people's mental and physical health, safety, business, relationships, and life without knowledge or experience. With huge popularity, but without knowledge or experience, the risks to consumers are huge.

THERE ARE MANY unseen and not widely known benefits to having the kinds of barriers to entry that have now fallen away on the internet. While building IT Cosmetics, we had to abide by the strict safety, regulatory, and quality control standards of many of our retail partners. We had to do extensive allergy and safety testing, as well as abide by FDA labeling and safety guidelines. In contrast, these days cosmetics companies are popping up everywhere online, and if they're attached to a popular personality, the products are selling like hotcakes. Many are completely unregulated—meaning they never go through safety testing—and the consumer has no idea what they're really putting on their face and body. This is even worse in the supplement and food industry, where consumers ingest these unregulated products.

Of course, there are government agencies charged with overseeing all of this, but they are spread way too thin and don't have the infrastructure to handle the speed with which companies pop up with a photo and sell the product directly to consumers. It's easy to get a fancy, credible-looking website and have bots promote a product with hundreds or even thousands of fake reviews. And the result is no one knowing that the product they're buying is overexposed and underdeveloped. This puts consumers' health and safety at risk.

THE SAME IS true in the categories of advice and services. Whether someone is an influencer, a thought leader, or an "expert" on something, when their popularity and community grow at a pace faster than their own real-life experience, knowledge, and true expertise, they find themselves in a tough spot. They start making money this way—through video views, ads, programs they're selling, online events, or product placement—and a vicious cycle ensues. They need to keep their likes and views high on every post so that ad money and sponsors keep coming in. But unlike an expert who spent decades acquiring the expertise that led to their fame, in this new world, the person can build that type of fame without any foundation of knowledge and experience to stand on. They're now overexposed and underdeveloped. Then to top it off, those watching these meteoric rises, both young and old, start to believe that putting in the hard work of gaining expertise is not necessary and that the dream of success and money coming easy, is now in fact . . . well, easy!

Behind the scenes, there are online relationship and love experts selling courses on marriage who are staying in unhealthy relationships to keep up a façade that they've promoted online. There are love and healing experts who are hiding that they are actually in the infancy of their own healing journey and haven't yet learned how to love themselves. They promote ideas that haven't been researched, tested, and that they haven't even experienced themselves. And behind the walls of technology, filters, and fancy websites, this can be difficult to detect.

With the quick exposure many are having in our new direct-to-consumer-via-technology world, it's so easy to fall into the trap of tasting success and then wanting as much of it as you can. Or feeling like you need to strike while the iron is hot. And not worry about if you have the infrastructure or development to sustain it long term. It's hard to say no to fame or to money or to people celebrating you. It's hard to say no to short-term success even if you know it's being built on a foundation with a lot of cracks and weak spots. It's hard to resist the lure of short-term wins that please investors and bosses and teams and peers and partners and family and social media followers.

You'll be overexposed and underdeveloped in love if you don't also love yourself.

WHILE I ENDURED the early years of building IT Cosmetics that came with the hundreds of rejections and frequent brushes with bankruptcy, the tides completely shifted when we started getting sales success. Suddenly, all of the retail stores who had told me no for years now wanted me. Right around that time, one of my mentors gave me strong advice on how to be a regulator of momentum. She told me several stories about other brands who grew fast in popularity and demand. They said yes to any and all exposure, signing deals with everyone who wanted to carry and sell their products. But because their own teams couldn't deliver on all the aspects needed to succeed, including operations, finance, safety, quality control, legal, hiring, marketing, and education support, they failed to deliver to the retail partners and eventually were discontinued in their stores. She told me that if I allowed too much growth before my infrastructure could keep up, it could all come crashing down.

Being in demand after years of rejections made it hard for me to tell the new surge of retailers who finally wanted me, *No*. It feels so good to be wanted. But I also knew that if I got into their stores too soon and too fast, I would be overexposed relative to how developed my company's infrastructure was at the time. And I also knew that if I didn't go into their stores and have sales success right away, I would be kicked out just as fast as I was finally welcomed in.

My mentor wrote me a note that said, "Winning in cosmetics is a game of perfect execution," and placed it on my desk. What she was saying was to make sure our development kept up with our exposure so that we could sustain it and succeed. So we decided to say no to all of the newfound demand to launch our products into the countless retailers that all of a sudden wanted us, and focus instead on delivering with full focus for retailers like ULTA Beauty who had believed in us early on and shared the vision of inclusivity and of celebrating every person's unique beauty. We built our team and infrastructure and worked hard to eventually grow to the top spot in their prestige department, and we waited until our development caught up with our demand before expanding into other retailers. My mentor taught me the critical lesson of being a steward of your own momentum. To this day, I believe that in order to have long-term success in our business, it was key to say NO to short-term wins, and to be keenly aware that our exposure matched our development at a healthy ratio.

So many companies nowadays spend all their money on exposure in the form of publicity and advertising and growing their social media platforms, and none on development—just like many "experts" online. Receiving the world's applause and equating exposure to success make it easy to slide down the slippery slope of ending up on the wrong side of the overexposed, underdeveloped equation. But long term, businesses won't last, art won't last, ideas won't last, and personalities won't last if they only focus on the exposure and ignore the development.

This lesson applies to your personal life and relationships too. It's hard to say no to what looks like love. It's tempting to prioritize finding a loving partner when you haven't yet learned to truly love yourself. **You'll be overexposed and underdeveloped in love if you don't also love yourself.** When you yourself are underdeveloped, you're more likely to find yourself attracted to someone who mirrors the lack of love you have for yourself. Or to someone who loves you more than you love yourself, in which case it is more likely that you sabotage it or that it doesn't last. Louise Hay originally taught that if you're looking for a loving romantic partner or friend, you should write out all the traits that you want in them. Then focus fully on BEING that person yourself, the one who has those traits. Because the kind of love we attract from someone else reflects the amount of love we have for ourselves.

THROUGH THE GIFT of meeting tens of thousands of entrepreneurs and thought leaders over the years, I've found patterns and through lines they have in common in their lives. When people build long-term, sustainable success either in the form of a business, talent, reputation, or ability to form lasting, loving relationships in their life, it's almost never an accident. It almost always comes from a commitment to hard work and ongoing development, no matter the level of success already attained.

Letting ourselves become overexposed and underdeveloped can quickly backfire, with feelings of imposter syndrome or incongruency. When we show up in a fake-it-or-make-it kind of way, we're pretending to be something we're not. It's okay to show up as a guide alongside others and lead them through in the role of partner or guide, but not to claim you know more than you do. You can show up and say here's my experience and **no matter what your experience is or isn't, it's beautiful when it's true. But when you prioritize the glory instead of the authentic journey, it won't last.**

> *When you prioritize the glory instead of the authentic journey, it won't last.*

IT'S IMPORTANT TO note: being overexposed and underdeveloped is a very different thing than the common excuse we make that we're "not ready" to pursue our dreams. You're always ready to show up authentically. Let's get granular here. Because believing you're ready doesn't mean you can now fly a plane, so you hop in the pilot seat of an airplane without training. It means you're worthy of and ready to start the pursuit of becoming a pilot. Being unqualified can be a lie, and it can also be a measured fact. It sometimes appears as a lie we tell ourselves. *I'm not qualified to share my story in a book. I'm not qualified to invent a product. Or launch a business. Or find unconditional love.* All lies. But when it comes to measurable factual qualification, like *I'm not qualified to fly a plane because I never have,* that's a truth. Self-awareness is so critical here.

People lie to others about being more qualified than they are and lie to themselves about being less qualified. Part of building worthiness and self-confidence is becoming acutely aware of how your development and experience parallel your actions and the story you tell the world about who you are. When they're congruent, you are free and in your power. When they're incongruent, you're living a charade. And those almost never last. **Most people didn't fake it 'til they made it, they just kept going until their preparation timed up with opportunity.**

Your Development Leads to Your Destiny

When you keep going, determination starts looking like talent, and hard work starts looking like genius.

— ERWIN RAPHAEL MCMANUS

It's important to do hard things. To focus on your development even when the exposure is more fun. To keep promises to yourself. To earn it for yourself. It doesn't mean you won't get lucky breaks or grace or divine appointments or miracles. It just means when they happen, you'll more easily believe you're worthy of them. A big part of believing you're deserving of them is knowing that you're showing up, putting in the hard work, giving it the best you can, and continuing to grow and develop.

Don't hold back from going after your goals and dreams with full confidence; just make sure to remember you're the steward of your own development and your own exposure in your journey. If you fail to develop the areas critical to your calling, you risk sabotaging your own success. Be the steward of your own momentum. Evaluate the areas where you need to level up your hard work, discipline, and development. This might mean developing a skill set, committing to daily habits, developing your mindset, strengthening your worthiness, beginning the path toward healing your trauma, or simply gaining more experience. Your soul will know what areas feel underdeveloped. And when you start developing them, it will feel good. Embracing your

People lie to others about being more qualified than they are and lie to themselves about being less qualified.

worthiness doesn't mean your greatest hopes and wildest dreams will miraculously just happen. Becoming aware of and committing to your own development along the way is critical. **Make sure to check in often with how your outward exposure and success match your inner developmental success.** Keeping them in alignment is key to building and maintaining self-confidence and self-worth that are unshakable.

CHAPTER 19

Transformations

*In the midst of winter, I found there was
within me an invincible summer.*

— ALBERT CAMUS

IF YOU READ inspirational, self-help, or transformational books, or have consumed that type of content online or in podcasts, chances are you've heard more than one inspiring author or speaker liken the journey of transformation to the caterpillar and the butterfly. Most people know that a caterpillar makes a cocoon and then emerges as a beautiful butterfly, and this analogy is commonly used to describe many types of transformational experiences. And that's about as detailed as these analogies get. The biggest and most important part, though, is a part of the metamorphosis that I haven't ever heard anyone talk about.

This is the good part. The part that is the most real and raw and applicable. The part maybe you've been through or are going through in your life right now. During metamorphosis the caterpillar completely dissolves into liquid inside of the cocoon. Yep, total liquid. It eventually develops and transforms. Its wings take shape, and it emerges through the cocoon. We picture it flying out as a beautiful butterfly, end of story, but in fact, at this stage, it actually enters a stage of tremendous vulnerability. A stage of great hardship, and one where its chances of survival are at stake. See, as if liquefying itself wasn't hard enough, it emerges from the cocoon with wet wings, unable to fly. It's tremendously vulnerable to falling to the ground and to predators. This is its phase that is hardest to survive. If it makes it through, and its wings dry and it spreads them and they can start to flap, it can fly away to its future.

When we go through our own chapters of transformation in life, it can easily feel like we're breaking down and liquefying. Then, even when we make it through that phase, our wings are wet, and we're not sure if they're fully formed or if they'll catch us when we fall or try to fly. When we feel wet, we feel vulnerable to friends and acquaintances who might actually try to stop us from flying. We encounter people who might not understand the transformational journey we're on and who might judge us. They might not even understand we're a butterfly at all. Because they might be a caterpillar for their entire life cycle.

They won't understand you're a butterfly if their entire life they remain a caterpillar.

See, when a butterfly lays eggs, only one or two out of every hundred actually survive to become butterflies. Nature, along with predators, disease, herbicides, and insecticides, kills 98 percent of them. This is not too dissimilar to the way it feels when our self-doubt and culturally conditioned belief systems keep us conforming, doubting our greatness, and playing life small. The majority of us stay in hiding, never going after our dreams, never feeling worthy, never becoming the full expression of ourselves.

Whenever I encounter a butterfly, I don't just marvel at its beauty. I think about all that it went through to get to where it is right now, as a fluttering, victorious, miracle in motion. I think about how it defied the odds as just one or two out of a hundred eggs to survive. I remember how it made it through the process of completely liquefying itself, and how it emerged from its transformation with wet, vulnerable wings that it wasn't yet certain would dry and spread and work. In the very moment we see a butterfly before our eyes, it's endured many hardships and vulnerabilities to emerge in its full glory.

Every time I see a butterfly, I experience awe and wonder and delight. I often take a photo of it and keep it in a folder on my phone, and I revisit the photos when I need to be inspired and reminded of how **so often our greatest beauty comes after our most difficult seasons of transformation.** Each butterfly we see has a story, perhaps not too dissimilar from yours and mine.

Do you give yourself grace and patience to let your wings dry? Do you give grace and patience to the people you encounter who might not understand the transformational experience? Do you question yourself or feel you don't have what it takes when what's really happening is your wings are still drying?

> *Change is incremental, and it is sometimes quiet.*
> *And it is happening. I promise you it is happening.*
> — GLENNON DOYLE

No matter what our past is, we can defy the odds in life. Just like the one or two out of a hundred butterflies who make it did. I think it's safe to say that if you think of a hundred people you might know or have come across in your life, likely one or two out of that hundred ever actually braved the path toward living the highest, truest expression of their souls. Are you going to be one of the one or two rare ones to spread your wings and fly in the full glory you were born to? Or are you going to be one of the other ninety-eight who don't? I believe in my heart that you have what it takes to courageously become the one or two out of a hundred who do. And if you know someone who's in a transition of liquefying in an area of their lives right now, share this story with them. Having perspective and hopeful meaning attached to it is so powerful.

In her memoir *Untamed*, Glennon Doyle impacted souls everywhere with a realization that she shared in one simple sentence: "I was staying in this marriage for my kids, but would I want this marriage for my kids?" I personally know people who decided to end their marriages after they read this. Glennon's truth ignited a truth in themselves. They were staying in unhappy relationships because they believed it was best for their kids. But it wasn't an example of marriage that they wanted to set for their kids. When they had the realization, like Glennon, they transformed their thinking and long-standing beliefs, and made different choices. Making the decision that you are worthy of a great relationship, and your kids are worthy of being shown an example of one, is easier said than done. It takes a strong sense of self-worth to let go of the label MARRIED. Society expects and celebrates marriage, and in some families and communities divorce is seen as failure. It takes incredible bravery, strength, resistance, and a pursuit of transformation to unlearn a belief that no longer feels right to you, and instead choose to believe that it's a victory to courageously end an unhealthy marriage rather than show your kids a definition of marriage you wouldn't ever want for them.

WE'VE TALKED ABOUT cracking the code to ultimate fulfillment in life and how the key ingredients to that are *self-worth, self-confidence, growth,* and *contribution.* This season of Glennon's personal evolution has all four of those ingredients, which is why, while her life-changing decision and transformation was surely liquefying and incredibly painful, it ultimately led to fulfillment. She began with a strong sense of self-worth, knowing she was valuable as she was, with or without her marriage. She then braved the season of growth, by tapping into courage and embracing uncertainty. This builds self-confidence along the way. When she realized that this marriage she wouldn't want for her kids would likely influence the benchmark they set for themselves in the future, she made a decision that was beyond and bigger than herself. This one season in her life of massive growth and transformation led to ultimate peace, happiness, and fulfillment in her life. And when you look at it from an outside, big picture perspective, you can see that all the ingredients for ultimate fulfillment were there: self-worth, self-confidence, growth, and contribution.

ONE OF MY best friends, Lia, has a story of what it's like to transform when you're the *first* in many ways. Lia was raised in a rough part of Philadelphia and spent her childhood living with her family between a homeless shelter and the projects. Her mom wanted a better life for Lia and her siblings but wasn't able to show them one. She always told Lia, "Your predicament doesn't determine your destiny." As Lia grew up, while others around her began to accept the limitations of their environment, Lia had different plans for herself. She began to dream of being the first person in her family to go to college, and maybe even one day to start a business. She talked with her mom about these bold ideas, and despite all the years of encouraging Lia in the past, her mom instantly shut her dreams down.

So often our greatest victories come after our most difficult seasons of transformation.

She told Lia that going to college was impossible, and there was no way they could afford to do something like that. Lia decided not to give up.

Even as a little girl and later a teenager, Lia made the conscious decision to focus on and allow any of the positive words spoken over her to take root in her identity around worthiness. She rejected the negative, fearful ones. She also leaned on what God's word says about our worth and chose to believe it. While many of us, including myself, weren't even aware of, much less able to do this until much, much later in life, Lia was the first and only in her immediate environment who believed in her own worthiness, and the way her path unfolded after is simply inspiring.

Lia worked multiple jobs and eventually paid her way through college, becoming the first, and to this day the only, person in her family and extended family to attend college, let alone graduate. Her mom always told her she sparkled and had a light inside of her. Lia took that belief and started designing jewelry. After many years of setbacks and rejections as a struggling entrepreneur, Lia eventually got her business—a jewelry, handbag, and lifestyle brand called Valencia Key™—off the ground. And after a few years of hearing no, she eventually got a yes from QVC, after entering and being selected in their nationwide competition called *The Find.* She was selected by their judges out of thousands of entrants to present her products live on-air, broadcast to more than 100 million homes across the United States.

Lia went from **homeless** to broadcasting live **to 100 million homes**. Lia is first.

And Lia won't be the last. As she continues to keynote speak globally and work hard daily to get the word out about Valencia Key, she also goes back to homeless shelters like the one she was raised in to speak to little kids and women there, showing them an example of what's possible. She wants to show others that, in the words of her mother, *their predicament doesn't determine their destiny.*

Lia is able to enjoy and truly feel fulfilled in her life, despite the setbacks and struggles that still come up, because, like Glennon, she was able to combine self-worth, self-confidence, growth, and contribution to find fulfillment. Lia chose to believe she was valuable and worthy as she was, and worthy of her hopes and dreams. Then she put in the hard work of building her skill sets and experiences, which fostered confidence. She garnered tremendous growth in the pursuit of both. And she's serving and contributing beyond herself by giving back to women in homeless shelters like the one she was raised in. Lia is still in start-up mode in her business and doesn't know with certainty if it will become the company she hopes it one day will, but her level of fulfillment is the highest it's ever been.

In fact, Lia's light shines so brightly that just this year QVC asked her to co-host one of their new shows. My prediction is that Lia's wings are still drying, and she has no idea of just how wide they'll be spreading in the future, just how beautiful the patterns on them are, and just how high they'll take her.

Your predicament doesn't determine your destiny.
— LINDA KEY (LIA'S LATE MOTHER)

Speaking of *high*, my friend Frederick checks this box in many different ways on his path of transformation. Frederick began selling drugs with other family members at a young age. That was the highest you could fly in the circle around him. He eventually joined the military, and while all parts of his life looked to be upstanding on the outside, behind the scenes he continued to run his side business selling drugs. Eventually his drug business grew in scale and Frederick became the middleman for much larger packages of drugs. He would receive them from one source, then drive, often to places in the middle of nowhere, to meet an unidentified person to hand the package off. As his operation expanded, he and his network began solving the *middleman* part in a different way. They began shipping the packages of drugs to a few specific zip codes and then paying off a network of delivery drivers who worked for large delivery companies. Those drivers would intercept the packages put onto their trucks for delivery and instead deliver them to a different address than what was on the package so that nothing could be traced. Frederick shipped each package from varying mailbox stores in cities surrounding where he lived, using a different sender name and address each time. Eventually, when he began to fear looking suspicious to the mailbox store owners, he bought and opened his own mailbox store.

As the owner of his own store, Frederick could manually change the sender's name and address in the computer each time a package was ready for shipment and could gain better control and certainty of the process. That is, until one of the drivers was caught and tipped off police. Frederick was busted as part of a major drug ring and went to prison for half a decade.

While spending much of his twenties inside prison, Frederick realized that the efforts to prevent outside contraband made it difficult for families to communicate with inmates. And it never seemed to improve no matter how much time passed. As Frederick was embarking on his life's greatest season of both liquefying and transforming, he also decided to turn his pain into purpose and considered that perhaps the worst days of his life might just be the catalyst for his best days of life ahead.

He decided to begin the work of reassessing his life and solving that prison communication problem at the same time. When Frederick was released, he started a company called Pigeonly, which scans mail for inmates, then prints it and gets it to them fast. This saves the prisons from the hassle of potential contraband, and it connects the inmates to loved ones much more efficiently. He's now the CEO of Pigeonly, has a board of extremely seasoned and sought-after investors, and his company has a multimillion-dollar valuation. Frederick is also a kind, generous, and loving friend. And he's the first in his family to transform his life. The first to believe he's worthy of putting in the hard work and determination to make it happen. He was the caterpillar eating every leaf in sight, he's been in the cocoon where he completely liquefied, he emerged with wet wings, and he survived the vulnerable season. He worried his past might hold him back from flying into his future, but he decided to believe he was worthy of flying, and he kept spreading his wings until he did.

Journeys of Transformation

In our journeys of transformation, our level of self-worth always becomes the upper limit we allow ourselves to fly. Which is why embracing the lifelong pursuit of continuing to build it is so important. **I have friends who are from overachieving families who only knew how to "do" but not to just "be," and they had to go on an intentional quest of learning to believe they're worthy of rest. To feel enough simply as they are. Not as they do. To be human beings, not human doings.** I've had friends that suffered excruciating physical health challenges because they were hiding their true self from their family. Then when they finally started living whole and sharing their truth, whether it was through revealing a way in which they identify that they were previously keeping secret, or sharing that they don't want to join the profession their parents desperately wanted for them, or any number of other examples, their physical health was restored. **Courageously embracing and building their worthiness and then living in authentic alignment wasn't without hardship. But the true success of the transformations we embark on in our lives isn't just the outcome of them. It's the strength and resilience we build along the way.**

When you're the first in your family or immediate peer group to embrace and set out on a journey of transformation in your life, and when transformation starts to take root on your way, sometimes you just can't describe it to the people around you. And no matter how hard you try, they just don't get it. And sometimes it can be hard to communicate your transformation with others, especially when your words haven't caught up yet with your changes. And if this describes you, or someone else you know who is in the midst of a transformational season (or about to talk themselves out of one), please share this book or the tools in it with them. Let them know they're not alone in all of the liquefying and vulnerable stages of transforming. Sometimes just knowing we're not alone is enough to keep us going on the path toward trusting ourselves and embracing our innate worthiness.

There are so many things in life—from our culturally conditioned belief systems, to our peer group, to the things we're not yet privileged enough to shed but are determined to one day—that keep us as a cater-pillar, keep us in environments that make us prey, get us off course, or have us believe we're never deserving of our wings. When these things happen to you, remember the stages of transformation. Know that with growth and change often comes liquefaction and vulnerability. It takes tapping into courage and embracing uncertainty.

You can be the one or two out of a hundred who believes, knows, and then lives the truth: You are more than worthy of spreading your most glorious wings. You were born to fly.

PART FOUR

KNOWING

You Are Worthy:

It's in You, It Is You

CHAPTER 20

Your Ticket to the Moon

The most difficult thing is the decision to act.
The rest is merely tenacity.

— AMELIA EARHART

I'M AFRAID OF going all in and then later learning I'm building the wrong rocket ship," I said to my friend Jason over coffee. He listened patiently to my wallowing. "I keep hoping, then trying to manifest, and then praying for clarity. I want to feel a knowing of exactly what direction to go in because once I go, I go all in."

I'd been contemplating an important professional decision for more than two years, and I still wasn't sure what direction to take. "I just feel like I should know. And I'll clearly know, once it's right. So if I don't have full clarity yet, I must not be ready."

While Jason had no idea I'd be debriefing him that day on just how stuck I felt (lucky him, haha), what happened next felt like a divinely orchestrated moment.

"I brought something for you, but I'll need to explain a bit," he said, pulling a clear acrylic square box from his pocket. It was lined with blue velvet and had what looked to be like a tiny, shiny golden-silver square reflective thing in the middle, about the size of a grain of rice.

"In JFK's famous speech to Congress in 1961, he set a bold agenda for the US to be the first country to land a man on the moon and return him to Earth, and he proclaimed it would happen within the next decade. He had no idea how it would happen. He just decided to declare it by faith and rally everyone's support of the vision. He gave direction to move forward anyway with nothing more than a vision."

I nodded as if I knew the details he was sharing astutely and tried to hide how fuzzy my recollection of some of them was. I continued to listen.

"Then in July of 1969, they did it! In one of the greatest achievements in human history, NASA's *Apollo 11* landed on the moon . . . remember when they said, 'One small step for man, one giant leap for mankind?'"

"Yes, of course," I said, nodding.

"Inside this box is an actual piece of foil from the *Apollo 11* command module. It's a mission-flown fragment of Kapton foil. I wanted to give it to you. Because you can go to the moon, Jamie. And maybe you're not sure how, and maybe you don't have all the answers yet, but you just need to take a step forward anyway."

I looked into Jason's eyes and started crying. I think I caught him off guard. He's used to me being strong for everyone else and in the role of serving others the best I can. But in that moment, he knew he was serving me. What a gift. I understood exactly what he meant: I didn't need to wait for total clarity to make my next move. I just needed to take a step out in faith. That next step that felt right and trust it. I placed the box with the piece of foil from *Apollo 11* on a special shelf in my bedroom, in a spot I'd be sure to see every day. I strongly believe in keeping visual reminders around that remind me of people, feelings, memories, or lessons that fill my soul, or inspire or empower me.

I am learning every day to allow the space between where I am and where I want to be to inspire me and not terrify me.

— TRACEE ELLIS ROSS

Leaps of Faith

Do you ever wait for clarity, to figure out exactly what to do and precisely how to do it, before you decide to actually do it? Do you feel like you need to have it all figured out before you proceed? Or like if you can't do it perfectly, you're not ready to do it? Perfect doesn't exist. And **perfectionism isn't something that's aspirational, it's the opposite. Since waiting on perfect is an impossibility, it turns into a never-ending justification for why we're not ready to move forward.** Do you feel like the smart thing to do is to cover all of your bases, troubleshoot ahead of time, and solve every possible problem that could come your way, before you take a shot? I default to all of these. If we're not careful, the things that we tell ourselves are a responsible strategy for success can leave us stuck and looking back at the days, weeks, months, and years when we still haven't done the thing. Still haven't created the product. Still haven't registered the business. Still haven't told a special person that you're interested in being more than friends.

Perfectionism isn't aspirational, it's the opposite. Since perfect is impossible, it becomes a never-ending justification for not moving forward.

Still haven't told a person the relationship isn't right for you anymore. Still haven't called the loved one to make amends or told the friend that your friendship needs new boundaries. Still stuck, because we're too busy troubleshooting our lives to one day hope to live them.

Sometimes we wait for the Universe to hand us an answer. For the door to magically open. We think if we envision it with enough focus and keep it on our vision board for long enough, it will appear. Or we pray for it, asking our Creator to bring it into our lives, and deciding if it doesn't happen, it's not meant to be. We tell our friends and loved ones that God clearly must not want it to happen right now. Or we give that advice to others when what they're hoping for isn't happening. And while

I wholeheartedly believe in the power of both manifesting and prayer, I've also learned that for either to be activated, you almost always have to add one critical ingredient to the mix: **action**. The part we play isn't to sit back and wait. It's to take action. Specifically, to take a step toward the thing we want. A step that feels most like **the next right one**. If you're not sure how to tell which next step feels right, get still, turn inward, and ask. Then take the next step that feels closest to right. After we take that first step, we get the clue, the knowing, of what step to take next.

> *Pray as though everything depends on God.*
> *Work as though everything depends on you.*
> — SAINT AUGUSTINE

By taking a step of faith, we put the energy of the miracle in motion into the universe. By taking that step, even before we have all the answers, we show our Creator we actually have faith. If we had all the answers ourselves, we wouldn't need faith.

And here's an idea I want you to consider:

Both self-doubt and self-belief take an equal amount of energy to manifest something that hasn't happened yet.

We can have self-doubt, pessimism, and fear . . . or we can have hope, faith, and belief. They each take an equal amount of confidence in something that's unseen. Something that hasn't happened yet. Something that's not even done. And we get to choose which one we put our energy into. Because neither's happened. Neither is proven. When we have self-doubt, pessimism, or fear, it's important to remind ourselves it's about stuff that hasn't even happened yet. It's about a future we worry about or a thing we're not confident in or a thing we don't believe we're capable of. All those things

Both self-doubt and self-belief take an equal amount of energy to manifest something that hasn't happened yet.

aren't proven. On the other hand, we can just make the decision to have hope. To have faith. To have belief. Yeah, maybe those things aren't proven either. But they take an equal amount of energy. And the one we give our energy to can change our entire life.

As humans, every single one of us is wired to give our energy to things like doubt and fear. But we also have the power to intentionally shift our energy to things like hope, faith, and belief. When we muster up the courage to intentionally give our energy to hope, to faith, to belief, it literally changes our entire life and the lives of the people around us.

A Giant Leap Forward

> *When you want something, all the universe conspires in helping you to achieve it.*
> — PAULO COELHO

After you take that next step that feels right, look around. Notice the view. See how the breeze feels from the new vantage point. Observe who shows up around you in this new place, and how they show up. Don't be surprised if once you've taken that next right step, new people come into your life at exactly the right time. New people you meet, or even old friends or colleagues that get back in touch. Or a sign that comes to you in the form of a dream, a gut feeling, a nudge, an overt occurrence out of nowhere, or even a friend in your life calling you with a thought they just felt like they had to share with you. Be open to see it and receive it. Sometimes it might come in the form of a whisper, or other times, in the form of someone handing you a piece of foil from *Apollo 11*. Don't be surprised if each step feels different from the last, or if you feel like a new person with each step you take. There might be moments or even seasons that feel like a whole lot of missteps. But if things unfold exactly as they should, then: **No step is a misstep. It either takes you to the next right destination or the next right lesson.**

No matter the results of each step, it will always feel more beautiful and fulfilling than the anguish, longing, and regret of standing in place, hesitating even longer.

> *It's important to be willing to make mistakes.*
> *The worst thing that can happen is you become memorable.*
> — SARA BLAKELY

The same day my friend Jason gave me that incredibly meaningful gift of the piece of foil from *Apollo 11*, I decided to make a decision on the issue I had been stuck hoping for clarity on for the previous two years. I took the first step, and then after that, the next step that felt right. Six months later, I found myself in a spot where I wasn't sure if I had even come close to feeling the kind of momentum I was hoping for yet. I was growing a bit weary. Not quite stuck yet, but almost.

AROUND THAT TIME, I was at a speaking event and joined by another friend of mine, a living legend, John C. Maxwell. We greeted each other in the greenroom before we headed to the stage to speak to the audience, and he said to me, "I brought a gift from home for you." In John's seventy-five years so far on this earth, he's written more than sixty books that have sold over thirty-five million copies. Whenever I see him, he brings me a book and signs it with a special message inside. I cherish these books. Now he pulled out a wrapped box, about the size of a book, and handed it to me. As I began to open it, I quickly realized it wasn't a book. It was a box with a pen inside. It was a special edition JFK Montblanc pen, designed and dedicated to the hopes and dreams embodied in JFK's Apollo space program. I quickly noticed that the gold tip of the pen was engraved with an image of the *Apollo 11* lunar module. The same one from which my friend Jason had given me a bit of space foil.

John then told me with conviction, "Jamie, you can go to the moon. You're the moon shot. You're here to do big things." My jaw fell open, and I began to tear up. What an incredible serendipitous moment, just when I needed the reminder. I didn't know the exact right move ten steps ahead of now, and I couldn't even predict how the next step would work out, but my job was to trust myself and take the next step that felt right, and then keep taking the one after that. I can go to the moon, and so can you. We just need to keep taking that next right step.

JOHN AND JASON don't know each other, I've never expressed any interest in space to either of them, and neither had any idea about each other's gifts to me. Also, it is not even common for my friends to get me gifts. This was very, very unusual. Some might simply write this off as a coincidence. I believe it's synchronicity and serendipity. **I believe the lesson we need to learn will present itself to us again, over and over, until we finally fully get it.** Sometimes it's a beautiful reminder, or lesson of encouragement like this one was for me. Other times it can be a harsh or painful lesson that we have to keep going through until we truly learn it. Like the years in my twenties when I continued to date the same type of "bad boy" who had lied and mistreated me. The same pain and disappointment and lesson continued to show up in every new relationship, until I learned the lesson that we are attracted to what we believe we're worthy of. That same lesson kept showing up over and over, just wearing a different cologne each time. And sometimes, the same cologne. Until I finally learned the lesson in a way that took root in my life. Until I finally decided to do the work on myself to change my own choices and to change what I believed I was worthy of.

> *The lesson we need to learn will present itself to us again, over and over, until we finally fully get it.*

272 Jamie Kern Lima

When we're willing to take action, to be scared and do it anyway, to not know where we're headed but to know where that one step is going and to just take that, then I believe the next right thing, or person, or lesson, or repeat lesson will always show up. In the exact moment, as many times as we need to learn and trust the lesson, exactly as it's all supposed to.

Your mind will generate thoughts that give you all the reasons you don't have what it takes or you're not ready yet. Your mind might insist that you don't have enough astronaut training to belong on the rocket ship. But you're not your mind. Those thoughts are not you. You are magical, born to be as bright and meaningful and inspirational as stars. You are a living, breathing miracle in motion.

Your mind will always want to dissect the telescope and the fuel storage scenarios and the rocket ship parts. But **your soul was created to go to the moon**. It's your time for liftoff. One brave next step at a time.

CHAPTER 21

Who Are You *Really* Doubting?

Faith is taking the first step, even when
you don't see the whole staircase.

— MARTIN LUTHER KING, JR.

I PROMISED YOU I would show up as the real me, even when at times it feels like I'm standing here naked. This chapter comes with a warning: it is bold. But if I didn't share it, I truly believe I would be doing a disservice to you, to my promise that I'm going to give you everything I've got on our journey of building worthiness together, even the real, raw, vulnerable stuff.

One thing I know for sure, beyond a shadow of a doubt, is that you are worthy, right now, exactly as you are. I know that I am as well. And the revelations and tools in this chapter have been the most impactful of all throughout my own quest of building self-worth. And in how I learned to believe I was worthy of the rooms I've walked into, and the businesses, friendships, and hopes and dreams that I've built. If, as you get into it this chapter it doesn't speak to you, then please feel free to skip it. I'm sharing this chapter with you out of pure commitment to give you everything I've got, including the revelations, shortcuts, and tools that when I started to apply to my life, have truly helped me build unshakable self-worth.

DO YOU BELIEVE in a power greater than yourself? God? The Universe? Your Creator? Do you believe in miracles? In divine energy? That we're all connected? Have you ever considered how what you believe impacts your sense of worthiness? I want to share with you one of the most profound realizations I've ever had as it pertains to worthiness. I've found this to be a secret weapon, and an instant, powerful shortcut to breaking through self-doubt and truly believing I am worthy in my life. I hope you can use it in your life too, right now.

I am going to share this powerful lesson on worthiness through the example of how it applies to me in my personal relationship with God. As I've mentioned, I intentionally spend my time around both people who share my beliefs and people who are very, very different from me. And I love them all unconditionally. My friends, family, and those I spend time around all pray differently (or don't pray or believe at all), vote differently, identify differently, and love differently. I don't judge them, and they don't judge me. And this chapter is truly a powerful, universal lesson and tool that you can apply to your life right now, no matter what you believe. If you happen to be in a spot where you feel like nothing you've done so far in life has led you to a place where you feel fully worthy and fulfilled, this chapter and the tools in it might be a complete revelation for you, as it truly dives into the one thing I know beyond a shadow of a doubt works for me and so many others I know—whether it's to find worthiness or to literally turn their entire life around. And even if you don't practice a specific faith, but you have friends, family, or colleagues who do, this is a powerful tool to have in your pocket to help them on their self-worth journey.

PERSONALLY, I BELIEVE God is love, and love is everywhere. Before I embraced my relationship with Jesus, I went through a long season of God-doubt, until I began praying and literally telling God I doubted He existed and then asking Him to prove me wrong. I did this almost every time I prayed, for many years. Until He did prove me wrong. And in my life, I now know, beyond a shadow of a doubt, that God is real and that it's through His grace that the miracles in my life have unfolded exactly as they have. (Note: I share this journey through decades of doubting God exists in more detail in my first book, *Believe IT.*) Some faiths teach you that you are made by God or in God's image. And that your God loves you. If you believe in the Universe, you likely believe that things are divinely orchestrated and unfolding exactly as they should, and that the Universe has your back. No matter what specific faith you follow, I'd like you to consider a few ideas on how what you believe, and if you in fact believe what you actually say you believe, can be a powerful tool in building your foundation of worthiness. *Please note, while I'll use verses from the Bible in my examples, please apply your own beliefs and the spiritual texts that you personally most closely connect with, so that you can apply this powerful tool right now to your own life in a way that speaks true for you.*

Two of my favorite Bible verses that inspire and empower me are *I can do all things through Christ who strengthens me* (Philippians 4:13 New King James Version [NKJV]) and *God created mankind in His own image* (Genesis 1:27 NKJV).

Self-Doubt and God-Doubt

Let's start with these two questions:

First question: God says you are wonderfully made in His image and that you can do all things through Christ, who strengthens you. Do you believe that? Do you *really* believe that to be true in your soul? Or, if you believe the Universe is divinely orchestrated, that there are no coincidences, that the Universe always has your back and things are unfolding exactly as they should, do you *really* believe that to be true in your soul?

Second question: Do you struggle with doubting that you are *enough*?

If you answered yes to both . . . then we have a paradox. See, one of them can't be true if the other is. How can you say you believe God's word about you but also doubt that you're enough? If this is the case, you're believing your own thoughts and doubting God. Or you're believing you can only trust your human mind and not the divine.

Yep, let me shout it from the rooftop for a minute: **when you call something self-doubt, what you're really doing is believing your own thoughts and doubting God's word.**

Your thoughts are in your mind, and your Creator is in your soul. It's up to you to decide which to trust when it comes to your worthiness. Your mind or your soul. In my life, while I've never heard God talk to me audibly, I hear Him in my soul, through my intuition. And when my culturally taught and conditioned, often BS beliefs talk to me, I hear them in my mind and thoughts. It's also where self-doubt lives. Self-doubt and unworthiness don't come from your soul or from your Creator who fills it.

When you call something self-doubt, what you're really doing is believing your own thoughts and doubting God's word.

Remember the infamous line in the movie *Sweet Home Alabama*, where Reese Witherspoon's character is torn between two loves, and her father, played by Fred Ward, says to her bluntly, "You can't ride two horses with one ass, Sugarbean." This line is based on the centuries-old proverb *You can't ride two horses with one behind.* Meaning you can't do two completely separate things at once. So in your life, right now, moving forward, who are you going to decide to believe? Your thoughts and limiting beliefs, or God and His word? Because every single time you're doubting you're enough, doubting you have what it takes, doubting you belong in the room, or doubting you are worthy of your goals and dreams, what you're actually doing is saying that your thoughts are true and God's word is not.

Where True Worth Lives

Many faiths talk about the importance of not worshiping false idols. They teach us that if we worship worthless things, we're left feeling worthless. And yet, we live in a society that worships external things that build temporary, fluctuating self-confidence—and none of the things that build true self-worth. Our society's mainstream form or worship is focused on achieving things like money, material possessions, job titles, physical appearance goals, and follower counts on social media. We worship and place on pedestals others who accumulate material possessions and accolades and reward them by following them online and buying any product they attach their name to. We do this in hopes that it will bring us closer to the feeling of fulfillment we imagine they have. Then, in our day-to-day lives, we devote our precious time, energy, and focus toward hustling to get more and more of what we hope will finally lead us to feeling enough. Because it sure looks like it will in those ads and highlight reel social media posts that the idols we often unconsciously worship share with the world.

And no matter how close we get to getting it all, it never feels like enough. We still feel empty. We tell ourselves it's because we don't have *enough* still, and that when we finally get *enough*, then we'll get the feeling of being *enough*. We convince ourselves that those other people who seem to have it all, surely must feel *enough*!

Remember the difference between self-confidence and self-worth, and how self-confidence alone doesn't lead to fulfillment. Almost all these things our society worships religiously only lead to boosting self-confidence at best. They never lead to self-worth.

I'VE HAD THE blessing of meeting some of the most famous people in the world, many who are liked by millions on social media daily. And guess what? Nothing is different in their lives than it is in yours and mine when it comes to self-worth and fulfillment. Some are fulfilled and have strong self-worth, and many others don't. Yes, they get the excitement and boosts of confidence that come from things like fancy cars and sold-out stadiums cheering their name. But none of those things bolsters true self-worth, and they are no happier or fulfilled because of the fame, monetary possessions, or external adoration. And in fact, many are extremely empty, unfulfilled, and have low self-worth. It can be hard to understand when a celebrity who seems to have it all sabotages it, or worse. And even though many celebrities have spoken out about how money or fame doesn't bring them joy and fulfillment, we're still in a society and economy that are both fueled by worshiping all things external.

> *I wish everybody could get rich and famous and have everything they ever dreamed of, so they can see it's not the answer.*
>
> — JIM CARREY

How much time and energy are you devoting in your life right now toward trying to achieve things that at best will only bring the feeling of self-confidence, but can't bring the feeling of true fulfillment?

Making the decision to believe God's word that you are wonderfully made and fully worthy exactly as you are, over the socially conditioned idea that material things can bring you fulfillment and worth, will equip you to make much more strategic decisions over what you trade your time for, what you deprioritize your relationships for, and what you choose to focus on and experience in this one precious, beautiful life.

When we realize that putting these external things on a pedestal never leads to feelings of worth and fulfillment, and trusting His word does, it can be the one thing that changes everything.

Humpty Dumpty

Perhaps you're familiar with the nursery rhyme Humpty Dumpty. It's one I read several times in my Mother Goose nursery rhyme book growing up, but this rhyme took on a whole new meaning when I heard Pastor Albert Tate use the story of Humpty Dumpty as an analogy in a keynote speech he gave at the Global Leadership Summit. In case you're unfamiliar with the rhyme, here's how it goes:

Humpty Dumpty sat on a wall,
Humpty Dumpty had a great fall;
All the king's horses and all the king's men
Couldn't put Humpty together again.

Like Humpty Dumpty, many of us have had great falls. And we strive and strive to put ourselves back together again. I've certainly had many great falls in my life. Falling off course many times in my rebellious teen years, falling into depression in my twenties, falling in love with people who mistreated me, and falling into the trap of thinking I could change them. Discovering by accident in my late twenties that I was adopted, embarking on a tiring multiyear search for my identity, being prescribed antidepressants, facing heartbreaks in relationships and friendships, experiencing cycles of addiction in my family, weathering professional seasons that just didn't feel like they were going my way, teetering on bankruptcy, and of course, the lifelong battle with self-doubt and striving to believe I'm worthy.

When we have falls, struggles, setbacks, unfair situations, disappointments, and heartbreaks, there are many different versions of how we try to put ourselves back together. Sometimes those versions start with just trying not to fall further. This can take the form of avoidance, numbing, disassociating, survival modes, and coping methods we default to in hopes that we don't crumble further. When we start putting ourselves back together, growth and healing can take many different forms. This of course depends on access, privilege, and other factors. If we're fortunate enough to have access to therapy and other resources, these can be so incredibly helpful in putting ourselves back together. But in my journey, even with invaluable therapy and a lot of personal development work, I was never able put myself back together again fully. It wasn't until I started trusting myself and my knowing, deepened my faith and my relationship with God, and started leaning into Him, that I was able to put myself back together in such a way that I felt fully alive.

In the nursery rhyme, notice that all the king's horses and all the king's men couldn't put Humpty back together again. They couldn't do it alone. In my life I've learned that when I only lean on the king's horses and men, or in other words, when I only lean on other people or things, it's not enough. I read the rhyme as only *the King himself* would have been able to put Humpty back together again. And what I've learned in my life is that all the man-made tools are so incredibly helpful. And to this day, I feel so incredibly blessed and grateful for the role that therapy, healing modalities including meditation, and personal growth resources play in my life. And I believe it's possible to put yourself back together again with these, but for me, this tool is the ultimate shortcut to worthiness: without the assistance of the king—for me that's the God whose image I'm made in, who resides in me, in my soul—I wouldn't be able to put myself back together again fully, and certainly not as fast.

Are you leaning on and trusting God to help put you back together? Or are you doubting that He can? Maybe today is the day you realize that all the king's horses and all the king's men are nice, and some are even super handsome, but if you depend on them and them alone, it might be why you still don't feel fully restored.

What I personally know with certainty is that there is nothing you can do, no mistake you've made, no flaw you have, no fall you've taken, no matter how much you've crumbled, that ever disqualifies you from God's love. God is love, and so are you. I believe God loves you exactly as you are, no matter your height, age, race, ethnicity, sexual preferences, gender identity, or family structure. I believe God loves you no matter how varying your current or past beliefs are, no matter your current or past mistakes, no matter what choices you make, no matter where you come from or what labels you put on yourself or other people put on you, no matter where you fall in all the spectrums of humanity, nothing disqualifies you from His love.

(Note: If you want to start or strengthen a relationship with God, all you have to do is ask Him for one. That's it. In my faith, you just say, "Jesus, come into my life." You can say it silently in your thoughts or out loud. It's that easy. And while I love the experience of certain churches, I don't believe you have to go to one to experience God. I believe He is there with you right now. And I believe He is all around you and me right now. In the beauty of every flower, in each ray of sunlight, in every drop of water, in every combination of the two that bends into a rainbow, in every caterpillar, cocoon, and butterfly, in every moment of grace. God is love, He is with you right now, and He is everywhere.)

Trust in a Higher Power

Every time I wonder who I should love and for how long I should love them, God continues to whisper to me: everybody, always.

— BOB GOFF

Okay, I am getting fired up right now. I wrote this book for you if you have some self-doubt to destroy and a destiny to fulfill. I wrote this book for you if you know deep down inside you have a light inside of you that's destined to shine brighter than it has been. I didn't come here to look cute. I am here with you, right now, if you know you have a beauty and a strength and a purpose inside of you that's destined to be expressed as its highest offering to the world. And I want to ask you today, who are you going to decide to believe? Your thoughts or your soul and Creator? When that guy breaks your heart and you're tempted to feel unworthy, who are you going to believe, your thoughts or God? When that friend hurts you and doesn't include you, and you're tempted to change who you are to fit in, who are you going to believe, your thoughts or God? When that boss doesn't promote you or value your ideas, who are you going to believe? Them or God? When that person you dated made you feel disrespected and devalued, who are you going to believe? Them or God? When the publisher, or countless publishers, reject your manuscript, who are you going to believe? Them or Him? (Thankfully, countless of the world's best-selling authors chose to believe their Creator over the many publishers that first rejected their now best-selling books.) When Oprah hands you her number and you're doubting that you are worthy of being her friend, so you don't call her, who are you going to believe? You or Him? I believed my thoughts for almost four years, and thankfully, I finally decided to believe what He says about me and what my soul knows to be true about me. Now Oprah is not only a mentor, she's a friend. Thank you, God. And thank you, growth. And thank you, courage.

So if the Son sets you free, you will be free indeed.
— JOHN 8:36 NEW INTERNATIONAL VERSION (NIV)

If you are someone who believes you have strong faith, in the moments you're doubting you're enough, you're believing your mind and doubting God. You might say you have self-doubt when really what you have in those moments is God-doubt.

Let's say, for example, you believe God's words in the verses I just shared. If you do, then:

Every time you believe you're unworthy, you're telling God, "I don't believe you."

Every time you believe you're unlovable, you're telling God, "I don't trust you."

Every time you say your body is flawed, you're doubting His art and vision. When you say your body is flawed, what you're really saying is He is flawed. You are made in His image.

Every time you decide you're not enough, you're saying, "God, I believe my doubts more than I believe you."

Every time you're feeling unqualified or like you don't deserve your hopes and goals and dreams, you're deciding to put people, and their or your opinions, on a pedestal instead of God.

Who are you going to believe? Whose hands and words are you going to trust your future with? Those of other human beings or those of God? Who are you going to trust with your hopes and dreams?

When you learn to trust your Creator over your own thoughts, then in moments of self-doubt and unworthiness you can ask yourself, *Who am I really doubting?* It's like having the secret ingredient that instantly solves the equation. For me it's the most powerful instant shortcut and life hack to worthiness. And if you know someone who values their faith but struggles with self-confidence and self-worth, please share this book and tool with them.

You might say you have self-doubt when really what you have in those moments is God-doubt.

I reflect on my life before I had this tool almost as if it were a latte missing the espresso. Imagine if everyone was running around with a Starbucks cup, filled with their choice of milk, stevia, even some fun vanilla cold foam, brown sugar shaken syrup, and cinnamon on top with caramel drizzle. But there was no espresso in the cup because they didn't know or believe it existed. The latte would still be the best thing to start the morning. It might taste a little bland with the espresso missing, but it would sustain you. Then imagine when all these oblivious latte drinkers discover espresso and add it to their favorite coffee drink. They've entered a whole new universe of power and goodness! That's what learning to embrace this secret ingredient feels like to me. I trust my Creator's word. I intercept my self-doubt and ask, *Who am I really doubting?* It's a whole new world of goodness. And the best part is, unlike a daily Starbucks habit, this secret ingredient is free.

Our thoughts, especially the limiting ones, are so easy to believe. Raised in a world where we're taught to dim our light to fit in, doubting ourselves is a lot more comfortable than trusting ourselves. Believing our own thoughts, which we hear loud and clear, feels safer than trusting our Creator, who we can't see or often easily hear. But when it comes to our destiny, we have three choices: **we can trust what other people say about us, we can trust what our negative thoughts tell us about us, or we can trust what God and our soul says about us.** The more I trust the third, the more I feel aligned with my authentic power and destiny.

> *We are not human beings having a spiritual experience.*
> *We are spiritual beings having a human experience.*
> — PIERRE TEILHARD DE CHARDIN

Learning to hear what your Creator says about you can come from different practices. And some might resonate more than others for you. You might look to a spiritual text and scripture. You might attend church to see if you hear or feel your Creator speaking to you through the pastor or the message or the music. You might just get still, meditate, or pray, and then listen to what comes to you. This is one of my favorite practices. When I hear whispers or sensations that feel like a still, small voice—one I can't hear, only feel—I trust it.

Martha Beck, author of *The Way of Integrity*, says, "Every truth makes us relax our muscles and every lie makes us tense our muscles." One of the ways I distinguish between something I am thinking in my mind versus a whisper, a knowing, and something I should actually trust, is I make sure it feels like the truth to me in my own body. It's also how I distinguish whether a thought or feeling feels like it's from the divine or from my own head. When we get still and check in, our actual physiology will give us clues if something is true or not. Our soul knows, even when our mind doesn't. This is also a great way to decide if a church, a religion or religious practice, or even a job, relationship, or friendship is right for you. How does it feel in your body? Does your body tense up like it does in a lie, or does your body relax and your nervous system feel peaceful, like when it's a truth?

I believe self-doubt kills more dreams than almost anything else, and **self-doubt is a weapon we've formed against ourselves.** When you stay in faith *no weapon formed against you shall prosper* (Isaiah 54:17 NKJV), and **when we don't feel worthy, we're not in faith.** The world has trained you your whole life to tell yourself you're not enough, but in a single prayer, in a single still, small voice, in a single knowing, your Creator and soul will tell you that you are. I've heard it said this way, that **His great *I Am* . . . is so much bigger than all of our *I'm nots.***

> *You'll never get intimidated walking into any room if you remember Who you're walking in with.*

> *The Spirit who lives in you is greater than the spirit who lives in the world.*
> — 1 JOHN 4:4 NEW LIVING TRANSLATION (NLT)

A question to consider . . .

What has doubting God's word about how you're *fully equipped* and *wonderfully made*—and instead believing your own thoughts of self-doubt—already cost you in your life? In your relationships? In your potential? In your ability to step into your purpose and calling? I know, I know, it's a lot to take in. But again, we're not here to play it small, we're here to build real worthiness.

> *Your relationship with your Creator is the*
> *only way to find out why you were created.*
> — SARAH JAKES ROBERTS

Right now, in my life, *every single time* I start to doubt myself, I interrupt my own thoughts and ask this question: *Who am I really doubting? Me or God?* And almost every single time it comes down to the fact that I'm doubting His word and trusting my own limiting thoughts. So right then, in that moment, I make the commitment to trust Him and my soul. And right then, in that moment, I literally decide that no matter what my mind might be telling me, my soul believes Him, and therefore I choose to believe that I have what it takes. That I am qualified. That I am equipped. That I am funny. That I am courageous. That I am smart. That I am kind. That I belong in the room. That I belong on the stage. That I belong in the hug. That I deserve the compliment. I know the answer. I am ready. I am enough. I am worthy. I now believe and know this: **you'll never get intimidated walking into any room if you remember Who you're walking in with.**

> *Jesus looked at them and said, "With man this is*
> *impossible, but with God all things are possible."*
> — MATTHEW 19:26 NIV

The number of times I've applied this worthiness tool is countless. Still, to this day, I can't believe I am blessed enough to sit down to coffee with some of the most incredibly kind and inspiring friends I could ever ask for. And when I am, I use this tool right before I enter the coffee shop to believe I'm worthy of being there. Still to this day, every time

I'm asked to speak on stage, I begin to doubt that what I say will be impactful enough, then I apply this knowing and instantly decide to believe that God wouldn't have orchestrated the invitation to speak if I wasn't fully equipped to serve. Still to this day, every time I look at myself in the mirror, my default thinking wants to notice all my self-perceived flaws. And I instantly decide to believe Him, that I am wonderfully made in His image. I would never criticize how God looks, that is absolutely absurd . . . and it is *just as* absurd for you and me to criticize how we look. No different.

Every risk I take, every idea I share, every room I walk into, every expression of myself and my soul I put out into the world is almost always at first met with a moment of me being tempted to doubt it's enough, and almost always, I intercept that moment with this tool. And I make the decision to stop doubting God. And I make the decision to believe Him. That I am remarkably and wonderfully made in my Creator's image. And you are too. Exactly as you are. **You are *enough* and fully valuable, and unconditionally lovable in this very moment, *exactly* as you are.** And what I've learned is that truly believing your Creator is the greatest and most instantaneous shortcut to truly believing you are worthy.

God will, very likely, give you more than you can handle. He will not, however, give you more than He can handle.

— HODA KOTB

NoteWORTHY: For a bonus collection of some of my favorite go-to Bible verses on worthiness, visit WorthyBook.com/Resources

CHAPTER 22

Solos

There are no mistakes in dance class, only solos.

— ANONYMOUS

MY HUSBAND, PAULO, was born in Brazil, a country known in part for beautiful rhythmic offerings to the world, including samba dancing, capoeira martial arts, and the beautiful game of football, or, as Americans call it, soccer. Walking through the streets of Rio de Janeiro, you can often hear music everywhere. Paulo says Brazilians are born dancing straight out of the womb. That is, *most* Brazilians are. He is an exception. Paulo isn't sure why, but despite his mom having impeccable rhythm and his brother being musically gifted, Paulo can't keep a beat. He has no rhythm. And I mean none. Not even two left feet. Those, at least, would be in sync. Paulo is one of the most brilliant, talented, kind, and funny people I've met in my life. He is not, however, a rhythmic dancer.

For the traditional first dance at our wedding, we decided we weren't going to do anything fancy. I set the bar low, hoping for a middle-school-style slow dance where we stepped back and forth. My only goal was for us to do it to the beat. Whenever he had any patience for this ambition of mine, like maybe during a commercial break while watching TV, or on a car ride, I would put on a song and start counting "One, two, three, four, five, six, seven, eight" over and over, then ask him to try counting to the beat with me. This might be his least favorite activity I've ever asked him to do. I'm pretty sure he would rather take the trash out, pick up dog poop from the yard, or perform literally any other chore or activity other than trying and trying to hear the eight-count.

After many practice sessions in our living room, my hope of a middle-school-style, two-step slow dance on the beat was dwindling fast. I had to take more drastic measures. So I invited over a friend who was a great dance teacher, and the three of us sat in the living room for many sessions, just trying to teach Paulo how to hear an eight-count in music. He eventually could hear it! And count to it! The next step was to add movement. First, we started by stepping to the beat. That wasn't going so well, so she changed it to clapping. All of us stood there listening to the music and clapping on the counts of two, four, six, and eight. It was going pretty well until she began asking Paulo to do it on his own. That's when the waters got choppy. He literally clapped on the half beat of any of those numbers, every time. Two and a half. Then randomly on five. I tried so hard not to laugh or make him feel judged. He wanted to get the dance down for our wedding so badly.

HAVE YOU EVER looked back at a moment in your life and thought: *I wish I knew then what I know now?* Trying to teach Paulo our first wedding dance is one of them for me. He and I would have been so much happier and had so much more fun if I had only learned a life lesson that I picked up in a dance class several years after our wedding.

A life-changing lesson, that happened in the middle of a twerking class. Yep, twerking. (Grandma, that is a dance style where you're bent over at the waist and you gyrate your backside, intentionally. It's now mainstream. And it makes the old mainstream days of Elvis's risqué hip gyrations seem like the minor leagues.)

My friends and I were in a dance class at a mindfulness retreat. The teacher was doing her best to wrangle a group of about twelve mostly women, of varying ages, levels of dance experience, and coordination, into formation. In the hour-long class, we were supposed to learn a routine that lasted about three minutes, and then at the end of the class, the goal was to perform that routine in unison, twerking and all.

About thirty minutes into the class, we collectively looked much more like a pack of wild rabbits than like Rockettes. No one was hopping or kicking at the exact same time. I noticed one of the women in the class was feeling really defeated. It seemed like no matter how many times the teacher had us start over with the opening sequence, she couldn't get the transition part right where you step, step, clap, spin on the first four counts—then whip quickly to bend down and twerk, twerk, twerk, twerk for the next four counts. She kept losing her balance in the spin and taking a big step out of line. The front wall of the classroom was a giant mirror, so every time we did the routine, the whole class could see who was out of unison. After three or four blunders, this woman looked like tears were welling up in her eyes. I started to wonder if she was going to leave class.

At that moment, the instructor stopped the class. With a giant smile on her face and all the patience in the world, she proudly proclaimed, "There are no mistakes in dance class, only solos."

We loved that idea, and all laughed together in relief. From that moment on, the class got really fun. Any time I decided to fully commit to the moves, even the ones beyond my skill set and coordination, and it didn't end so well I would yell out, "Did you see my solo?" My friends started doing the same.

"I loved that solo," one would say to another.

"I'm a solo artist," another would share with a smile.

I had a moment, midclass, where I realized the beauty and the power of how the energy shifted in the room, all from the simple shift in perspective. I had been in gymnastics and dance classes as a little girl, and when anyone fell out of unison or made up their own move intentionally, it was deemed a mistake. It was embarrassing. The goal was to make sure you never veered from the beat or from formation. The goal was for the whole group or class to flow in perfect synchronicity. To all be the same.

But I watched as joy and freedom took over that adult dance class, and I had a much bigger shift in perspective, one that stretched far beyond the walls of that room.

> **The solos of life are where the true beauty is.**
> **It's in the solos that creativity sparks.**
> **It's in the solos that ideas are birthed.**
> **It's in the solos that strongholds are broken open.**
> **It's in the solos that generational cycles end for good.**
> **It's in the solos that novel ideas are born.**
> **It's in the solos that businesses are birthed.**
> **It's in the solos that your soul feels its own expression.**
> **It's in the solos where authenticity thrives.**
> **It's in the solos where authenticity shines.**
> **It's in the solos where aha moments happen.**
> **It's in the solos where the dance with the divine is most intimate.**
> **It's in the solos.**

If you're spending your life in a dance class where solos aren't celebrated, especially the spontaneous or unplanned kind, it's time for a new class. **There are no mistakes in dance class or in life, there are only solos.** And the solos are the moves only you can do, only you can feel, and on whatever beat of your life's music you choose.

You were never a bad dancer. You were born to do solos.

Have you ever noticed how the best dancer on the party dance floor is rarely the one who is most technically trained? It's rarely the one who knows the latest dance trend or is most perfectly on the beat. **The best dancer on the party dance floor is almost always the one who most fully commits!** Whether it's at the company holiday party, the family or community gathering, or the wedding dance floor (you know the one I'm talking about). The one who just absolutely unequivocally goes for it. Holds nothing back. Has no shame in their game. And with every step and slide, point and

You were never a bad dancer. You were born to do solos.

posture, jump and gyration, and soul-first expression, they confidently take up space with palpable, infectious, admirable energy.

They're the person everyone most admires and secretly longs most to be like, because despite lack of skill, they show up in their full glory anyway. They exude abundant confidence and little worry. They're filled with joy, and void of doubt. The one who is most fully alive. The one who is most free.

BECOME THE BEST dancer of your life. The one who most fully commits to your dreams. The one who feels the solo coming and meets it with arms flung wide open, legs moving to a beat only your soul knows, and with soul-singing wild abandon dances to the beauty of your life. Dance full-out.

You don't need permission to do a solo. You are on this earth to do one. You don't need a teacher to evaluate it. Only your soul is qualified to do that. You don't need a dance class to dance. The whole world is your dance floor.

CHAPTER 23

You Are Worthy—Your Victory Lap Starts Now

Que la vida me perdone las veces que no la viví.
May life forgive me for all the times I did not live it.

— UNKNOWN

IN TWO SEPARATE moments, my mom Nina changed my entire life. First, when she adopted me the first day of my life, and equally as powerfully forty-five years later on the last day of hers. She shared words with me that hit me to my core. And a lesson that I instantly knew my life would never be the same after learning.

Let me give you some context. See, I believe in the power of being a lifelong student, of always learning and growing and serving others and giving and creating and ideating and evolving all with the intention of, as Oprah would say, becoming the "highest, truest expression" of yourself. And to feel ultimate fulfillment, we always have to be growing ourselves, and contributing to others, at least in some area of our life.

My mom, Nina, pronounced her name like the number nine with an "a" after it. From the day I was born, she was my real-life superhero. She was the one who held it all together when my adoptive dad didn't. She was the rock during his multidecade battle with alcoholism, gambling, and infidelity. And while my adoptive father Mike had many admirable qualities too and loved me with all of the capacity he had to love, it was my mom Nina's capacity to love big, and way beyond herself, that blessed me most my whole life. I was six when she had endured enough broken promises and finally divorced my dad. It was the first example I witnessed of a person deciding she was worthy of something more and making the hard decision to do something about that knowing. She later married my stepfather Dennis, who became another loving rock in my life. My mom was the one who taught me the value of hard work, and she taught me that all things are possible when you work hard enough and make the decision to believe that they are, in fact, possible. My entire childhood she worked a lot. Often seven days a week.

Growing up I used to fantasize about one day making so much money that my mom wouldn't have to work so hard. That I could take care of her, the way she had worked so hard to take care of me. My whole life I wanted to make her proud. My dad Mike didn't want me ever to know I was adopted, so they never told me . . . until I found out by accident at age twenty-seven. After years of processing it all, my love for my mom Nina only grew deeper. She wanted me. She chose me. She is the person I am the closest to in the entire world. And I let her know I would always choose her too.

By the time I had reached professional success building IT Cosmetics and could afford to help her retire, she had already spent decades of her life working way too hard. And it had impacted her health tremendously. She was diagnosed with the autoimmune disease scleroderma, in addition to a number of other ailments. Instead of the life of retirement I had dreamed of for her, the focus became finding the best doctors and medical care possible. For her last decade, my mom split her time between the ER, ICU, hospital, and then recovering back at home.

If you've ever had a sick parent, maybe you can relate to the moment when the roles reverse. All of a sudden, we're the ones who are up all night worrying, instead of the other way around like it often was growing up. The role reversal can be overwhelming. I did everything in my power and spent every penny I could trying to fight for my mom. Trying to extend her life. Trying to do whatever might help her feel the best she possibly could. In the last handful of years, she often spent more days in the hospital than out. I hung on to hope each time, and she would make it through and come back home. She kept telling me she wanted to fight longer to live. That she didn't want to leave Dennis, whom she was still deeply in love with after forty years of marriage. She wanted to see her grandbabies grow up. She wanted to keep fighting, so we fought together. And it was hard. So, so hard. Every time the doctors would remind me, "You know your mom is not going to get better, right?" I would simply reply to them, "What can we do to change that?" and "That's not true if she has any say in the matter." **It was hope, grit, and sheer will to live that fueled her light, even as her body was breaking down.**

IN 2022, I spent every moment I could at the hospital by her side. When the time came where the doctors said she only had a few days left, and there was absolutely no way around it this time, we decided to take her home. We set up a hospital bed in her living room, so she could see the sunlight out the window. At night, Dennis slept in the recliner in the same room. I lined up several dining chairs in a row and slept on them, right next to her bedside so that I could hold her hand all night. When she made eye contact with me, I would smile, and only when she looked away did I let myself cry. She was my mommy. The one who chose me the day I was born. And I didn't want to let her go. The pain of letting her go felt unbearable at times. My identity was always to be the *strong one*. The one who spoke up to anyone I needed to at the hospitals to make sure she was taken care of. The strong one in so many areas of my life. But now I felt like the weakest one. The one in absolute anguish, with no control over anything, losing the person I've loved most my entire life. The person who loved me most in her entire life. It knocked me to my knees.

I knew from talking with hospice workers and many doctors that it's important to let your loved ones know it's okay for them to go. Otherwise, people keep fighting, sometimes in great pain, because they're trying to hold on to life at that point solely for their loved ones. If they get the blessing of their loved ones to pass, they are better able to peacefully transition. Dennis and I both did this with her, in one-on-one moments. I knew when he had done it because he left the room weeping in anguish. I had never heard him make sounds like that before.

In her final days, she joyfully filmed some sweet video messages for her grandbabies, and I asked her every question I could think of. When she had the energy, we had deep conversations about her life. Most of all, I just tried to comfort her however I could. During a moment where she seemed to be particularly alert and energetic, she was looking deep into my eyes, and I asked her this question: "Mom, what are your hopes and dreams for my future? What do you hope most for me?"

I anticipated her reminding me that all things are possible, that I could do anything I set my mind to, and that she hoped I would continue to work hard, impact and inspire others, and raise my children with great values and by great example. I anticipated her sharing her hope that I continue to achieve all my goals and dreams. But that's not what she said. Not at all. In fact, in a way, she said quite the opposite. When I asked her, "Mom, what are your hopes and dreams for my future? What do you hope most for me?" She looked me straight into my eyes, and a feeling of ultimate knowing, complete confidence, and total truth filled the air. "I hope you don't change," she said. "That's my ultimate wish for you. It would be so terrible if you ever change."

Without a moment to even process these words, "don't change," tears started streaming down my face. My mom was saying to me loud and clear: *Don't ever change the real you. You are enough and worthy, exactly as you are. All this other stuff—goals, dreams, growth, achievements—is all fine and good and an exciting part of the journey, but the only thing that truly matters in this life is the truth of your beautiful soul. The real you.*

And the real you, your soul, is all that matters. I had never in my entire life, truly felt like I was enough, exactly as I was, until I stood there, a forty-five-year-old woman, crying as my mom, knowing that her time on this earth was ending, said those words.

This was a total breakthrough for me. A moment where my true knowing surpassed my learned, conditioned belief system. My soul over-rode my mind. I knew what she was saying was true. I am worthy and enough exactly as I am. Without ever having to have done, or needing to do, another thing. And so are you.

MY ENTIRE LIFE, I just wanted to make my mom proud. And then later, I wanted to make the world proud. Then God proud. My whole life, I confused approval with love. And achievement with love. And affection with love. And applause with love. And the world's definition of success with love. All in a single moment, my mom emphasized that none of that matters. I knew that she was saying, *Yeah, sure, keep growing in the areas you want to, like career, goals, hopes, and dreams, but don't change your heart, because you, alone, truly are and have always been enough.* She knew the real, true me, even the parts I'd hidden in the past or deemed shameful, and she was saying not to change the real me. **The me that is me is enough.** Without achieving or striving or accomplishing. And that her greatest hope for my future is that I don't change the me that *is* me. She has no other hopes for me. Nothing else. "I hope you don't change. That's my ultimate wish for you. It would be so terrible if you ever change."

A long pause filled the air. I could only feel, not think. And then I said, "Okay, Mommy, I won't. I promise," as she glanced up at me to see the tears I could no longer hold back. "I'm going to share these words with so many others too, okay?" I tried hard to let her feel that these tears were ones of overwhelming gratitude, not fear. I rested my chin on our interlocked hands. In her last days I would only let go of her hand if I absolutely needed to step away for a moment. "Mommy, thank you for loving me. Even in the times I wasn't so easy to love. Thank you for adopting me the day I was born. Thank you for choosing me. I love you. So much."

THIS REVELATION, "DON'T change," hit me to my core. And I've been processing it every day since. It feels like a billion-pound weight of expectations and *not-enoughness* that I had placed on my shoulders my entire life is lifting. I still have the same ambitions and hopes and dreams and goals and inspiration and motivation, but I now don't see them as tied to my own worth. I see them as the joy of the journey. As accompaniments. They are my Creator's calling *in and through* me. But they are not the worth *of* me. This revelation sings like sunshine to my soul. It tastes like truth. It feels like freedom.

I am someone who at my core cherishes and celebrates growth and change. It's beautiful and powerful to be on a lifelong mission to grow, impact, serve, and change in all the ways that make our lives, the lives of others, and the world around us better. But when it comes to the core of who you truly are, your soul, the real you, it is already fully worthy, and it is already love. There is absolutely nothing you should strive to change. So this might be the first time in my entire life I've ever wished this for myself or for someone else, but right now I wish it for me and for you. When it comes to the real you: Don't change. You are already everything you need to be. Full love. Full worth.

On her final day on earth in her physical form, as I continued to play my mom's favorite songs on loop on a playlist I'd made for her, she woke up with a big smile on her face. She squeezed my hand tightly, and she said to me, "Jay Jay, it's all so beautiful." She looked like she was transcending beyond what Dennis and I could see or understand.

"What do you mean, Mommy?" I asked.

"I wish I knew this sooner," she said. "All the stuff people fight about, none of it even matters. It's just all so, so beautiful." After she said those words, she looked to have a peace around her that filled the room.

"How are you feeling?" I asked her.

She just smiled at me but didn't answer.

Then I said, "Are you scared at all, Mom?"

She smiled, shook her head back and forth, and said no. I knew this moment was different. She rested for a while and when she woke up the next time, she strained to whisper to me, "I love you. And it's a love that will never go away." A while later, while I was holding her hand tight on her left side, and Dennis was on her right side with his hand on her forehead, she took her last breath on this earth.

MY MOM'S WORDS—"DON'T change"—felt like truth. Like a love poem from her soul to mine. And I'm sharing them with you as a love poem from my soul to yours.

I'm not sure why in her seventy-four years this was the first time she said these words to me. Perhaps it's because it's the first time I asked the question. Or perhaps it's because she was now transcending into a greater understanding of what really matters and what's really true.

My mom Nina loved the color yellow. She loved hummingbirds. And butterflies. And See's candy. She believed in me, even on the days I didn't believe in myself. I spent most of my life trying to make her proud, not realizing she already was, in the only way that mattered. I've spent most of my life trying to make God proud, and I now know beyond a shadow of a doubt, there's nothing I could do to make Him otherwise. And I've spent most of my life trying to make myself feel proud and worthy and loved, not realizing that there is nothing I can do or achieve or attract that will ever arrive at that lasting feeling. **The only way to achieve that lasting feeling of love and worthiness is to know that it already exists within us. In full power, at our core, it *is* us.** I'll say it again: **Who you truly are is LOVE. It's already all inside of you and IS you.** The rest of it all is just the human experience, the adventure we go on, that if we're fortunate, eventually leads us to the one thing that we already are.

My mom gave me everything she had in her, her entire life. She truly gave it her best shot, to raise her only living baby the best she could. For all the heart and soul that she had poured into me her entire life, this moment, when she shared the words "don't change" and imparted this lesson that you, exactly as you are, regardless of anything else, are enough, felt like her *victory lap* in her journey of choosing and raising me as her daughter. A victory lap she wasn't even intending or planning. It just was. The ultimate moment and lesson came through her in her final moments on this earth, and she left it with me. And I'm keeping it alive. Through me and now, if you choose, through you. No matter the relationship you may or may not have with your mom right now, if my Nina were here right now, she'd wrap you in her arms and say these exact words to you too. With full unwavering love for you, exactly as you are . . .

I hope you don't change. That's my ultimate wish for you.
It would be so terrible if you ever change.

— NINA MARIE DAUGS (MY LATE MAMA)

Your Victory Is Knowing You're Enough

When we lose a loved one, it has a way of making us think not just about death, but about life. What truly matters. How we want to intentionally live the rest of our precious days on this earth. The dictionary defines the term *victory lap* as a celebratory extra lap run around the track or sports field, made by the winner or winning team after the conclusion of a race. After this experience with my mom, where my soul literally shifted into command over my mind, I know this to be true: **the moment we realize and believe we are truly and fully worthy, exactly as we are, is the moment we've won.** The unremitting and absolutely exhausting weight of unworthiness many of us have been carrying our entire lives lifts. And in that moment, it opens us to embrace the infinite, expansive joy, love, and possibility that life has to offer. The moment we know it to be true, and begin embracing our innate worthiness, is the moment our victory lap of life can begin. It's the moment we realize we've won the victory inside. And now we can be even more powerful in all of the things we want to do on the outside.

When you win the victory *inside*, you're infinitely more powerful in all that you want to do, create, give, serve, build, ideate, love, change, and impact on the *outside*.

The term *victory lap* ordinarily applies to something that happens *after* you win. Or at the *end* of something. But what if there's a second and even more powerful way to define a victory lap? See, I now believe the moment you begin to lift the heavy burden of unworthiness and begin to believe, then know, that you are fully worthy is the moment your *lifelong* victory lap can begin! Instead of waiting until the end to run one, what if we can make our entire life, from this point forward, for decades to come, feel like a victory lap?

The moment we realize and believe we are truly and fully worthy, exactly as we are, is the moment we've won.

Begin your victory lap now, with the goal of running it for decades and decades to come. This doesn't mean life won't still be hard, often too hard. It doesn't mean you won't stumble and fall and face setbacks. It doesn't mean you're no longer ambitious. It doesn't mean you're even close to doing or giving or serving or creating or building or offering all your talents, gifts, passions, businesses, and ideas with the world that you still plan to. It simply means that when you do all these things as part of your victory lap, you're no longer trying to carry the billion-pound weight of unworthiness at the same time. When you know you are truly enough, exactly as you are, your self-worth is secure. You're now going after your hopes and dreams from a place of security and freedom. And when you truly feel worthy, and have solid self-worth, it becomes your foundation. The foundation that fuels your resiliency to keep going when you fall down. And the strength to know that whether you stumble and get shamed by the world, or you achieve and get flooded with adoration from the world, it doesn't impact your internal unshakable worthiness that you alone, regardless of any of it, are fully worthy.

LIFE IS SO much more beautiful, and you can fight even harder for the good stuff and recover even faster from the bad stuff when you don't have the weight of unworthiness on your shoulders on top of it all. You still find great self-confidence in working toward becoming the highest, truest version of yourself, while your self-worth is fully intact independent of it all.

When we begin nurturing and growing our worthiness, and the unbearable weight of *not-enoughness* we've been carrying our entire lives slowly lifts, that's when we've taken the first step onto the victory lap track. Our future ahead, in all of its ups and downs, seems less foggy, clearer, and infinitely more possible. Because our knowing now knows with certainty, and even surprise, that we ever doubted it, that we are in fact worthy of all our greatest hopes, wildest dreams, and all of the unconditional love in the world. Knowing you're already fully worthy doesn't decrease your hunger or drive, it allows you to feel fulfilled and actually enjoy the things you're driving toward and achieving. And while you might still have an unremitting fire inside of you for all that you still want to do in this world in the decades to come, you'll be running your race from the freedom of the *Victory Lap Track*, versus the *Not-Enoughness Treadmill*.

My mom gave me the gift, in the end of her life, of me not waiting until the end of mine to learn this lesson. Let's not wait until the end of our lives to embrace or share it. First, to allow it to take root deep inside ourselves. Then bring another person with you who's got some self-doubt to destroy and a beautiful, powerful destiny to fulfill. Let's start running our victory lap of life knowing we're fully worthy today . . . and when we do, we have a much longer track ahead that we get to lap for the rest of our lives. The greatest victory is realizing there is nothing that needs to change for us to embrace it fully.

The victory lap will still come with ups and downs, with moments that knock us flat on our face, or moments that take our breath away in their beauty. But when we know we are fully worthy exactly as we are, we live with a peace and knowing that **no matter what happens** *around us,* **we have unshakable worth** *within us.*

> *When you know your worth, you move different.*
> — UNKNOWN

Just remember, you're now beginning your victory lap, and there are no rules! You can solo dance in full commitment and celebration that you're one of the *free* ones on the track. You run at your own pace and with full grace, even when you might get off track, trip and tumble, or start jogging backward for a minute. It's okay if you walk it at times, or perhaps even crawl. Naps are permitted on the victory lap too. On this lap, you don't need anyone else to feel fully complete, but you'll also never be alone. You'll feel your Creator with you, in the breeze on your skin, the sunlight on your face, the wind at your back, the blades of grass and wildflowers on the side of the track. And in the soul-filling spirit that tastes like divine purpose every time you help another runner get back up from a fall, or help them to remember that they are seen, valuable, and enough exactly as they are. As for me, I'll be running my lap too, right there with you. If you wanna take a break for chocolate or Cheetos or snuggle up under a blanket on the sidelines just to take in the view, I'll share my favorite cozy blanket with you, anytime. We can sip coffee or tea together, or even drink some celebratory wine in our WORTHY coffee mugs together (no judgment).

And on our victory lap, while we're all running at our own pace our own race, we're also all running together, in full love. The most beautiful part is that we each have the power to pass a baton and invite and inspire others to start their own victory lap, knowing they're worthy exactly as they are, right now. We have unlimited batons to pass, continuously inviting other runners on the victory lap of their lives, where they are realizing their innate *enoughness* exactly as they are. And when we do that, our own run becomes even more purposeful. Let's welcome as many others to the victory track as we can.

Together, with all our might, let's leave no girl, no woman, no person behind.

Maybe your whole life you felt like victory and winning was something that happens to other people, but not you. Maybe you've felt like you have a long way to go, so much more to prove, so much smarter to become, so much harder to work, before you'd ever consider the thought that you've won. But those are all lies. Lies that keep us hustling and striving to a never-possible-to-reach and always unfulfilling path to nowhere. Lies don't ever lead to love. Truth does. And the truth is: **you, exactly as you are, are the victory.**

You, exactly as you are, are the victory.

You have the power to cast off the weight of *not-enoughness* from your shoulders for good and begin running your victory lap, beginning today! Maybe your victory lap begins by deciding you'll no longer hide in plain sight. By believing your new definition of rejection, one that says, *Hey, Rejection, you might be tempted to underestimate me, but let me save you some time . . . don't.* Maybe your victory lap begins today by deciding you're not crazy, you're just first, and that there is greatness inside you! Maybe it begins by forgiving that person who hurt you, or by forgiving yourself and embracing fully that you are not your past mistakes. Maybe it begins by deciding to break free from the cage and start forming a new circle. Or by deciding to unlearn one of those lies of unworthiness that's been holding you back. Maybe you're going to decide to stop waiting on your weight, or stop waiting on the hero to show up, and realize you are her! Or you're going to decide, starting today, to speak your truth, to share your art, your ideas, your message, your story with the world, and no longer cancel yourself out of your calling. To take your next right step on your own personal mission to the moon, and to fully commit on that dance floor in your one beautiful solo of life. Maybe it begins with wearing the swimsuit, or jiggling your cellulite confidently with joy, or getting on the dating app, or getting a tattoo of the word that you're going to choose to believe as your new label. Perhaps it starts with deciding to start a new morning routine where you look in the mirror, deep into your own eyes, and say, *You are worthy, and I love you.*

In this moment, it is so very powerful to embrace that everything that happened before in your life was all happening *for* you. All divinely orchestrated. Even the hard parts. Even the ones you'd never want to go through again. But you made it through. Perhaps so that you can now be a living, breathing example of wisdom, perseverance, and strength for how others can make it through similar situations too. I believe you'll have many, many more victorious peaks to come on your journey, ones the world around you will celebrate, but you'll know deep down inside to enjoy the joy, and go for it with full gusto, but that your worth doesn't waver with the world's celebration and approval, just like it doesn't waver with the world's judgment, criticism, or shame. You, your soul, the real you is separate, unbound, untethered, independent, and free from all of that. You are valuable beyond measure, with or without any of it.

You are worthy. You are love. It is already you. The real you. Exactly as you are. Your soul. Your innateness. From the moment you were born. It's not something you have to earn, seek outside of yourself, or acquire, despite how many times the world tells you otherwise. And it's not something you can ever lose. You can have the fear that you'll never find it, and the fear that you will lose it. But it's impossible. When you realized **you already are it**.

The more you know this to be true, the more the power *in* and *of* you expands.

What will you do with the power that is you?

I can't wait to cheer you on as you live that answer, fully, soul first.

I see you. I believe in you. I love you. You are love.

You are . . . WORTHY!

From my soul to yours,

Your victory lap partner for life, starting now,

Jamie

WORTHY DOESN'T END HERE

WORTHY DOESN'T END here—we're now victory lap partners for life! If you're on social media, come say hi to me. I'd love to hear your story! And please post and share your favorite quote, tool, lesson, or takeaway from the book, and be sure to tag me, along with the hashtags #WorthyBook and #JamieKernLima, so I can repost yours on my page! If you'd like ongoing weekly inspiration and encouragement on your worthiness journey, I'd love to invite you to join my free email newsletter at JamieKernLima.com.

And together, let's promise this is just the beginning! In the spirit of no girl, no woman, no person left behind in knowing they're worthy, I'm passing YOU the baton to positively impact someone's life by passing this book on to them. Whether you give *your* copy of the book to someone else, or you pay it forward and gift them one, let's each get a full Victory Lap Card! (Find your Victory Lap Library Card on the page just inside of the back cover of your book!) Inspired by a traditional library card (where you added your name and the date you checked out a book), a Victory Lap Card lists and celebrates all the people you pass the baton to, who will be reading this book after you. Ask each person you pass your book on to, to add their name and date next to yours, and then to pass the book on, like a baton on their next victory lap. If you want to keep this copy for yourself and order one for someone else, you can hand write the name of each person you "pass" a copy on to on your Victory Lap Card right next to yours. If you choose to send one or more to an organization that would love to receive and share it, you can add their name to your card as well. Together, we can change the world, one girl, one woman, one person knowing they're WORTHY at a time.

And remember, you can pass the baton to yourself as well. I love reading a book more than once, as I always take away different things each time. I also love rereading a book a few months after the initial read, as a great sign of growth is when you read the same book more than once and have a different experience because you've changed and grown!

I always read a book at least twice. The first time
I highlight it. The second time it highlights me.

— JOHN C. MAXWELL

NoteWORTHY: For additional WORTHY resources, including free tools, worksheets, meditations, and more, visit WorthyBook.com/ Resources

NoteWORTHY: Experience the audio/video version of me reading this spoken word poem, from my soul to yours, at WorthyBook.com/Poem or scan this code.

You're Not Crazy, You're Just First

Who do you think you are, they say.
Things like that aren't for people like us.
Why are you going around changing?
Planning to leave us in the dust?

Are you forgetting where you come from?
Are we not good enough anymore?
And just like that the temptation to play life small
Feels more comfortable than before.

If you're doubting you're enough . . .
Your thoughts, their words, have got you down . . .
It's time for your soul to tell your mind
There's a new boss in town . . .

See—there's no one else quite like you
In the entire universe . . .
And what your soul knows is . . .
You're not crazy, you're just first . . .

The first to have your hopes and dreams.
The first *you* there's ever been.
So don't be surprised if they don't get you
Or try to shame you to fit in . . .

They call you odd, strange, different
For having dreams bigger than they can see.
Because those dreams weren't given to them
They see them through fear and anxiety.

And even the well-intentioned people
Who love you to the bone
Can see you pursuing your dreams as a reminder
Of them not fulfilling their own.

If people like people who are like them
Hiding your true self is a comfort zone.
But a calling unexpressed inside of you
Leaves you feeling anguished and alone—
Even . . .
Inside . . .
Of your own home . . .

They call you words like *crazy*, and say
We stick together, for better or for worse.
But what your knowing knows is
You're not crazy, you're just first.

The first to launch the business,
To dust your dreams off the shelf.
The first to believe you're worthy
Of betting on yourself.

The first to beat addiction,
To live life sober and awake.
The first to end the generational cycle
That you know you're born to break.

The first to start healing.
The first to forgive so you'll be free.
The first to love others for who they are
Not for who you wish they'd be.

The first to be a visionary,
To dream up the screenplay that you'll write.
The first to recognize your gifts
And stop hiding in plain sight.

The first man in your family to say
I deal with self-doubt too.
The first mom to say *No, I'm not okay,*
And I don't know what to do.

The first in generations to love your body
And celebrate it joyfully to prove it.
To know that it's a Miracle in motion
And what a gift it is to move it.

The first to risk rejection,
To speak your truth with vigor
Knowing the opposition might be big
But your Creator is bigger.

The first to cheer yourself on
And truly believe it, not just fake it,
Knowing most people won't cheer for you
Until after you make it.

In class they used to pick you last . . .
And now they're at a loss . . .
Because instead of calling you employee
They now call you Boss.

The first to stand up for the outcast
And say *Stop teasing, I just won't* . . .
You might be tempted to underestimate me,
But let me save you some time . . . don't.

The first to say *You broke my heart . . .*
You gave up on me for something else . . .
And it took me awhile to know I'm worthy
Of believing in myself

And what I know is yeah, you hurt me
But I'm not rejected, see . . .
God just hid my value from you because
You're not assigned to my destiny.

The first to recognize your circle
Looks a lot more like a cage.
The first to say, *Dad, will you love me for me?*
And *Grandma, I was born this way.*

The first to turn your pain into your purpose
Using the parts that were most rough,
To help guide others on their journey
Of feeling less alone and more enough.

The first to say, *Let's agree to disagree.*
We all have the right to free speech too.
Stop trying to cancel and hate on others
Just because you're hurting too.

The first to believe in your dreams
Even when others might not get you,
Then one day love them anyways
When they're bragging to people how they met you.

The first to unlearn the lie *you're not enough*
Unless you keep striving and achieving.
That's a lie that leads to nowhere,
And one it's time to stop believing.

The truth is accomplishments are great,
But to know you're worthy, you don't need 'em.
And when we know something is true,
It feels like joy and tastes like freedom.

You are not your successes.
You're not how many times you fail or fall.
You are how big you love . . .
And love is free for all . . .

See, when we fear we're not enough
And fear even more we won't be loved,
It's so tempting to shrink in size
And trade in our purpose for their hugs.

When you're feeling like you don't fit in
Or that you never quite belong,
Your uniqueness is your superpower;
Your truth is never wrong.

And when they criticize to hold you back,
Cuz your dreams aren't what they're used to,
And they're afraid that you'll outgrow them,
Leave them behind, and that they'll lose you.

Stop asking for their advice
If they've never been there themselves.
When you people-please for others
You end up betraying yourself.

When doubt tempts you to dim your light
Always remember this verse . . .
Your soul knows you were made for more . . .
With so much purpose it could burst . . .

You're born with greatness in you,
And whether it's a blessing or a curse . . .
The world won't be better
Until your greatness is dispersed.

See, there is only one of you
In the entire Universe,
And your knowing knows, *deep down*,
You're not crazy . . . You're just first.

ACKNOWLEDGMENTS

THE CREATION OF this book wouldn't have been possible without the love, contribution, and encouragement of so many. First, thank you to the loves of my life, Paulo, Wonder, and Wilder. And to my family (adopted, birth, extended, and chosen). And especially my late mom Nina. Thank you for adopting me the day I was born. Thank you for loving me. Thank you for teaching me that we are all worthy exactly as we are. A lesson that changed my entire life, and one that now lives on through this book and the lives of everyone it touches. Thank you to my friends and family mentioned in the stories in this book, and the many, many more who are not, but who are equally to thank for being part of my story, my strength, my character, and my heart. I cherish you and am grateful to have the gift of doing life with you. Thank you for loving me. I love you.

This book is the result of many people showing their belief in this *WORTHY* mission and in me through the most precious gift I could ask for: their time. I would specifically like to thank the following people for their mentorship, their leadership, their friendship, and their championship of me and my intention for this book to touch as many lives as possible: Thank you, Oprah Winfrey, for the blessing of your time, your always candid feedback, and your invaluable mentorship. Thank you for showing me what strength, resilience, intention, and living in divine alignment looks like. A special thank-you for your support, wisdom, friendship, and encouragement to: Ed Mylett, Robin Roberts and Amber Laign, Prince EA, John Maxwell, Ellen DeGeneres and Portia de Rossi, Brendon Burchard, Joel and Victoria Osteen, Tony and Sage

Robbins, Steven and Holly Furtick, Dr. Nicole LePera, Mel Robbins, Kate Redding and Aaron Silverman, Mallory Ervin, Danielle Canty, Lisa and Tom Bilyeu, Glo Atanmo, Craig and Amy Groeschel, Trevy Wragg, Rory and AJ Vaden, Craig Clemens and Sarah Anne Stewart, Sarah Jakes Roberts and Toure Roberts, Maria Shriver, Bob and Maria Goff, Erwin and Kim McManus, Glennon Doyle, Sara Blakely, Darrin Powell, Dean and Lisa Graziosi, Jenna Kutcher, Jon and Kathryn Gordon, Joel and Kat Marion, Trent Shelton, Natalie Ellis, Jim Kwik, Randy Garn, Mel Abraham, Kacia Ghetmiri, Mally Roncal, Miles and Vanessa Adcox, Brooke Thomas, Karissa Kouchis, Erin Skye Kelly, Edward Enninful and Alec Maxwell, Margaret Riley King, Jen Hatmaker, Rachel Luna, Russell Brunson, Lori Harder, Candy Valentino, Dan Fleyshman, Jason Jaggard, Koya Webb, James Clear, Lewis Howes and Martha Higareda, Matthew Hussey and Audrey Le Strat, Sarah Robbins, Don Miller, Michael Hyatt, Luvvie Ajayi Jones, Isabel Alysa, Heidi Powell, Emily Ford, Amy Porterfield, Jasmine Starr, Paula Faris, Evan Carmichael, Drew Hitchcock, Jay Shetty and Radhi Devlukia-Shetty, Denise White, and to my fellow Henry Crown Phoenix Class family, I love you.

And an extra special thank-you to my team and close friends who read more drafts of *WORTHY* than what they signed up for: Sarah Witt, Jacquie Finnan, Lia Key, Desiree Zirolli, and Olivia Daugs. And completing the original Worthy Circle and Worthy Weekend team, a special thank-you to Trevy, Summer, Danielle, and Olivia A. To my Lost Valley Circle of Trust, Paula, Annie, Hillary, Danielle, Candace, Rachel, I love you. To the many, many more friends too numerous to list, who have helped support me in writing this book, thank you for sharing your encouragement, ideas, inspiration, contacts, advice, endorsements, prayers, and thank you most of all for your belief in me.

The creation and launch of this book was only made possible by a true dream team. Thank you to Dupree Miller, especially Jan and Shannon. Thank you to Nicole Perez-Krueger, Diandra Escamilla, Taylor Rodriguez, Gabby Yuen, and the entire team at Align PR. Thank you to Trevina Wragg, Elizabeth Kadar, Zazu Larrinaga, Janna Yu, and the whole Prestige social team. Thank you Hilary Liftin for your abundant talent and partnership. When the two of us walk into a bar we make magic, it's a gift to walk into any bar with you. Thank you Daniel Decker for your advice, passion, friendship, leadership, and expertise. Thank you Kelly Madrone for your expert research and thank you Pete Garceau for the beautiful *WORTHY* cover. Thank you to my IT Cosmetics family, we are family forever. And thank you to the many retail and business partners for your belief in IT Cosmetics, especially L'Oréal, QVC, and ULTA Beauty, for your commitment to inclusivity, diversity, and celebrating the beauty in every person!

Thank you to my publisher, Hay House, to the legendary Reid Tracy for believing in me and in *WORTHY*, and to my amazing editor Anne Barthel. Thank you to the entire Hay House team for your passion, talent, and belief in *WORTHY*, including Margarete Nielsen, Patty Gift, Lizzi Marshall, Lindsay McGinty, Diane Hill, John Tintera, Betsy Beier, Monica O'Connor, Tricia Breidenthal, Julie Davison, Kirsten Callais, Marlene Robinson, Danielle Monaco, Celeste Johnson, Kathleen Reed, Lisa Bernier, Brianne Bardusch, Toisan Craigg, and Devon Glenn. And to each and every person who in many ways big and small contributed their talent to the book, thank you!

If I've missed including anyone who's contributed to *WORTHY*, I'll be sure to update the acknowledgments with each reprint of the book. And THANK YOU from the bottom of my heart to each and every person who has been part of my journey so far, part of this book, and part of the WORTHY mission.

BIBLIOGRAPHY

Adam, Jamela. "What Is Toxic Positivity and How Is It Bad for Your Workplace?" *U.S. News*, March 15, 2023. https://money.usnews.com/careers/articles/what-is-toxic-positivity-and-how-is-it-bad-for-your-workplace.

"Advancing the Future of Women in Business: The 2020 KPMG Women's Leadership Summit Report," KPMG, 2020. https://info.kpmg.us/content/dam/womensleadership/pdf/2020/2020wlsstudy.pdf.

Alavi, Hamid Reza. "The Role of Self-Esteem in Tendency Toward Drugs, Theft and Prostitution," *Addiction and Health* 3, no. 3–4 (Summer–Autumn 2011): 119–124. https://www.ncbi.nlm.nih.gov/pmc/articles/PMC3905528/.

"Amelia Earhart – Quotes," Goodreads, accessed August 21, 2023. https://www.goodreads.com/quotes/123820-the-most-difficult-thing-is-the-decision-to-act-the.

Angelou, Maya (@drmayaangelou). "Nothing will work unless you do," Twitter post. January 13, 2017, 2:33pm. https://twitter.com/DrMayaAngelou/status/820021073727160320?lang=en.

Ballard, Jamie. "Women Are More Likely than Men to Say They're a People-Pleaser, and Many Dislike Being Seen as One," YouGov, August 22, 2022. https://today.yougov.com/topics/society/articles-reports/2022/08/22/women-more-likely-men-people-pleasing-poll.

Beck, Martha. "How to Know It's Real Love," Oprah.com, March 15, 2002, https://www.oprah.com/relationships/how-to-know-its-real-love-advice-from-martha-beck/all.

Branch, Marsha. "Loving Me! – May the Space Between Where You Are and Where You Want to Be Inspire You!" Marsha Branch, accessed August 21, 2023. https://marshabranch.wordpress.com/2014/01/05/may-the-space-between-where-you-are-where-you-want-to-be-inspire-you/.

Brown, Brené. "In You Must Go," Brené Brown, May 4, 2018. https://brenebrown.com/articles/2018/05/04/in-you-must-go-harnessing-the-force-by-owning-our-stories/.

Butler, Kristen. *3 Minute Happiness Journal*. Carlsbad, CA: Hay House, 2023.

Camus, Albert. *Summer*. New York: Penguin, 1995.

Carter, Christine. "What We Get When We Give," *Greater Good* magazine, February 18, 2010. https://greatergood.berkeley.edu/article/item/what_we_get_when_we_give.

"Catechism of the Catholic Church," *Catholic Culture*, accessed September 24, 2023. https://www.catholicculture.org/culture/library/catechism/cat_view.cfm?recnum=7199.

"C.G. Jung – Quotes – Quotable Quote," Goodreads, accessed August 17, 2023. https://www.goodreads.com/quotes/10933615-the-world-will-ask-who-you-are-and -if-you.

Chapata, Billy (@iambrillyant). "being loved feels warm. loving yourself feels like/ the entire sun inside of you." Twitter post. August, 9, 2021, 9:06am. https://twitter.com /iambrillyant/status/1424748858614108165.

Coelho, Paulo. *The Alchemist*. New York: HarperOne, 2006.

Coelho, Paulo (@paulocoelho). "If you live to please others, everyone will love you except yourself." Twitter post. June 2, 2013, 6:55am. https://twitter.com/paulocoelho /status/344800100599623680?lang=en.

Davis, Tchiki. "Four Steps to Feeling Better About Yourself," *Greater Good* magazine, October 19, 2016. https://greatergood.berkeley.edu/article/item/four_steps _to_feeling_better_about_yourself.

Dickrell, Stephanie. "More Than 1 in 2 Americans Will Get STD in Lifetime," *SC Times*, August 22, 2015. https://www.sctimes.com/story/life/wellness/2015/08/21 /americans--get-std-lifetime/32123427/.

Doyle, Glennon. *Untamed*. New York: Dial Press, 2020.

Doyle, Glennon. "IF YOU DON'T KNOW WHAT TO DO – START HERE. HERE'S WHAT TO DO." Instagram. May 26, 2022, accessed August 21, 2023. https:// www.instagram.com/p/CeBpLTzlK-J/?hl=en.

Economy, Peter. "17 of the Most Inspirational Quotes from Beyoncé—Business Genius and Music Superstar," *Inc.*, June 4, 2019. https://www.inc.com/peter-economy /17-of-most-inspirational-quotes-from-beyonce-business-genius-music-superstar.html.

Economy, Peter. "Sara Blakely's Most Inspiring Quotes for Success," Inc., March 20, 2015. https://www.inc.com/peter-economy/sara-blakely-19-inspiring-power-quotes -for-success.html.

Gibson, James L., and Joseph L. Sutherland. "Keeping Your Mouth Shut: Spiraling Self-Censorship in the United States," *Political Studies Quarterly* 2023 (June 1, 2020). http://dx.doi.org/10.2139/ssrn.3647099.

Gillett, Rachel, and Madison Hoff, "Gender Bias Could Make It Harder for Women to Become CEO, According to a Recent Study," *Business Insider*, April 17, 2020. https:// www.businessinsider.com/why-women-almost-never-become-ceo-2016-9.

Goff, Bob (@bobgoff). "Every time I wonder who I should love & for how long I should love them, God continues to whisper to me: Everybody, always." Twitter post. July 2, 2018, 11:39am. https://twitter.com/bobgoff/status/1013839515088138241 ?lang=en.

Graham, Steven M., and Margaret S. Clark. "Self-Esteem and Organization of Valenced Information About Others: the 'Jekyll-and-Hyde'-ing of Relationship Partners," *Journal of Personality and Social Psychology* 90, no. 4 (April 2006): 652–665. https:// doi.org/10.1037/0022-3514.90.4.652.

Gray, Emma. "11 Ways Maya Angelou Taught Us to Be Better Women," *HuffPost*, May 28, 2014. https://www.huffpost.com/entry/maya-angelou-women-quotes_n_5404284.

Gross-Loh, Christine. "How Praise Became a Consolation Prize," *The Atlantic*, December 16, 2016. https://www.theatlantic.com/education/archive/2016/12/how-praise-became-a-consolation-prize/510845/.

Hanh, Thich Nhat. *The Art of Power*. New York: HarperOne, 2007.

Heggeness, Greta. "44 Ellen DeGeneres Quotes to Make You Laugh, Cry & Stay Motivated," Yahoo!, October 11, 2022. https://www.yahoo.com/video/44-ellen-degeneres-quotes-laugh-161600383.html?guccounter=1.

Homer, Nakeia. *All the Right Pieces*. New York: Thought Catalog Books, 2022.

"How to Feel Better About Yourself," interview by Dacher Keltner, June 22, 2023, in *The Science of Happiness*, podcast, https://greatergood.berkeley.edu/podcasts/item/how_to_feel_better_about_yourself_rene_brooks.

Kaur, Rupi. *milk and honey*. Kansas City, MO: Andrews McMeel Publishing, 2018.

King, Martin Luther, Jr. "Martin Luther King's Sermon: The Drum Major Instinct," filmed February 4, 1968, YouTube, April 2, 2028. https://www.youtube.com/watch?v=Mefbog-b4-4.

Knight, Rob. "Eight in 10 Young Adults Feel They Are Not Good Enough, Poll Claims," *The Independent*, November 1, 2019. https://www.independent.co.uk/news/uk/home-news/millennials-mental-health-love-young-adults-social-media-poll-alpro-a9181296.html.

Kotb, Hoda. *I Really Needed This Today: Words to Live By*. New York: G.P. Putnam's Sons, 2019.

Lachmann, Suzanne. "10 Ways Low Self-Esteem Affects Women in Relationships," *Psychology Today*, December 17, 2013. https://www.psychologytoday.com/us/blog/me-we/201312/10-ways-low-self-esteem-affects-women-in-relationships.

Leary, Mark. "Emotional Responses to Interpersonal Rejection," *Dialogues in Clinical Neuroscience* 17, no. 4 (December 2015): 435–441. https://doi.org/10.31887/DCNS.2015.17.4/mleary.

Lynch, Alison. "80% of British Women Don't Feel Good Enough, According to New Survey," *Metro*, August 25, 2015. https://metro.co.uk/2015/08/25/80-of-british-women-dont-feel-good-enough-according-to-new-survey-5360444/.

Mann et. al. "Self-Esteem in a Broad-Spectrum Approach for Mental Health Promotion," *Health Education Research* 19, no. 4 (August 2004): 357–372. https://doi.org/10.1093/her/cyg041.

"Martin Luther King, Jr. – Quotes," Goodreads, accessed August 21, 2023. https://www.goodreads.com/quotes/16312-faith-is-taking-the-first-step-even-when-you-can-t.

Maryfield, Keyanna. "77 Know Your Worth Quotes and Sayings to Boost Your Confidence, Happiness and Success," Inspired Life, accessed August 21, 2023, https://www.inspiredlifehq.com/know-your-worth-quotes/.

Maxwell, John C. *The Power of Significance: How Purpose Changes Your Life*. New York: Center Street, 2017.

McManus, Erwin Raphael. *The Way of the Warrior: An Ancient Path to Inner Peace*. Colorado Springs, CO: WaterBrook, 2019.

"Mindy Kaling – Quotes," Goodreads, accessed August 17, 2023. https://www .goodreads.com/author/quotes/194416.Mindy_Kaling?page=16.

"Misty Copeland – Quotes," Goodreads, accessed August 21, 2023, https://www .goodreads.com/author/quotes/7155409.Misty_Copeland.

"New Dove Research Finds Beauty Pressures Up, and Women and Girls Calling for Change," PR Newswire, June 21, 2016. https://www.prnewswire.com/news -releases/new-dove-research-finds-beauty-pressures-up-and-women-and-girls-calling-for -change-583743391.html.

Okura, Lynn. "Iyanla Vanzant on Breaking the Body-Shaming Cycle and Accepting Your Lumpy, Bumpy Body," *HuffPost*, December 6, 2017. https://www.huffpost.com /entry/iyanla-vanzant-help-desk_n_5813356.

Orth, Ulrich, Richard W. Robins, and Keith F. Widaman, "Life-Span Development of Self-Esteem and Its Effects on Important Life Outcomes," *Journal of Personality and Social Psychology* 102, no. 6 (June 2012): 1271-1288. https://doi.org/10.1037/a0025558.

Oxford English Dictionary, accessed August 23, 2023, https://www.oed.com/search /dictionary/?scope=Entries&q=impostor%20syndrome.

Palmer, Mario. "5 Facts About Body Image." Amplify, accessed February 24, 2014. http://amplifyyourvoice.org/u/marioapalmer/2013/05/21/byob-be-your-own-beautiful. Quoted in "11 Facts about Body Image." DoSomething.org, n.d. https://www .dosomething.org/us/facts/11-facts-about-body-image.

Pandya, Charmaine. "The 17 Second Rule That Changed My Life," Charmaine Pandya, accessed August 21, 2023. https://www.charmainenlp.com/single-post/2016 /02/15/The-17-second-rule-that-changed-my-life.

Parton, Dolly (@dollyparton). "Find out who you are and do it on purpose. #Dolly-ism." Twitter Post. April 8, 2015, 1:40pm. https://twitter.com/DollyParton/status /585890099583397888?lang=en.

Pentreath, Rosie. "What Are the Origins of 'Humpty Dumpty Sat on a Wall' and What Do the Lyrics Mean?" Classic FM, July 30, 2021. https://www.classicfm.com /discover-music/humpty-dumpty-sat-on-a-wall-lyrics-history/.

Petrocchi, Nicola, Cristina Ottaviani, and Alessandro Couyomdjian. "Compassion at the Mirror: Exposure to a Mirror Increases the Efficacy of a Self-Compassion Manipulation in Enhancing a Soothing Positive Affect and Heart Rate Variability," *The Journal of Positive Psychology* 12, no. 6 (July 2016): 525–536. https://doi.org/10.1080 /17439760.2016.1209544.

Robbins, Mel. *The High 5 Habit: Take Control of Your Life with One Simple Habit*. Carlsbad, CA: Hay House, 2021.

"Salma Hayek – Quotes," Goodreads, accessed September 24, 2023, https://www .goodreads.com/quotes/109192-people-often-say-that-beauty-is-in-the-eye-of.

Schnall, Marianne. "Dolly Parton on Her Latest Projects, the Power of Love and More," *HuffPost*, November 29, 2016. https://www.huffpost.com/entry/interview-with-dolly-parton-on-her-latest-projects_b_583da37ee4b0bb2962f178cb.

"Sexually Transmitted Infections Prevalence, Incidence, and Cost Estimates in the United States," CDC, January 25, 2021. https://www.cdc.gov/std/statistics/prevalence-2020-at-a-glance.htm.

"67 Maria Shriver Quotes on Parenthood, Motherhood and Inspiration," Quotes. pub, accessed September 24, 2023. https://quotes.pub/maria-shriver-quotes?page=2.

"Spiritual Awareness / Awakening Quotes," Xavier University, accessed August 21, 2023, https://www.xavier.edu/jesuitresource/online-resources/quote-archive1/spiritual-awareness-quotes.

"Steven Furtick—A Troubled Mind and an Open Door," Sermons.love, accessed August 17, 2023. https://sermons.love/steven-furtick/8712-steven-furtick-a-troubled-mind-and-an-open-door.html.

Stone, Jay. "Carrey—Being Rich Not the Answer," *The Ottawa Citizen*, December 16, 2005. https://quoteinvestigator.com/2022/11/09/rich-famous/#f+442218+1+1.

"The Confidence Kit," Dove, accessed August 23, 2023. https://assets.unileversolutions.com/v1/81511615.pdf?disposition=inline.

"13 Times Taylor Swift Was the Wisest," *Marie Claire UK*, October 16, 2015. https://www.marieclaire.co.uk/entertainment/music/best-taylor-swift-quotes-33427.

Thomas, Brooke. "Your Predicament Does Not Determine Your Destiny – with Lia Valencia Key, Ep 215," *The Live Out Loud Show*, accessed August 21, 2023. https://www.brookethomas.com/your-predicament-does-not-determine-your-destiny-with-lia-valencia-key-ep215/.

@tinybuddha. "If speaking kindly to plants helps them grow, imagine what speaking kindly to humans can do." Twitter post. June 25, 2021. 11:30am, https://twitter.com/tinybuddha/status/1408477701585899526?lang=en.

Twain, Mark. *Mark Twain on Common Sense: Timeless Advice and Words of Wisdom from America's Most-Revered Humorist*, Stephen Brennan, ed. (New York: Skyhorse, 2014).

"Ulta Beauty Launches the Joy Project to Ignite a Movement for the Next Generation," *Business Wire*, September 25, 2023. https://www.businesswire.com/news/home/20230925298587/en/.

Weiner, Brian. "Lessons from the Mountain," Brian Weiner, February 18, 2022. https://brianweiner.com/the-only-people-who-get-upset-about-you-setting-boundaries-are-those-who-are-benefitting-from-you-having-none/.

Williamson, Marianne. *Everyday Grace: Having Hope, Finding Forgiveness, and Making Miracles.* New York: Riverhead Books, 2004.

Williamson, Marianne. *Return to Love: Reflections on the Principles of "A Course in Miracles."* New York: HarperOne, 1996.

Winfrey, Oprah, and Bruce D. Perry. *What Happened to You?: Conversations on Trauma, Resilience, and Healing.* New York: Flatiron Books, 2021.

Zorn, Eric. "Without Failure, Jordan Would Be False Idol," *Chicago Tribune*, May 19, 1997.

ABOUT THE AUTHOR

Jamie Kern Lima is a *New York Times* best-selling author, a leading voice in personal development and transformation, a guest teacher of "The Life You Want" class live with Oprah, and Founder of IT Cosmetics, a company she started in her living room and grew to the largest luxury makeup brand in the country. She sold the company to L'Oréal in a billion-dollar deal and became the first female CEO of a brand in its 100+ year history. Her love of her customers and remarkable authenticity and belief eventually landed her on the *Forbes* America's Richest Self-Made Women list. She's been a Denny's waitress, a struggling entrepreneur, lived a lifelong journey of rejections, and has battled her way through years of self-doubt, body-doubt, and God-doubt. She was placed into adoption at birth and has been on a journey of learning to believe she's here with purpose, on purpose, and for a purpose and is worthy, lovable, and enough. She's a mother of two and an active investor, speaker, and thought leader who is passionate about inspiring and elevating women. She's also an active philanthropist who has funded leadership training in more than 100 prisons and women's shelters across the United States and has donated over $40 million in product and funds to help women face the effects of cancer with confidence. She's donating 100 percent of her author proceeds for *WORTHY.* You can get free Worthy Bonuses and more info at **JamieKernLima.com** and **WorthyBook.com** and on social media **@JamieKernLima**

CONNECT WITH JAMIE

WWW.JAMIEKERNLIMA.COM

 youtube.com/@jamiekernlimaofficial

 @JamieKernLima

 facebook.com/JamieKernLimaPage

 www.linkedin.com/in/jamiekernlima/

 @jamiekernlimaofficial

To get regular weekly inspiration, tips, lessons, and encouragement, join Jamie's free inspirational email newsletter at JamieKernLima.com

We hope you enjoyed this Hay House book. If you'd like to receive our online catalog featuring additional information on Hay House books and products, or if you'd like to find out more about the Hay Foundation, please contact:

Hay House, Inc., P.O. Box 5100, Carlsbad, CA 92018-5100
(760) 431-7695 or (800) 654-5126
(760) 431-6948 (fax) or (800) 650-5115 (fax)
www.hayhouse.com® • www.hayfoundation.org

———

Published in Australia by: Hay House Australia Pty. Ltd.,
18/36 Ralph St., Alexandria NSW 2015
Phone: 612-9669-4299 • *Fax:* 612-9669-4144
www.hayhouse.com.au

Published in the United Kingdom by: Hay House UK, Ltd.,
The Sixth Floor, Watson House, 54 Baker Street, London W1U 7BU
Phone: +44 (0)20 3927 7290 • *Fax:* +44 (0)20 3927 7291
www.hayhouse.co.uk

Published in India by: Hay House Publishers India,
Muskaan Complex, Plot No. 3, B-2, Vasant Kunj, New Delhi 110 070
Phone: 91-11-4176-1620 • *Fax:* 91-11-4176-1630
www.hayhouse.co.in

———

Access New Knowledge.
Anytime. Anywhere.

Learn and evolve at your own pace
with the world's leading experts.

www.hayhouseU.com

NOTES

NOTES

NOTES

NOTES

NOTES

NOTES

NOTES

NOTES

NOTES

NOTES

WORTHY VICTORY LAP PARTNER LIBRARY CARD

Pass your baton! Share your book with, or send a book to, another person who you know needs these stories, lessons, and tools, and to know just how worthy they are! We are all Victory Lap partners together—no girl, no woman, no person left behind! In the spirit of the traditional library card, write your name in the **From** column and write the name of the person you're passing your book on to in the **To** column. Then ask them to pass it on to another person when they're done reading! Let's get full library cards! And if you give a new copy of the book to someone as a gift, write your name in the **From** column and then the name of each person you give a copy to in the **To** column. Please send me a snapshot of your card every time it changes hands . . . tag me, I'll post it! And if you need an extra card to print out, you can get one at WorthyBook.com/Resources

YOU ARE WORTHY!

VICTORY LAP PARTNER LIBRARY CARD

FROM	TO	DATE
Jamie Kern Lima		